DAVID JAMES PRITCHARD

FEEL

the

RAIN

AN INTRODUCTION TO THE COMPLEXITY
AND EXPANSION OF CONSCIOUSNESS

FIRST EDITION

Print ISBN: 978-1-09837-840-0

All profits from this book will be donated to Friends Without A Border
www.fwab.org or similar charitable organization.

Some people feel the rain.
Others just get wet.
—Unknown[1]

This book is dedicated to my father, Raymond,
who always modeled an open and loving consciousness.

I forever value and thank my wife, Joan, who has always supported and inspired me. I cannot thank enough my friend, Jan Deutsch, who for more than four years patiently and professionally helped me prepare the drafts and final manuscript of this book.

I appreciate and thank the friends who volunteered to read, edit, and comment on particular drafts of this book: Manfred Jantzen, PhD; John Sullivan; Mark Pritchard; Peter Turner; and Keith Logie, MD. In particular, I thank and appreciate Phil Kenny, PhD for his many hours of patient editing and scholarly input. Special thanks to my friends: Jessica Tampas for her professional help with all photographs; and Bruce Kerr for his anatomic drawings.

I am in awe of and thank my indispensable music muses who eased me through the stark times of writing and into the flow of creativity: Regina Spektor, Megon McDonough, Rita Yahan-Farouz, Bob Dylan, W. A. Mozart, and especially Michael Hoppé.

---

1 There is both a scholarly and an emotional dispute as to the author of this perfect quote that so beautifully reveals the nature of an open consciousness. Most attribute the quote to Bob Dylan, many to Bob Marley; but the best evidence of authorship points to Roger Miller, an American singer-song writer known for novelty hit songs like "King of the Road" and "Dang Me". See, quoteinvestigator.com.

TABLE OF CONTENTS

INTRODUCTION

The unexamined life
is not worth living.
—Socrates[1]

Tradition holds that these were among the last words spoken by Socrates (470-399 BCE) before being sentenced to death. Although this quote seems quite apt to introduce a book on the complexity and expansion of consciousness, I hesitated to use it because of its tinge of egoism. Socrates argued that it is only the pursuit of wisdom (philosophy) that raises human beings above animals that live only through instinct. Does this mean those of us struggling and overwhelmed by work, bill paying, and child raising are not leading lives worth living? Of course not. So what makes life worth living? At least for me, it doesn't get any better than the welcoming smile of a grandchild, a cold beer after working a long day in the yard, or the embrace of my wife at night. It is a promise of this book that these precious life pleasures as well as life's challenges will become more vivid, less fearful, and more meaningful as your consciousness expands.

Understanding the nature of consciousness and expanding its temporary and false boundaries provides the potential for you to see and relate to yourself and to the world as if from a new dimension. You discover new values, new realities. . .a more authentic plane of awareness and existence. This is accomplished in large part through a new freedom from habits and fears. These are often deeply penetrating habits and fears of which you are not even aware. This new freedom of expanded consciousness welcomes you into an accessible lightness of being.

The promising benefits of meaningful expansion of consciousness certainly sound awe-inspiring, and indeed they are. Yet they cannot be achieved by the widespread "magical thinking" of our so-called New Age. If we hope to change/expand our consciousness, a bit of academic rigor is first required to get a better understanding of the enigmatic nature of consciousness. After all, the essential first step in attempting to change something is to first try to understand how that "something" operates. Understanding the nature of consciousness is no easy task. For example, it may surprise you to learn that the definition and significance of the nature of consciousness have been disputed for more than three thousand years. The disputed theories about consciousness are numerous and contain extreme differences. At one end, there are those who believe there is no such thing as individual human consciousness, and that we are all essentially biologic automatons responding only to our instinctual evolutionary needs. At the other end, there are those who believe that the entire universe is the manifestation of one, singular, and omnipresent consciousness; and that humans, animals, plants, minerals, and even a grain of sand share in this singular consciousness. Many dozens of theories on consciousness fall between these two extremes.

Many of the topics covered in this book are complex, subtle, and constantly evolving. These are ideally topics for academic scholars who dedicate their time, energy, and lives attempting to better understand phenomena such as: the societal understanding of consciousness throughout history; the neuroevolutionary origins of consciousness; the developmental levels of human motivation; the neurophysiology of the brain; meditative and other "altered" states; and even whether there is a "Transcendent" reality distinctly separate from our commonly accepted understanding of existence. Mystics also serve an invaluable role in investigating and describing their deep immersions into the nature of consciousness and reality itself. While I am by nature (and by years of disappointing experience) a skeptic who strongly prefers so-called "scientific" proof of all claims regarding reality, to dismiss the wisdom of mystics is to foolishly miss out on some of the deepest and most beautiful insights about life. This book will include the findings of both leading academic scholars and mystics, which I will refer to collectively as "scholars and mystics" with "scholars" referring to the academic professions and "mystics" referring to the spiritual/transcendental practitioners.[2] Citational footnotes are provided should you wish to consult original sources or investigate further.

This book, however, was not written for scholars or mystics. I wrote this book for myself and for people like me. People who are blessed (or as my mother once said "cursed") with a compelling need to understand how life works. Maybe even begin to understand a few of the so-called mysteries of life. I know there are people out there like this because I have been fortunate to meet and even become friends with many. By no means do I call myself a mystic or an academic scholar on consciousness. I am a searcher with a decades long passion for investigating, practicing, and learning about these matters. Quite frankly, the more I think I learn, the more I appreciate how very much I will never really know. Yet hopefully, I have an ability to communicate to other like-minded searchers an understandable yet penetrating introduction/overview of the key issues, challenges, and practices regarding the nature and expansion of consciousness.

We will explore together both the fundamental challenge and the hopeful promise of consciousness expansion. The fundamental challenge is that, while most scholars and mystics agree that endeavoring to expand your consciousness is arguably the most authentic and worthwhile of human endeavors, actual progress at consciousness raising is extremely difficult. This difficulty is due in large part to six major filters which affect how we take in information, process that information, and act upon that information. Those filters are:

1. ignorance;
2. genetics;
3. the non-conscious;
4. culture;
5. emotions; and
6. circumstances of the moment.

The hopeful promise is that the very fact that you are reading this book is an important sign that you are considering making the difficult changes necessary to begin to expand your consciousness and begin to bring deeper and more authentic meaning into your life. To counter-quote Canadian rapper, Drake, "If you're reading this, it's not too late".[3]

It is a primary premise of this book that discipline, courage, and radical humility are each absolute requirements to help see past the filters and begin to expand consciousness. It takes "discipline" because meaningful growth of personal consciousness may be the most intense work/challenge you have ever undertaken. It takes "courage" because to expand your consciousness, you will need to leave the conscious and non-conscious comfort of your own culture, habits, beliefs, and even your genetics. It takes "radical humility" because the most fundamental belief you must question and eventually abandon is that you are a separate, independent, and permanent self who is in total control of your own consciousness. These absolute requirements are not only mandatory first steps, but they will continue to be constant and challenging requirements to strive for during the quest to see and understand yourself and the world other than through a glass darkly.

This book is divided into two sections which are entitled: "Recognition" and "Transformance". These are the most fundamental steps for any attempt at consciousness expansion. Each section takes a different approach to intro-duce and assist you in understanding and expanding your consciousness.

Section I "Recognition" introduces you to the highly disputed and ethereal nature of consciousness. Chapter One addresses the question, "What is consciousness?" This first chapter describes the evolution of human understanding of consciousness from the animism of Paleolithic times to the latest neuroscientific discoveries, and even onto claimed "Transcendent" the-ories based on phenomena such as quantum entanglement and wave-func-tion collapse. This fascinating look reveals how each otherwise advancing society was still unable to grasp the true nature of consciousness. This reveals a deep truth that must be understood and accepted to expand consciousness in a meaningful way: No matter how brilliant they were, no society nor any brilliant individual thinker of their historical time period ever had the final understanding of consciousness. When a person or a society believes it has all the answers (on any subject not just consciousness), then they have closed and limited their consciousness. There is no expansion of consciousness without an open mind, period. Chapter Two takes a lighter look at why we should want to expand our consciousness. Chapter Three examines the historically evolving understanding of distinct "levels" of consciousness from the introduction of the concept by Freud, through Maslow's "Hierarchy of Needs Theory", and onto the argument for multiple "Transpersonal" levels beyond the current scientific understanding of reality. This third chapter presents compelling reasons why it is so difficult to expand consciousness to a new level. Chapter Four helps to identify and explain the almost insurmountable power of the main filters to our individual receptacles of consciousness, all of which are habit and fear based. Chapter Five concludes Section I by exploring the optimistic promise of brain plasticity.

Section II "Transformance" presents powerful and proved practices for expanding consciousness. Such practices almost always involve following roads less traveled, yet return again to share wisdom and compassion. Chapter Six compares the need for a therapist or so-called guru versus going on your own. Chapter Seven examines simple practices for changing your perspective. Chapter Eight looks at both the science and the mysticism supporting the long honored practice of meditation. Chapter Nine explores the rich complexity of forgiveness. Finally, Chapter Ten touches on Buddhist insights specifically relevant to consciousness expansion in the modern era.

The enigmatic nature of consciousness is precisely why this book is called an "introduction" to the complexity and expansion of consciousness. Each chapter is designed to introduce you to an area of thought which you may not have previously considered, but the challenge and the journey are all yours.

Thank you for your time and trust.

DJP

April 19, 2021

---

1 See Plato's Apology 38a.

2 The phrase "scholars and mystics" is simply used as a heuristic device. . . recognizing that there are scholars who are mystics, mystics who are scholars, and brilliant and insightful individuals who cannot neatly be described as a scholar or a mystic.

3 In 2015, Canadian rapper, Drake, released a mixtape entitled "If You're Reading This, It's Too Late". It debuted at number one on both the U.S. and Canadian music charts with over 17 million streams in the first three days of its release. Drake was the most streamed artist of the 2011-2020 decade, and surpassed even the Beatles for most ever top 10 hits.

SECTION I

RECOGNITION

The essential first step in attempting to change something is to try and understand how that "something" operates.

CHAPTER ONE

WHAT IS CONSCIOUSNESS?
(An Overview of the "Hard Problem")

Consciousness operates in mysterious ways.
One of those ways is that the old paradigm suddenly starts to die.
—Deepak Chopra

The definition of "consciousness" has been in dispute for millennia, and remains in dispute through the present day. Why is it so difficult to come up with a simple and agreed upon definition of consciousness? If you went up to any random person on the street and asked, "What is consciousness?", you would most likely get the following response: "It's like being awake, not asleep, not unconscious". If you asked a more reflective person, you might get a response like: "It's the degree of your awareness of yourself and the world around you." And if you asked a really thoughtful person, that person might add: "and your ability to be knowingly responsive to your internal and external environment".

The degree to which a person is aware of and knowingly responsive to their internal and external environment. . . actually not a bad definition of consciousness,[1] It would certainly serve for most conversations in life. But once you bring in the learned scholars and mystics. . . the varying definitions, theories, and schools of thought seem to expand exponentially.

In researching this chapter, I discovered more than fifty different types and theories on the nature of consciousness,[2] although several schools split hairs so finely that it was hard to tell the difference without careful study.

For example, there is a theory of consciousness called Monism; but this was soon followed by the development of Absolute Monism, Attributive Monism, Eleatic Monism, Neutral Monism, Numerical Monism, Priority Monism, Reflective Monism, and Substantial Monism. Don't worry, there won't be a test; and more importantly, it is not necessary to understand all these fine scholastic distinctions to begin to expand your consciousness.

In our current stage of human knowledge, this longstanding and contentious dispute over the specific nature of consciousness is not resolvable. In fact, most participants in the dispute recognize this impasse by referring to this dispute as the "hard problem".[3] While the so-called "easy problems" involve discovering and explaining the "objective" neural mechanisms of the brain, the hard problem involves an attempt to determine both the cause and the nature of the "subjective" experiences that each individual person feels.

Perhaps the simplest way to understand the general nature of the hard problem is by considering the following questions: Who or what is perceiving, analyzing, and acting upon information received by an individual through the human senses? Who or what is experiencing the subjective feelings/ emotions an individual person has? Is it the flesh and blood brain itself, or is there something else outside the physical human brain? Is there a separate "self" or "mind" (as opposed to the physical brain) that perceives, analyzes, feels, and decides? If there is a separate self or mind, how independent/ free is that self or mind to accurately perceive and then knowingly respond? Finally, are such questions even answerable?

This book cannot resolve the hard problem. It will, however, provide a meaningful and comprehensive introduction/overview of consciousness, which is necessary to begin to recognize and understand the enigmatic nature of consciousness. In Chapter One, we will explore together such topics as:

1. the four very general theories of consciousness;
2. the historical understanding of consciousness;
3. the evolutionary emergence of consciousness;

4. the latest science on the neuronal correlates of consciousness;

5. the power of non-conscious forces; and

6. claimed "Transpersonal" consciousness.

At the end of this chapter, I will offer my own working understanding of the nature of consciousness. It is not necessary to agree with me or to have any settled definition of consciousness to begin to take on the challenges of understanding and then expanding your own consciousness. Let's begin.

Although many scholars will be rightly horrified by what I am about to say, perhaps the simplest way to get an overview of this complex dispute of the hard problem is to very artificially divide these numerous theories about consciousness into four very general (admittedly reductionist) categories. These categories could be described as: 1) Dualism; 2) Monism; 3) Mysterianism; and 4) Way Out There.[4]

Dualism. . . Although there are numerous versions of Dualism, theories in this category essentially hold that while our brains are material, our consciousness is not. Rather, our consciousness is something "transcendent" beyond the range of merely physical human experience. Dualism contends that our consciousness is not made of matter. It is something outside of the material universe. There are physical objects and there are spiritual objects, and an insurmountable chasm stands between the two. In modern times, often the word "mind" is used to describe this claimed transcendent consciousness as opposed to the word "brain" which is used to describe the physical brain itself. Often the term "mind-body dualism" is used to refer to Dualism. It is not an overstatement to claim that Dualism has long been the conscious perception of reality in Western culture and religions.

At least the seeds of Dualism have been implicit in the thoughts and culture of humankind since the Paleolithic Period (Stone Age) which occurred 2.4 mya (million years ago). It is first found in the rise of Animism. The term Animism comes from the Latin word "anima" which means breath or soul.[5] Animism holds that all objects, places, forces (such as weather), and creatures possess and are animated by a spiritual essence.

Scholars suggest that Animism arose as prehistoric humans attempted to explain seemingly uncontrollable phenomena such as day and night, heat and cold, available food or starvation, life and death. It was likely dreams that gave rise to the animistic belief that such phenomena were each controlled by a living essence or spirit that could be persuaded/influenced by petition or ritual. This was not yet Dualism, nor even what could be considered a religion. Prehistoric humans did not distinguish between spiritual and physical, nor was there yet a concept of a creator or overlord god. Yet the first seeds of religion and Dualism were sown.

As civilization expanded and coagulated, so did dualistic concepts such as the eternal soul. In Ancient Egypt (c. 3000 BCE), belief in a transcendent/eternal human soul was well established in both the religious and the civic customs. Dualism (although obviously not yet called "Dualism") was the reality in both individual consciousness and in the consciousness of the state and the culture. Let's start with how the ancient Egyptians looked at the soul.

In simplified terms, the ancient Egyptians believed there were five component parts to the human soul: Ren was the name given to the person at birth, and which survived as long as the living remembered the name. Bo was the unique personality of the person. Ka was the vital essence which animated the body, and which left the body at death for the eternal afterlife of darkness or the radically more desirable Field of Rushes depending on whether the person lived a just life; the component somewhat similar to the Christian understanding of the soul.[6] Sheut involved a vague shadow component of the person. Finally was the Ib, which was literally the human heart, said to be formed from one drop of blood from the mother at conception. Given our discussion, it's interesting to note that it was the heart and not the brain that played such a central role in Ancient Egyptian death ceremonies, for it was believed that the heart was the organ of thought and emotion. Again, not yet Dualism, but now a consciousness of the duality of a material/earthly life and an eternal/non-earthly life.

The next step in the evolution of Dualism involves the Ancient Greek Philosophers, which broadly speaking occurred from c. 600—300 BCE. Essentially, both leading Ancient Greek philosophers and the Greek populace

in general agreed with their Animist predecessors that a type of soul emanates all living things including animals and plants. If it was an animate
object, it had some type of soul. Philosophers argued that there were different
types of souls for men, women, slaves, animals, and plants. There was also
wide acceptance of an afterlife for at least the human soul. Some type of
quasi-person lived on in another realm: a heavenly place; a hellish place (my
adjectives not theirs); and/or within some system of transmigration of souls.
There was a widely held belief that souls were composed from some type of
ethereal stuff. Accordingly, there was also an underlying fear by some that,
although the soul survived the death of the body, that soul might eventually
dissipate after the death due to its ethereal nature.[7]

One of the Ancient Greek philosophers' key evolvements to the concept of Dualism was to add attributes or functions to the human soul. They
began by attributing certain emotions to the soul. These were emotions such
as pleasure and sexual desire such as in the metaphoric expression, "The
meadow filled my soul with a sense of beauty." In particular, "courage"
especially in battle was believed to be a function of the soul. This is not
surprising since these were societies often involved in war. Next came moral
qualities, and finally cognitive qualities such as thinking and planning were
also attributed to the soul.[8]

These are all "dualistic" functions because they attribute certain functions to the inanimate soul rather than to the physical body. Yes, they believed
the soul emanates the body to give it life; but the soul was conceived of as
distinct from the body possibly due to its ethereal and/or inanimate nature
as well as its potential immortal existence. That distinction between body
and soul is Dualism.

Before we leave the Ancient Greeks, let us explore a somewhat related
warning important for understanding consciousness. Socrates (470-399 BCE)
and others of his stature consistently taught that sensory data (for example,
things we believe we see, hear, and smell) was potentially misleading to a
person's understanding of the world (consciousness) due to the inherent
limitations of the senses. For example, did you just see a snake in the river,
or was it a stick? A person should not rely on their senses for truth. But like

all self-assured Greek philosophers of that era, Socrates believed there was a "rational" part of human consciousness that could tap into the wisdom inherent to the soul and allow a person to determine the truth of things. . . especially if that person had the privileged position of being a philosopher.

Fortunately, we can leave the esoteric philosophic distinctions of the Ancient Greek masters to the scholars since they are not essential to consciousness expansion. The important "macro-point" here is that these foundational philosophers of Western thought all seemed to be proponents of mind-body dualism. (Note: Throughout this book I will use the made-up term "macro-point" to give special emphasis to what I believe is a fundamental/critical point in understanding the nature and expansion of consciousness.) This dualistic fundamentalism of all things Western (including Philosophy, Theology, Canon Law, Civil Law, and even the understanding of the Cosmos[9]) continued for almost two thousand years, well into the Renaissance (c. 1300-1700); and only began to abate with the coming of the Scientific Revolution (c. 1550-1700).

The next major step in the evolvement of Dualism involved geographically moving the claimed transcendent nature from the soul to some claimed transcendent part of the brain. Perhaps the most well-known proponent regarding Dualism (certainly in the modern age) was Rene Descartes (1596-1650). Descartes was the first philosopher to coin the term "dualism". He developed what is now called Cartesian Dualism. Descartes' Dualism consisted of the material world of matter, which Descartes labeled "res extensa", and the immaterial world of human thoughts and emotions, which he labeled "res cogitans". Many scholars believe that Descartes was the first person to use the term "conscientia" (consciousness) to mean mental ideas of awareness. Prior to Descartes, conscientia had only referred to moral feelings such as when one speaks of having a guilty conscience or of doing something unconscionable.

Many scholars refer to Descartes as the "Father of Modern Philosophy". Descartes' most famous pronouncement is: "I think, therefore I am." This iconic sentence was first published by Descartes in 1637 in his "Discourse on the Method".[10] The great prominence of this sentence in philosophical circles is such that it has been awarded its own title: "The Cogito" from the Latin translation for Descartes' famous pronouncement: "Cogito ergo sum".[11]

Like his Ancient Greek forbearers, Descartes doubted the absolute certainty of any information coming from the senses; but Descartes is best known, not only for doubting sensory information, but for doubting the absolute veracity of most all mental thoughts. For example, Descartes argued that one could never know for sure that he was not dreaming or being controlled by an evil demon. For Descartes, the only proposition he could be certain of was "The Cogito". Descartes was certain he was thinking, so therefore he must exist. The absolute truth of all other mental thoughts was suspect.

Yet we can reasonably discern that Descartes was also "certain" of one additional fundamental and unassailable proposition. . . Church Doctrine on the existence of the eternal and transcendent individual soul. As such, Descartes' consciousness was already irrevocably filtered by a dualistic belief in the soul which Descartes did not even consider doubting. In Descartes' consciousness this Doctrine came from God; and as such, was beyond question.[12] Descartes was unshakable in his belief that the human soul was immaterial and immortal. For Descartes, the soul was part of the res cogitans just like the mind. Descartes' consciousness was such that it did not seem to have occurred to him to question Church Doctrine to the extreme degree (or to any degree) that he questioned both information from the senses and information from most thinking. Knowing this, perhaps we can understand in hindsight Descartes' unwavering defense of Dualism.

Descartes' life, accomplishments, and personality are so fascinating that it is well worth further reading on these topics.[13] Descartes' brilliance was not only in philosophy, but in Canon Law, optics, military engineering, anatomy, astronomy, helping to develop (what is now known as) the "scientific method", and especially in mathematics where he made several seminal developments in algebra and analytic geometry. Through his (new yet limited) knowledge of science, Descartes claimed to have discovered the specific location in the brain where material sensory input is converted into transcendent consciousness. He chose the pineal gland for this distinguished role.

There was actually some misplaced logic in this decision. Descartes chose the pineal gland because he concluded that it was the only anatomic portion of the brain located equally between the two hemispheres of the brain.

Knowing what we know today about brain anatomy, one would think that there would be few if any scholars who believe there is a particular part of the brain that converts material sensory data (such as vision, hearing, touch) into transcendent consciousness. However, although there are probably no current thinkers who believe in such a majestic role for the pineal gland, Cartesian Dualism remains alive and well and continues to this day.[14]

The often overwhelming emotional need to salvage Dualism is completely understandable. This is a macro-point in understanding the evolving cultural understanding of consciousness: The consequences of denying some transcendent (beyond the physical) aspect to our consciousness are just too high of an emotional price to pay within the consciousness of most people, especially as they face the inevitable trials of tragedy and mortality in this life. Consciously or non-consciously, such persons simply must cling to a belief in an eternal and transcendent connection beyond this earthly/material life. . . whether that connection be the heavenly afterlife of Western religions, reincarnation, or any number of so-called "New Age" and/or "Spiritual" beliefs.[15]

Monism. . . Theories in this category essentially hold that there is only one substance throughout reality. There is no individual transcendent "mind" or consciousness. There is no transcendent anything, because everything in reality is made from only one kind of material stuff. The numerous schools of thought within Monism vary greatly, and essentially involve disputes over the individual degree of free will. A small number of schools hold that there is no free will, and believe that individual human beings are essentially automatons/robots activated and motivated solely by evolutionary drives/needs. Many other schools see consciousness not as a static thing, but as a dynamic changing phenomenon. They see consciousness as real, but only as an experience. Still others (originally and largely in the Eastern cultures, but slowly and steadily increasing in the West) hold that the entire universe is all one big material consciousness from which all things in the universe emanate.[16]

The philosophers who subsequently challenged Dualism in favor of Monism are too numerous to include here, but let's take a look at the historically evolving thinking of a few key players. Although he did not use the term "Monism", one of the first highly regarded philosophers to specifically deny Cartesian Dualism and espouse Monism was Thomas Hobbes (1588-1679) who argued: Only matter exists. There is no mind as a mental substance. Thoughts are just motions of brain matter.[17] Quite an insight in those times especially given the power and influence of Christianity at that time.[18]

A paradigm shifting monist well worth studying in more detail on the nature of consciousness is William James (1842-1910) (also one of my personal deep thinking heroes). James was both a psychologist and a physician. He taught the first course in psychology in the U.S., and eventually received the moniker "Father of American Psychology". In 1904 James published "Does 'Consciousness' Exist?"[19] Like all good monists, James rejected Cartesian Dualism absolutely. James was adamant that "there is only one primal stuff or material in the world, a stuff of which everything is composed". But his more paradigm shifting insight into the understanding of the nature of consciousness was to describe consciousness as "pure experience". For James, consciousness was the experience of a process not an object. It is equally important to note that while James denied that consciousness existed as a material thing, he never denied the existence and reality of consciousness as a valid human experience.

The significance of this insight by James cannot be overstated in the historical evolution of understanding consciousness because it exploded the longstanding myth that consciousness was a static "entity" as opposed to a dynamic ever-changing "experience". James saw consciousness more like a verb than a noun. James wrote that he did not like to use the word "consciousness" in his writing or in his teaching, but he recognized that it would be harder to communicate if that word was totally eliminated. So (at least in Western culture) James coined the term "stream of consciousness" to use instead.[20] This is an excellent metaphor for explaining the nature of consciousness. You can think of a stream as a static entity such as in the sentence, "I will need to cross the stream to get into town." But you can also think of a stream as an ever-changing experience. You can stand by a stream, and watch as the stream ever flows and changes. If you put your foot into that flowing stream at two separate times, the stream where your foot enters will be different on each occasion. It is not a great leap to recognize that one's consciousness is also in constant flux.

A somewhat more modern British Philosopher, Gilbert Ryle (1900-1976), is often credited with putting the final nail in the coffin of Dualism. In a paper published in 1949 entitled "The Concept of Mind"[21], Ryle summarily dismissed Cartesian Dualism by describing the proposed transcendent mind as "the ghost in the machine". This phrase has since often been used by subsequent scholars belittling Dualism, and was even made more popular in 1993, when 20th Century Fox released the science fiction horror film "Ghost in the Machine".

Perhaps the most prolific and highly regarded of contemporary philosophers on the topic of consciousness is Daniel Dennett. To be sure, Dennett has many critics (some quite heavy-handed in their attacks); but to Dennett's impressive credit, it is rare to find a contemporary book on consciousness of academic quality that does not contain multiple references to Dennett's research and writings. In 1991, his 500 plus page tome entitled "Consciousness Explained" made the New York Times "Ten Best Books of the Year" list.[22] Dennett's book is often cited as a demolishing attack on Dualism, or what Dennett calls the "Cartesian Theatre Model of Consciousness".

Dennett provides a detailed neuroanatomic description of the human brain and central nervous system that definitely proves three macro-points regarding the nature of consciousness. First, (not surprisingly) there is no pineal gland nor any other part of the brain that transmits sensory data to claimed transcendent consciousness. There is zero evidence for any such dualistic claim. Second, there is no specific part of the brain that directs consciousness. There is no central theater of command, no homunculus, no brain boss or general directing the constantly changing emergence of consciousness. As we will explore in more detail later in this chapter and book, this is because consciousness emerges from numerous heterogeneous sources, not only throughout the brain, but from portions of the central nervous system remote from the brain. Finally, not only is an individual unable to completely direct consciousness, but an individual cannot even witness the emergence of all aspects of consciousness. This is in part because many critical aspects of consciousness operate below the level of conscious human awareness.

Admittedly, Dennett had a decided advantage over Descartes because Dennett is not only a philosopher, but a modern day cognitive scientist with a seemingly encyclopedic understanding of many of the academic fields related to the brain including: neuroanatomy, psychology, evolutionary science, linguistics, and genetics. Not surprisingly, Dennett was able to describe (in what some commentators call interminable detail) the massively complex assembly of "nonlinear" processing components throughout "separate" areas of the brain and central nervous system that "each" potentially contributes to a single conscious thought. Neither you as a person, nor any specific/singular part of your brain is in total control of your consciousness. Multiple, separate, distinct, and even unknowable contributions into individual human consciousness are so "heterogeneous" and without a completely "conscious" (awake, aware, and knowingly responsive) self-director that the Cartesian Theatre Model of consciousness is an anatomic impossibility.

Dennett's demolition of any belief in a single/independent director of either the human brain or human consciousness is indeed a key macro-point for understanding consciousness expansion. Yet (at least to me) perhaps a more intriguing and pertinent aspect of Dennett's attack on Cartesian Dualism is Dennett's concept (macro-point) of "Cartesian gravity", which he develops in his (much more non-scholar accessible) subsequent book on consciousness entitled "From Bacteria to Bach and Back"[23]. While it is not difficult for us so-called scientifically enlightened folks from the 21st century to claim we understand the neuroanatomic flaws in Cartesian Dualism, Dennett also warns us about the hidden and reality distorting force of "Cartesian gravity" which arises out of our egos.

Dennett explains how narcissism can create an almost existential anxiety in an individual and in a culture when there is some suggestion that a person is not an independent master (director) of their own consciousness. Dennett correctly observes that there seems to be something not only special, but something almost sacred about the concept of consciousness. Consciousness can be a topic where a person does not want to be told their understanding of self is being questioned. As Dennett points out, who doesn't feel like an "expert" regarding one's own consciousness? Even when a person can suppress their ego and is open to new ideas about the brain and consciousness, the compelling power of Cartesian gravity just keeps pulling that person back to the emotional safety net of Dualism. We want to believe we are in control.

At least to me, even more compelling than the power of narcissism that consciously and unconsciously distorts our emotions and beliefs about the nature of consciousness, is the power of "fear". The often overwhelming power of fear should never be underestimated. No doubt others before me have previously said the same or similar, but I have for decades used the following statement to empathize the awesome negative power of fear.

> The opposite of love is not hate.
> The opposite of love is fear.
> Fear closes consciousness.
> Love opens. . .

There are so many human fears regarding how we understand consciousness: fear that you are not in control; fear that your life has no meaning; fear that you are alone; fear that there is no God; and fear that you are not eternal. . . just to name a few. Each of these fears pulls us back into the need for some form of transcendent Dualism. That Dualism does not have to be a "religious" belief. It could be a so-called "spiritual" belief, a so-called "New Age" belief, or any belief in a transcendent idea of individual self. It is fear that generates the narcissism of a separate sense of self in control of consciousness. Another key macro-point that will be discussed in further chapters is: If you want to expand your consciousness, you must first fully recognize that the power of these fears can and often does overwhelm and effectively control a person's consciousness.

Dennett is most certainly a monist who believes all brain activity is of one material substance. Unfortunately, while Dennett does an impressive job of addressing the so-called "easy problems" of the neural mechanics of the brain, Dennett's explanation of the "hard problem" of explaining subjective human consciousness has caused some critics to suggest his book should be renamed "Consciousness Unexplained". This is because Dennett concludes that consciousness is nothing more than a "user illusion".

Dennett takes the term "user illusion" from computer jargon which describes what the user sees on the computer terminal as an "illusion" because the vast majority of computer users can't tell or don't care how the computer is using the numerous underlying programs to generate what is seen on the screen. For example, when you click with the mouse and words just appear or disappear from the screen, it is much more than your conscious finger clicking of the mouse that causes this magic.[24]

There is no doubt that Dennett has successfully used (what is currently called) modern science to expose the inappropriateness of the dualistic meta-phor "Cartesian Theater" for explaining how consciousness functions. There is doubt, however, that Dennett's metaphor of "user illusion" is a completely satisfying answer to the "hard problem". In fact, this is a criticism to which even Dennett agrees:

> My explanation of consciousness is far from complete. One might say it was just a beginning, but it *is* a beginning because it breaks the spell of the enchanted circle of ideas that made explaining consciousness seem impossible. . . All I have done, really, is to [trade] in the Theater, the Witness, the Central Meaner, the Figment, for [the metaphor of] Software. . . but metaphors are not just metaphors; metaphors are tools of thought. No one can think of consciousness without them,

so it is important to equip yourself with the best set of tools available.[25]

Dennett's claim that consciousness is an illusion is of course correct in the sense that consciousness is a result of many heterogeneous systems within the human brain and remote central nervous system which produce the "experience" of consciousness. So if you want to call consciousness an illusion, in that sense you can. However, while I recognize that I'm just splitting semantic hairs here, it's troubling that the term "illusion" implies consciousness does not exist. Perhaps I'm unknowingly being pulled down by Cartesian gravity, but I believe any understanding of consciousness must begin by acknowledging the reality of consciousness if only as an experience. We may not (yet) be able to explain where a particular experience of consciousness specifically comes from, nor will we ever be in complete control of that experience, yet who can deny that the experience is occurring in reality?

The never ending complexity/disputes regarding the nature of consciousness is aptly demonstrated by an insightful and pithy story that I particularly enjoyed from Dennett. It involves a joke he told on himself during a Feb. 2003 TED Talk entitled "The Illusion of Consciousness".[26] Dennett explained that when he goes to a party of "lay" persons and explains he is a professor, peoples' eyes glaze over. When he goes to an academic party of "professors" and explains he is a philosopher, peoples' eyes glaze over. But when he goes to a party of "philosophers" and explains his specialty is understanding consciousness, no one's eyes glaze over. Rather, their lips snarl in total derision because they know *consciousness can't be explained.* This amusing story indicates the need for our third general category of theories of consciousness . . . Mysterianism.

Mysterianism. . . . Theories in this category essentially hold that questions involving the cause, existence, and nature of consciousness are simply unanswerable. Mysterians speak of an "explanatory gap" between the physical properties of the brain and the subjective inner-world of personal consciousness. For Mysterians, asking a learned scholar or mystic to explain the hard problem is essentially like asking an otherwise very bright dog to explain the theory of relativity. Mysterians believe that the human

21

brain is simply not capable of understanding the specific nature of human consciousness, and so they dismiss all such analysis and discussion.

The Mysterians got their name in 1991 from an insightful book on consciousness by Owen Flanagan called "Science of the Mind".[27] Flanagan describes two types of Mysterians. There are the "Old Mysterians" who are dualists, and who believe that consciousness cannot be understood because it operates according to transcendent non-material principles. There are the "New Mysterians" who are monists who readily acknowledge that the conscious mind is nothing separate from the brain, but argue that the hard problem will always be a mystery.[28]

Flanagan points out that perhaps the most relevant argument of the New Mysterians against any unified understanding of consciousness is what we have been referring to as the "heterogeneity" of the conscious mental processes. After all, the New Mysterians are quite correct that consciousness emerges from such diverse experiences as: input from each of our five senses; numerous types of emotions which can often be conflicting in nature; planning; contemplation; and moods just to name a few. If you add to that: altered mental states through drugs, meditation, dreams, and psychotic states, you have what Flanagan readily admits is a "hodgepodge" of consciousness which is not yet possible to fully understand.[29]

As a child of the 60's, I got a kick out of the fact that Flanagan got the name "Mysterians" from the 60's rock group, Question Mark and the Mysterians.[30] As an adult in the 21st century, while I can sympathize with the frustration of the Mysterians, at least with regard to their valid concerns about the heterogeneous nature of consciousness, I am more than a bit disappointed that they have given up the battle of trying to understand consciousness without giving future scientists a chance to better understand the complex workings of the brain. As a writer, I'm envious of and totally agree with the turn of phrase Flanagan uses to dismiss the New Mysterians as "mischievous reactionaries [whose] main trick involves setting impossibly high standards on explanation and intelligibility that keep us from continuing to investigate and learn".[31]

Yes, comprehensive understanding of consciousness remains a mystery; but what this mystery really boils down to is "subjectivity" or what the scholars refer to as "qualia". Almost every scholarly publication on consciousness in the last couple of decades addresses in detail the phenomenon of qualia. At first, the word qualia sounds both exotic and esoteric; but qualia are simply "subjective" mental images that an individual forms in their brain regarding such things as the color green, the smell of a skunk, feeling depressed, or falling in love. Qualia are private to the individual, and cannot be accurately communicated to another person except by such things as metaphor. For example, how do you tell another person what the color red looks like to you? When complaining of pain to your doctor, the best you can do is describe where it hurts, how long it has hurt, and perhaps give a personal intensity rating on a scale of 1-10; but is your level 5 pain the same as your doctor's level 5 pain? You will never know, because there is an "explanatory gap" between how you experience the pain and how a third-person tries to understand your subjective feeling of pain. Determining exactly what subjective qualia are and how they are created from the objective brain and central nervous system is exactly what the hard problem entails.

Yes, the Mysterians are correct that scholars (and even mystics) have not (yet) completely solved the hard problem of human qualia, but impressive scientific leaps have recently occurred. For example, neuroevolutionary scientists have determined how consciousness emerged on earth in stages during evolution. These same scientists have also identified when the first elemental stage of consciousness occurred in animals. Other scholars have taken the first preliminary steps in identifying the specific "neuronal correlates of consciousness" in humans. . . in other words how qualia arise from electrical activity on the vast neural networks of the human brain. Let's take a brief look at both these impressive developments in the understanding of consciousness.

"Neuroevolutionary Science" is a term used by Todd Feinberg and Jon Mallatt in their groundbreaking book "*The Ancient Origins of Consciousness*".[32] These scholars combine recent discoveries in the academic fields of brain science, animal behavior, and evolution (especially analysis of ancient fossils) to discover how and when consciousness first appeared on Earth in the chain of evolution. Feinberg and Mallatt do not claim to have solved the hard problem of human consciousness. They do claim, however, to have determined when consciousness first appeared in animals. They show how consciousness developed in stages beginning during the "Cambrian Explosion" of animal diversity, which occurred c. 560-520 mya when all animal phyla came into existence. Not surprisingly, this is when evolution had progressed to the point where the first complex nervous systems and brains appeared in animals.

When discussing the potential influence of evolution/natural selection on consciousness, it is important to first stop and ponder the vastness of "time" involved. Most scientists agree that life began on earth four billion (that's billion with a "b") years ago! I freely admit that my consciousness is such that I am unable to comprehend that amount of time, but I do understand that billions (or even tens of millions) of years seem like a good long time for natural selection to work its seeming magic.

Feinberg and Mallatt are hard-core monists as revealed by their statement that "whenever consciousness begins, it depends on life and thus ends with the death of the brain".[33] They then begin their definition of "life" with the statement that all living organisms made of cells (including one-cell organisms) share the following distinct traits: use energy to sustain and organize themselves; are responsive to stimuli; have genes; reproduce; are "embodied" with a boundary with a distinct interior separate from external surroundings; are chemically complex enough to have emergent features; and have the potential to evolve by natural selection.[34]

Scholars are in agreement that the first organisms to meet Feinberg and Mallatt's criteria for "life" were one-celled bacteria and archeans.[35] Did such organisms have consciousness? Well that depends on how you define consciousness. Feinberg and Mallatt define (at least the beginning of) consciousness as existing when a living organism can create an inner-world of qualia. . . mental images of the external world as obtained through the senses.[36] While a single cell organism, such as an amoeba, can respond to its environment by distinguishing between edible and noxious food sources, light and dark, hot and cold, these are "reflex" responses which are not qualia because these reflex responses do not create an inner-subjective world. We know this from the fossil evidence which shows that the first microorganisms did not have the most rudimentary neuronal correlates (brain architecture) to create an inner-world.[37] Therefore, these first microorganisms did not have consciousness.

Feinberg and Mallatt determined that sufficient neuronal correlates of consciousness did not appear until billions of years later, sometime during the Cambrian Explosion. More important to our overview of consciousness, these initial neuronal correlates had only evolved to the extent sufficient to produce the initial evolutionary stage of consciousness which Feinberg and Mallatt call "mapped exteroceptive" consciousness. Other scholars (including Feinberg and Mallatt) also call this first stage: sensory consciousness, primary consciousness, phenomenal consciousness, or perceptual consciousness.[38]

Mapped exteroceptive consciousness gets its name because the inner-world or qualia created by this first consciousness comes from outside (extero) the organism, and is more of a mapping of sensory input from "distance receptors" in the organism such as smell, taste, vision, and touch. This evolutionary development allowed the organism to react, flourish, and survive natural selection. Feinberg and Mallatt declare this to be first stage of consciousness because an "inner-world" and not just a reflex response is created in the organism from the outside sensory input; although this inner-world of rudimentary qualia was no doubt initially fleeting and completely without any response in the animal that we would understand as emotional.

(It should be noted that the evolutionary advancement of consciousness during hundreds of millions of years of evolution was not linear nor stairstep. It advanced differently through different animal phyla; and as occurs during evolution, some stage developments were sustained, some further evolved, while others did not survive natural selection and/or natural disasters. For example, at least seven human-like species evolved from the "hominid" (great apes) family. In addition to our species of homo sapien, there were: homo heidelbergenis, homo rudelfensis, homo abilis, homo floresiensis, homo erectus, and homo neanderthals.)

According to Feinberg and Mallatt, the second evolutionary stage in evolving sensory consciousness occurred as the number and type of neural receptors in the organism allowed for the emergence of something like "feelings" of pain and chemical changes associated with hunger. This was now "interoceptive" consciousness because the qualia are coming (in part) from biological processes "within" the organism/animal. Feinberg and Mallatt describe this interceptive process as adding "affective valence" (forming a mental representation of what is being perceived) to the qualia.[39]

The third evolutionary stage in sensory consciousness occurred with the evolution of the limbic system of the brain, a complex network associated with very basic and primal emotions and drives such as pleasure, hunger, sex, and dominance. The internal-world of the animal now had what Feinberg and Mallatt describe as "affective" consciousness. The animal had conscious awareness of its emotions and drives.[40]

Feinberg and Mallatt do not claim to completely understand the eventual (modern day) inner-world of the human brain. . . or what could be termed "higher" consciousness which has such features as meta-awareness (awareness of being aware), thoughts about the self, and thoughts about thoughts.[41] However, Feinberg and Mallatt offer some intriguing theories on the primary causes of this further evolution of consciousness. In particular, they suggest the evolution of the "predator" put tremendous evolutionary pressure on the prey species to adapt or perish. These adaptations of prey species in turn pushed the predator species into a reciprocal arms-race to evolve in strategies and behavior.[42] Yet even more critical to the evolution of higher consciousness may have been the neural correlates of "memory", which play such a critical role in survival strategies based on experience.[43]

"The Quest for Consciousness" by Christof Koch takes us to the next step in our investigation of consciousness by exploring the latest data on how the human brain physically works.[44] In the Forward to Koch's book, Francis Crick (co-discoverer of the structure of DNA) describes consciousness as "the major unsolved problem in biology". Koch takes on the challenge of attempting to solve this problem by investigating and trying to discover the minimal neural mechanisms jointly sufficient to generate a conscious perception, which Koch

calls the "neuronal correlates of consciousness" or "NCC". Koch asks, "How do qualia arise from the electrical activity of the vast neural networks of the brain?" This, of course, is the hard problem put in scientific terms. How do the 100 billion nerve cells called neurons interact through the electrochemical process of synaptic transmission to create qualia?

Koch and his colleagues have made some remarkable discoveries regarding the NCC for visual stimuli in mammals. But can Koch identify the particular NCC for how a person decides what to have for dessert, or how a person perceives the particular pangs of love or depression? No, at least not yet. Koch can, however, show us some important recent insights into the general process of the NCC, which are helpful in understanding consciousness expansion, and which we will now consider.

The human brain is quite complex... of that there is no doubt. With its 100 billion neurons and thousands of kilometers of synaptic connections, commentators have often described the human brain as "the most complicated object in the universe". As we learned from Dennett, multiple complex assemblies throughout the human brain as well as from the central nervous system remote from the brain all contribute to conscious thought through interconnections and influence on each other. In Chapter Five we will go into more detail on the brain anatomy of consciousness; but for now, let's briefly consider just three areas of the human brain particularly relevant to consciousness: the brain stem, the limbic system, and the cerebral cortex. These three areas are associated with three evolutionary stages of the human brain. Non-scholars sometimes metaphorically refer to these stages as the emergence of the gut, the heart, and the head. It is fascinating to note how long ago these brain aspects began to emerge, and even more fascinating to understand that these ancient evolutionary developments still influence our consciousness so many millions of years later.

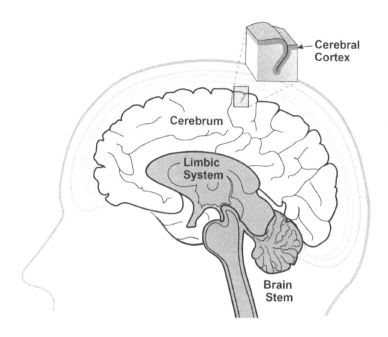

The *brain stem* is the oldest and innermost part of the brain. It is the junction of the top of the spinal cord and the rest of the brain. The brain stem is also referred to by scholars and non-scholars as the hindbrain, the central core, and as the "reptile" brain. Although this type of brain first evolved in fish c. 500 mya, it reached its full evolution in reptiles c. 250 mya. . . hence the name.[45] The reptilian brain not only controls non-conscious bodily functions such as breathing and temperature, but works with the amygdala (not part of the brain stem) for primitive flight or fight survival instincts such as fear and aggression. It is an important macro-point for anyone on the difficult path of consciousness expansion to know and remember that these primitive instincts remain part of our modern day consciousness 250 million years later!

The *limbic system* first evolved in small mammals about 150 mya, and brought with it both emotions and value judgments.[46] For those treading the path of consciousness expansion, it is important to know and remember that the power of emotions can both consciously and non-consciously influence our judgment and behavior. More on this in Chapter Four.

The *cerebral cortex*, which evolved "only" 2-3 mya, could be considered the most important part of the human brain. It is the most highly evolved part of the brain, and essentially what makes us human because it is responsible for the higher thought processes. It is only 1.5 to 5 mm thick, and lays like a spongey, wrinkled, gray blanket on the top of the brain. The cerebral cortex is densely packed with neurons. A neuron is a specialized, electrically excitable cell that both receives and sends information through electrical and chemical signals. Koch describes neurons as "the atoms of perception, memory, thought, and action".[47] Neurons are connected to each other by synapses. A neuron never works alone. Rather, it functions in the brain through a neuronal network sometimes referred to as a "coalition" of neurons. Koch explains that each coalition has specialized neurons designed for different aspects of perception including highly specific "feature detectors" for such things as orientation, motion, faces, etc. These coalitions have a loose hierarchal organization, with the lower coalitions subordinate to the higher coalitions. . . each sending information from their specialty.[48]

According to Koch, the sensory coalition systems in the brain can handle an almost infinite variety of images, sounds, smells, etc. When sensory information comes into the neuronal coalitions, often that information is insufficient to lead to an unambiguous interpretation of the data. Koch describes how neuronal coalitions then "fill in" their interpretation of the data with their best guesses, and the brain then seems to "jump to a conclusion" about the significance of the data. This process then involves the firing of neurons in the forebrain which produces spikes or action potentials that contribute to decision making. (Warning: My grossly oversimplified description of how the neuronal correlates of consciousness function may inaccurately make this process sound linear, or that the neurons in the forebrain are some type of a director of consciousness. As we will see, neither is correct.)

This process of decision making is both fascinating and quite revealing regarding the potentially inexact and misleading nature of consciousness. Koch explains how the temporary coalitions of neurons coded for particular events or objects compete against one another. A particular coalition eventually emerges victorious based on the strength of its firing activity. Rightly or wrongly, the winner is now the current content of consciousness! Koch explains that this battle for consciousness continues until the winning coalition fatigues, adapts, is superseded by a novel input, or is vanquished by a new victor.[49] Koch suggests the metaphor of a parliament to describe such decision making, but warns that the metaphor of consciousness as a political process must not be mistaken for a mechanistic model.[50]

It is important to understand how the omnipresent power of evolution comes into play during the NCC process. It's no surprise to learn from Koch that evolution provides a strong selective advantage to rapid reaction in decision making. Better rapid, intellectually wrong, and alive than pensive and eaten by a larger carnivore. As awesome as the brain is, conscious thought can be surprisingly slow. According to Koch, components of the brain involved in "switching" consciousness can occur at speeds a million times slower than transistors. Accordingly, evolution has a multi-parallel method for reaching a conscious decision. In simplified terms, this involves relying on detecting common correlations with prior experiences, and almost automatically reacting in a previously established pattern. Again, better wrong and alive than right and dead. This can result in essentially wise decisions such as slowing your car down without any deep thought or conscious awareness just because part of your consciousness has sensed the traffic light has turned yellow. This process can also result in a racist decision such as automatically and without "thinking" walking to the other side of the street due to an approaching person of another race. It's not difficult to appreciate that an awareness of and reflection about this rapid and habit based brain function is absolutely essential for consciousness expansion.

Perhaps an even more critical insight essential for understanding consciousness is an understanding of the power and scope of the "unconscious".[51] It should now come as no surprise that the terminology and concepts regarding the nature of "unconsciousness" are in as much dispute among scholars as the nature of consciousness itself.[52] All of us have heard the terms "unconscious", "subconscious", and "preconscious" which (even among scholars) are often (somewhat incorrectly) used interchangeably to mean ideas, desires, memories, etc. that are present in the brain but are not immediately accessible to consciousness even though they cause significant influence on our thoughts, beliefs, emotions, and actions. These "nonconscious" phenomena are of such importance in the understanding of consciousness that they are featured in Chapter Four of this book. But let's begin by learning from Koch on this topic.

Koch prefers the term "nonconscious" instead of the term "unconscious". This is largely because such nonconscious neurobiologic processes are not only present in the brain, but also present in the central nervous system remote from the brain. Moreover, the term "unconscious" comes with the semantic baggage of also referring to a person being knocked out or in a coma, which has nothing to do with our inquiry into the nature of consciousness and consciousness expansion. So this book will use the term "non-conscious" (artificially hyphenated for emphasis) to include the following three phenomena: the psychological "Freudian" understanding of the unconscious; the "habit formed quick responses" of our brain which we just explored; and the "reflex" input both from the brain and the central nervous system which we will now take a quick look at.

Koch uses an entertaining metaphor of "zombie agents" to explain the vast amount of reflex activity that occurs in everyday life without our conscious awareness.[53] Koch gives the example of jerking your hand away from a hot burner "before" you consciously feel the heat. Koch explains how this zombie action is not because you have consciously felt pain, and in fact is not even a "brain" activity. Rather it is a spinal reflex which has been scientifically reproduced even in decapitated animals.[54] We each have numerous zombie actions throughout our day which are not consciously under our control.

The macro-points of our overview of the current understanding of brain function regarding human consciousness are as follows: There is no neuroanatomic support for Dualism. There is no part of the human brain that converts matter into immaterial and transcendent consciousness. There isn't even a particular part of the brain that specifically directs or controls thoughts, emotions, or actions. Our thoughts, emotions, and actions come from at least three primary sources: non-conscious (Freudian) forces; a somewhat non-conscious quasi-parliamentary decision system with multiple data input from such things as our reptile brain and often incorrect value judgments (prejudices) learned by various neighborhood coalitions of neurons through past experience; and non-conscious zombie agents. Bottom line. . . you are not and never will be in total control of your consciousness!

The scholarly work in beginning to understand both the evolutionary development of consciousness and the neuronal correlates of consciousness is impressive. Although there is still much more research to do, scholars have made great progress in responding to the ultrahigh standards raised by the Mysterians. Yet given what we learned from Dennett about Cartesian gravity, as well as our discussion about the power of fear, it is perhaps not surprising that we find so many "Way Out There" theories on consciousness. All such theories seem to be grasping to justify something/anything eternal or transcendent about our individual consciousness.

Way Out There. . . As you might guess from my title for this final category of theories on consciousness, these are theories that at first blush do not seem to merit serious consideration. While it may be entertaining to review some of the extreme theories such as Scientology with its beliefs in thetans, engrams, cellular memory, and dianetic reverie, that is not the purpose of this book.[55]

Our so called "New Age" is rife with theories on consciousness most of us would politely describe as crazy stuff. Yet let's stop and observe an accomplished scientist like Dr. Robert Lanza[56] who has used his considerable knowledge of quantum mechanics, neurobiology, and astrophysics to postulate his new theory of "biocentrism". The fundamental holding of biocentrism is that consciousness is not a byproduct of reality. Rather, consciousness creates reality. Sounds a little way out there; but if I dismiss biocentrism, am I a modern day flat-earther because I refuse to open my consciousness to this possibility? Perhaps Dr. Lanza is the next Galileo or William James eventually guiding the rest of us slackers onto the next paradigm of understanding consciousness. Even though I place biocentrism in the category of Way Out There, who am I to judge? So let's take a look at biocentrism.

In 2009, Dr. Lanza published "Biocentrism. . .How Life and Consciousness are the Keys to Understanding the True Nature of the Universe".[57] This book was lauded by mystics such as Deepak Chopra, and by scholars such as Nobel Prize winner E. Donnall Thomas. While, in general, I don't accept Dr. Lanza's "Principles" of biocentrism, there are three reasons why biocentrism will be considered in this chapter. The first reason is that taking the time to listen to, think about, and try to understand someone or something with which you don't agree is a tried and true technique for consciousness expansion. This is because it pushes you outside of your individual consciousness box. Second, biocentrism is a prime example of a Way Out There theory of consciousness, and so considering biocentrism in detail is a good way to complete a chapter entitled "An Overview of the Hard Problem". Third, the most interesting argument for biocentrism involves "quantum theory"; and in particular why matter/energy does not always behave as expected. Variations on this "quantum phenomena argument" seem to be at the heart of so many New Age theories on consciousness (and New Age "spiritual" practices) that a careful look now may be helpful in future investigations of New Age theories you might undertake. So let's look at the key specifics of biocentrism.

Lanza presents a three-part presentation in defense of his theory of biocentrism:[58]

1. The scientifically accepted underlying worldview of how consciousness came into being (the Big Bang Theory) is fundamentally flawed.

2. Quantum theory is a wake-up call for questioning what we think we know about reality.

3. The missing component is biocentrism (life consciousness) because life consciousness creates reality.

1) The accepted underlying worldview of almost all scientists is the Big Bang. Lanza summarizes the Big Bang in an essentially accurate but overly simplified, reductionist, and intentionally pejorative way as. . . lifeless particles that attract and repel each other, obeying predetermined and set laws of physics, which eventually through randomness produce consciousness. Lanza does not expand on what he means by "consciousness" other than to equate consciousness with "subjective experience" which is a fair enough definition; but as we have learned, a rather limited definition of consciousness.

Biocentrism holds an almost opposite understanding of the origin of the universe from the Big Bang. It does not deny that a Big Bang may have occurred. It simply states that the randomness of the universe could not eventually create consciousness on its own. Therefore, the reverse must be true: An eternal consciousness created the universe, including the Big Bang, assuming a Big Bang occurred. Randomness had nothing to do with it.

Lanza's initial dismissal of the potential creative power of randomness is surprisingly disappointing in substance:

> . . . who in their right mind would say that it was all conjured by imbecilic billiard balls slamming each other by the laws of chance? No observant person would be able to utter such a thing, which is why it always strikes me as slightly amazing that any scientist can aver, with a straight face, that they stand there at the lectern – a conscious, functioning organism with trillions of perfectly functioning parts – as the sole result of falling dice.[59]

Lanza provides no rebuttal nor even any discussion of the work of neuroevolutionary scientists like Feinberg and Mallatt. Moreover, Lanza ignores the potential effects of the more than 13 billion (again, that's billion with a "b") years that his "imbecilic billiard balls" have had to "slam" around and evolve. Lanza seems to dismiss any such scholarly investigation by an overreaching statement in the extreme:

> As for how consciousness could arise in the first place, no one even has guesses. We cannot fathom how lumps of carbon, drops of water, or atoms of insensate hydrogen ever came together and acquired a sense of smell. The issue is apparently

too baffling to raise at all. Merely to bring up the topic of the origin of perception is to brand oneself a kook.[60]

Lanza's next argument regarding the undeserved sacredness of the Big Bang Theory is to correctly point out how little scientists actually know about an exceptionally vast part of the universe. Lanza correctly states that everything in the universe that has form, plus all known energies, constitute only 4% of the universe. The remaining 96% of the universe consists of 24% dark matter, of which we know precious little, and 72% dark energy, which is an utter mystery.[61] The implication intended by Lanza is that scientists don't know enough to have confidence in their Big Bang belief that the universe was created by randomness. This is a curious argument since, like most of Lanza's arguments, it implies Lanza himself does know enough about astrophysics, evolutionary biology, and every other intellectual area of inquiry to "know" that random universal action over 12 billion plus years "cannot" possibly create conscious life or any life. This argument by Lanza also fails for the same reason Flanagan dismisses the New Mysterians. . . Lanza is a provocateur (albeit a highly educated and interesting one) who's main trick involves setting impossibly high standards on explanation that keep us from continuing to investigate and learn.

Lanza's next argument against Big Bang/randomness is that the currently known laws of physics are exquisitely balanced to allow life/consciousness to exist as we know it; and with even the tiniest change, life as we know it would not exist. Lanza writes:

> . . . if the Big Bang had been one-part-in-a-million more powerful, it would have rushed out too fast for galaxies and life to develop. If the strong nuclear force were decreased 2 percent, atomic nuclei wouldn't hold together, and plain-vanilla hydrogen would be the only kind of atom in the universe. If the gravitational force were decreased by a hair, stars (including the Sun) would not ignite.[62]

The implication here is that there must be something special behind a design so perfectly suited to life as we know it. Such an argument is of course repackaged "Intelligent Design", which argues that some force such as the Christian God must have created the universe. To his credit Lanza admits that he may be suspected of this, but then Lanza simply summarily dismisses (ignores) this discussion by stating that whether God is or isn't the original designer is irrelevant to biocentrism.[63] Lanza then simply replaces "God" with his own "biocentrism".

Not sure what I'm missing in Lanza's argument that an "exquisitely balanced" universe must have intelligence behind it, whether that intelligence is God or consciousness. My admittedly untrained response is: Why does it require pre-existing intelligence? Doesn't any existing universe need to be exquisitely balanced; i.e. perfectly suited, in order for it to exist? If a universe wasn't perfectly suited for its own existence, it wouldn't exist. At least for me, it's just as reasonable (if not more reasonable) to postulate an eternal and always existing universe as it is to postulate an eternal and always existing transcendent creator, whether that creator be God or consciousness. Yet who knows for sure?

2) *Quantum theory* and the legitimate and fascinating questions it raises are Lanza's next argument supporting biocentrism. Quantum theory is essentially the theoretical explanation of the behavior of matter and energy at the atomic and sub atomic levels.[64] Lanza presents a scientific yet readily understandable explanation of three key and perplexing phenomena in quantum theory: quantum entanglement; complementarity; and wave-function collapse. His fascinating presentation is well worth reading (much more so in his more accessible second book "Beyond Biocentrism").[65] Any one of these three phenomena is well worth learning about since such consideration quite readily lifts most people out of their customary consciousness box of how they understand the world. The claim by Lanza that quantum theory is a wake-up call for questioning what we think we know is absolutely correct. The three phenomena in quantum theory that Lanza raises are not new,[66] but are nonetheless still intriguing. However, his conclusion that biocentrism explains these phenomena is simply not supported by Lanza. Let's look

at the three phenomena: quantum entanglement, complementarity, and wave-function collapse.

"Quantum entanglement" is a phenomenon that can occur when "entangled" particles are created by firing a laser beam through a crystal to split an individual photon into a pair of entangled photons. When such particles are then separated by large geographic distances (even hundreds of kilometers) actions performed on the first split-particle affects the geographically remote second split-particle. "Complementarity" basically holds that you can't know both position and speed of a quantum particle at the same time. "Wave-function collapse" arises out of the reality that certain quantum particles such as photons can behave like both a wave and a particle; but what is emphasized by Lanza (as well as by many "New Agers") is the famous "double slit experiment" which showed that mere observation of the particles can affect whether the photons behave as waves or particles. This became known as wave-function collapse.

3) Lanza's biocentrism argues that these quantum phenomena prove that space, time, location, and even existence are never certain; and that mere "observation" (the consciousness of an observer) plays an indivisible role in the phenomena. From this Lanza makes the giant leap to conclude that consciousness creates reality a/k/a biocentrism. Fascinating, but hardly convincing. Again, my response to Lanza would be the same as Flanagan's response to the New Mysterians. While Lanza raises some intriguing issues, he is yet another "mischievous reactionary [who's] main trick involves setting impossibly high standards on explanation and intelligibility that keep us from continuing to investigate and learn".

Summary Macro-Points on the Hard Problem. . . The purpose of this chapter was simply to provide a meaningful introduction/overview regarding the longstanding and still unresolved dispute over the hard problems of understanding the nature of consciousness. As stated at the beginning of this chapter, it is not essential to answer the hard problem in order to attempt to expand one's consciousness. So what have we learned from our overview of the history and disputes over the nature of consciousness?

We learned that after thousands of years of debate, there is still no agreed upon answer to the hard problem of consciousness. We learned from the Ancient Greeks that our consciousness can be fooled by our senses. We learned that some form of Dualism has prevailed in human culture since the Stone Age; that Dualism arises out of belief in some transcendent and eternal human spirit/soul; and that Dualism was a fundamental (if not commanding) part of Western culture, which only began to be questioned with the coming of the Scientific Revolution. We learned about the development of Monism which became the scientific norm, especially after the cultural acceptance of evolution.

In more contemporary times, we learned from James that consciousness should be thought of as a dynamic experience rather than a static thing. We learned from Dennett that there is no homunculus nor general within the brain that directs consciousness, much less converts matter into transcendent Dualism. We also learned from Dennett that, despite all our newly acquired scientific knowledge about both evolution and neuroanatomy, the power of Cartesian gravity to suck us back to Dualism can be overwhelming. We learned how the often overwhelming power of fear can keep us clinging to some type of Dualism under the guise of organized religion or so-called New Age thinking. We learned from Flanagan that, although there are multiple and complex heterogeneous aspects to consciousness, we shouldn't give up looking for answers just because there are yet unsolved mysteries. We learned from Feinberg and Mallatt how and when sensory consciousness first evolved into existence; and at least theoretically, how sensory consciousness further evolved into higher consciousness. We learned from Koch about the developing scientific discoveries regarding the neuronal correlates of consciousness, the way our consciousness works like a quasi-parliament with all its strengths and weaknesses, and about the vastly unappreciated power of the non-conscious. Finally, we learned from Lanza that there is still so much we don't know about reality, and that maybe we need to keep an open mind.

My working definition of individual human consciousness is just as suggested in the first page of this chapter: the degree to which you are aware of and knowingly responsive to your internal and external environment.

One might argue that my two-part "working" definition of consciousness goes beyond the common understanding of consciousness when it includes "action" rather than just observation/thinking/awareness. While that argument may be semantically correct, I believe our "working" definition of consciousness must include action in order to be operational in the real world. What good is merely observing/thinking/being aware if you are unable to "knowingly" act due to any of the many heterogeneous forces that affect your consciousness? As we will see in further chapters, expanding one's consciousness requires more than mere observation and thoughtful reflection. It involves interaction with the world. That being said, we now recognize both the challenge and the irony that a vast amount of the input into our consciousness is not only beyond our control, but unknowable.

For what it is worth, I am a Monist. I don't (currently) believe human consciousness is transcendent. I (currently) believe that consciousness is a dynamic experience that results from multiple heterogeneous systems within the human brain and remote central nervous system. I suppose you could also call me an "Optimistic Monist" because I believe (especially after learning from scientists like Koch) that science will eventually find the neuronal correlates of consciousness. But an important macro-point is that, even if I was a Dualist, Mysterian, or Way Out There, it makes no difference regarding my desire and ability to expand my consciousness. As will be discussed in the next chapter, expansion of consciousness is needed, not only to better know ourselves, but also to better communicate and interact with your spouse, children, boss, co-worker, enemy, or friend. The scope of your consciousness affects your perception, your emotions, and your actions. You don't have to be on a search for the meaning of life to want to improve your understanding of yourself, others, and the world. You just need to understand and accept how critical expanded consciousness is to navigating the world in which you live. Machiavellian motivation alone should be reason enough to want to expand your consciousness; and if you end up becoming a better person in the process, so much the better.

---

1 As will be further explained later in this book, I use the singular form of the word "environment" instead of the plural form due to the inseparable yin/yang nature of a person's internal/external environment.

2 Examples of the various schools and theories on consciousness include the following: absolute monism, access consciousness, anomalous monism, anti-constructive naturalism, attributive monism, behaviorism, biocentrism, biological naturalism, Cartesian dualism, cognitive neuroscience, computationalism, conscious inessentialism, eleatic monism, eliminativism, emergentism, empiricism, epistemological relativism, epiphenomenalism, computational functionalism, hard monism, idealism, identity theory, interpretation information theory, intentionality, interactionism, materialism, mind-body dualism, monism, mysterianism, mysticism, nativism, naturalistic dualism, neurobiological naturalism, neural Darwinism, neurophilosophy, neutral monism, new mystery anism, non-reductive materialism, numerical monism, orchestrated objective reduction theory, panpsychism, parallelism, personality identity theory, phenomenal consciousness, phenomenology, physicalism, primary consciousness, priority monism, property dualism, quantum-mind theory, reductionism, reflective consciousness, reflexive monism, revisionary materialism, solipsism, substance dualism, substantial monism, teleological functionalism, and theory of the mind.

3 Although this dispute now called the "hard problem" has existed for millennia, David Chalmers coined the term "hard problem" in 1995 in "Facing Up to the Problem of Consciousness" published in the *Journal of Consciousness Studies* 2(3); 200-19, 1995. This paper can be easily found online by searching "Chalmers the Hard Problem". Chalmers correctly points out that "there is nothing that we know more intimately than conscious experience, but there is nothing that is harder to explain". Chalmers states there are two major problem areas in understanding consciousness. There are the "easy problems" which involve discovering and explaining the neural mechanisms of the brain. There is the "hard problem" of explaining why each individual person has his/her own "subjective" experience of such things as the color red, the sound of a clarinet, and the smell of mothballs.

4 Just to complicate matters further, please know that there are theories that inconsistently seem to combine Dualism and Monism; but not to worry, this complicates matters not regarding the key premises of this book.

5 Although he was not the first scholar to use the term animism, English Anthropologist, Sir Edward Burnette Tylor (1832-1917) is universally credited with bringing the term into scholarly anthropology in his book "Primitive Culture".

6 For those readers with a religious/faith belief in an eternal soul, it is important to make the point here that belief in a transcendent "soul" does not automatically make you a dualist. Soul and consciousness are not necessarily the same thing, even though they could be; and even though most people may non-reflectively assume the two to be the same or at least closely related. This issue will become more apparent as we explore the historical understanding of consciousness.

7 There was significant and often confusing debate among Ancient Greek philosophers on dualistic subjects such as the nature and function of the soul. Even the writings of leading philosophers such as Plato (428-348 BCE) appear to be self-contradictory. For example, Plato's conceptualization of the soul in "Phaedo" seems to be in contradiction to his conceptualization in the "Republic". See , "Ancient Theories of Soul" from the highly regarded online Stanford Encyclopedia of Philosophy, first published 10-23-03, but continuously revised.

8 Another informative and lay-accessible source on these topics is: "Ancient Greek Philosophy" from the online internet Encyclopedia of Philosophy.

9 See Margaret Wertheim's "Phthagoras' Trousers. . . God, Physics, and the Gender Wars" for her historical analysis on the evolving understanding of the Cosmos in Western culture. W.W. Norton & Company, New York 1997.

10 The complete title of this work is actually "Discourse on the Method of Rightly Conducting the Reason and Seeking Truth in the Sciences", although it is typically now referred to as "Discourse on the Method". Search that brief title online for numerous sites setting out this extensive paper as well as numerous commentaries.

11 This iconic phrase was first published in French as "as je pense, donc je suis", and later translated into Latin to reach a larger audience.

12 It should come as no surprise that Dualism is deeply rooted in Christian tradition. Recall that the Old Testament speaks of the Creator God forming man out of clay of the ground, and then blowing the "breadth of life" into that material body to create a living being. Genesis 2:7 While the New Testament has the Son of God proclaiming in a loud voice, into your hands I commend my "spirit". Luke 23:46.

13 You can get a quick but interesting summary of Descartes' life online at "Descartes Stanford Encyclopedia of Philosophy". Hatfield, Gary, "Rene-Descartes", The Stanford Encyclopedia of Philosophy (Summer 2016 Edition), Edward N. Zalta (ed.), URL=https://plato.stanford.edu/archives/sum2016/entries/descartes/7.

14 It is interesting to note the relatively recent and continuing interest by some in what is known as the "cortical homunculus" or "little person inside the brain" that supposedly perceives and makes decisions. For an entertaining discussion of the "homunculus fallacy" see "The Quest for Consciousness – A Neurobiological Approach" by Christof Koch; Roberts and Company Publishers; Englewood, Colorado (2004). Here and after "Koch". Koch at p. 298-299. You can also find online Christopher Babcock's article in Psychology Today entitled, "Come Back Hommunculus – All is Forgiven!"

15 Advancements in science, and in particular advancements in neuroanatomy have created theological (or at least semantic) challenges for belief in a transcendent and immortal soul for the various Christian sects. From both a religious and an emotional point of view, it is easy to understand why a Christian wants to preserve a belief in the transcendent human soul, while still being open to the continuous and developing understanding of the neuroanatomy of human consciousness, which has increasingly disproved Dualism, especially in recent decades with developments in brain scanning. Various Christian sects have handled this challenge differently. . . some remaining with Dualism, while others accept Monism while reconceptualizing their faith belief in the transcendent soul as not being the same as individual transcendental consciousness. This book takes no position on this issue other than to say its resolution is not a prerequisite to consciousness expansion.

16 Although it is correct that Dualism monopolized Western thought and culture well into the 17th century, Monism also has its ancient roots in Western philosophy. Scholars point to Parmenides of Elea (c. 500 BCE. . . dates regarding his birth and death vary widely, but all agree he lived pre-Socrates). The only writing that survives Parmenides are fragments from one poem known as "On Nature". From these fragments most scholars have agreed that Parmenides was a monist who taught that all that exists is being; and being is one, unchanging, and eternal. If you are interested in getting deep into the weeds regarding the types of Monism, simply search online for "Parmenides Monism", and have at it.

17 The term "Monism" was first used by the German philosopher, Christian von Wolff (1679-1754). Hobbes' position on Dualism can perhaps best be found in Part 1 "Of Man" in his book Leviathan.

18 It is perhaps interesting to note that Hobbes' extreme position against Cartesian Dualism and in favor of Monism did not prevent Hobbes from believing in the eternal human soul. See Chapter

XXXVIII "Of the Signification in Scripture of Eternal Life, Hell, Salvation, the World to Come, and Redemption" from the book "Levinthan" by Thomas Hobbes which can be found on the internet at ebooks.adelaide.edu.au. Although I have not done an exhaustive search of Hobbes' writings, I have not found any such writings where Hobbes addresses the potential intellectual conflict between Monism and an eternal soul.

19 A PDF of William James "Does 'Consciousness' Exist?" first published in 1904 can easily be found online.

20 It is interesting to note that Mahayana Buddhism described consciousness as a "stream of water" more than a thousand years before this paradigm shifting metaphor occurred to James. See, "Transformation at the Base" by Thich Nhat Hanh, Parallax Press, Berkeley, CA 2001 at Footnote 2, p85.

21 Ryle, Gilbert, The Concept of Mind (1949); University of Chicago Press, Chicago, 2002, p11. The full text can be found online at archive.org.

22 "Consciousness Explained" (1991) by Daniel C. Dennett, Back Bay Books/Little, Brown and Company, New York, NY. Here and after "ConEx".

23 A PDF of "From Bacteria to Bach and Back: The Evolution of Minds" by Daniel Dennett (2018) is available online.

24 ConEx at p216.

25 ConEx at p455.

26 This TED Talk can easily be found online.

27 "The Science of the Mind" by Owen Flanagan (1991), MIT Press p313. Here and after "Flanagan".

28 The most referenced New Mysterians are Thomas Nagel and Colin McGinn. Nagel's most referenced publication is "What is it like to be a bat?" See "the Philosophical Review" October 1974. McGinn has several lectures/interviews that can be easily accessed on YouTube.

29 Flanagan at p361.

30 Flanagan at p313.

31 Flanagan at p365.

32 "The Ancient Origins of Consciousness" by Todd E. Feinberg and Jon M. Mallatt; (2016) MIT Press, Cambridge, Massachusetts. Here and after "F&M".

33 F&M at p17.

34 F&M at p18.

35 Archbacteria or archeans are basically bacteria type micro organisms with different aspects to their chemical structure.

36 F&M at pviii, p130.

37 F&M at p13.

38 F&M at pp130-131.

39 F&M at p130-138. For an interesting scholarly article on valence, see, "Micro-valences: perceiving affective valence in everyday objects" by Sophie Lebrecht et al; Frontiers in Psychology; Volume 3, Article 107, April 2012.

40 F&M at pp138-147.

41 F&M at p215.

42 F&M at pp62-63.

43 F&M at pp114-115, 124, 215-217.

44 See footnote 14 for citation.

45 See "The Brain from Top to Bottom" online at thebrain.mcgill.ca.

46 Id.

47 Koch at p22.

48 Koch at pp22-25.

49 Koch at pp47-48.

50 Koch at p25.

51 The term "unconscious" was first introduced by German philosopher, Friedrich Wilhelm Joseph von Schelling (1775-1854). The term was subsequently introduced into English by English poet and philosopher, Samuel Taylor Coleridge (1772-1834). But it was Austrian neurologist and founder of psychoanalysis, Sigmund Freud (1856-1939), who truly popularized the term in the field of psychology.

52 Although scholars contend that the term "subconscious" was first introduced by French psychologist, Pierre Janet (1859-1947), it's common usage more likely began years later when Austrian neurologist, Sigmund Freud, began using the term "subconscious" interchangeably with the term "unconscious" even though these words in German have a slightly different emphasis. According to scholar, Michael Craig Miller, M.D., Freud soon stopped using the term "subconscious" to avoid confusion. Nonetheless, the cat was out of the bag, and these two terms are still today (somewhat incorrectly) used interchangeably, much more so by lay persons. See "Unconscious or Subconscious?" by Michael Craig Miller, M.D., which can be found online at Harvard Health Blog (2010 updated 2016).

53 Koch at p213.

54 Koch at p213.

55 Conduct an online search of "Scientology Theory of Consciousness", and you'll have more to read than you ever wanted.

56 Robert Lanza, M.D. has been described as one of the world's leading scientists. In 2014, Time Magazine described Lanza as one of its 100 most influential people. While his knowledge of physics, neurobiology, and basically all things science is impressive. He is best known as a leading stem cell pioneer. Lanza was also part of a team that cloned the world's first early stage human embryo.

57 "Biocentrism" by Robert Lanza, M.D.; BenBella Books, (2009). (Here and after "Biocentrism".) Also see Lanza's much better presented second book "Beyond Biocentrism" BenBella Books (2016). (Here and after "Beyond Biocentrism".)

58 I apologize in advance to Dr. Lanza for any reductionist errors in my summary/analysis of biocentrism.

59 Biocentrism at p45.

60 Beyond Biocentrism p3.

61 Biocentrism at p6.

62 Biocentrism at p7.

63 Biocentrism at p83.

64 Another benefit of reading Lanza is his clear and excellent summary of the history of Quantum Theory as well as its current key issues.

65 Quantum Theory has been around since the early 20th century. Quantum Theory essentially involves how matter and energy behave at the atomic and sub atomic levels. Einstein is considered the founder of Quantum Theory by describing aspects of light as "quanta" and for which he received the Nobel Prize in 1921. Max Plank (1858-1947) was the first scholar to create a mathematical equation involving units of energy called "quanta" for which he received the Nobel Prize in 1918.

66 Lanza correctly acknowledges that Quantum Theory has been around for more than a century. Moreover, as previously noted earlier in this chapter, Eastern cultures have posited for millennia that the entire material universe is of one consciousness.

CHAPTER TWO

(Individual Receptacles of Consciousness)

Quidquid Recipitur
Ad Modum Receipentis Recipitur.
(A receiver receives like a receptacle receives.)
—Thomas Aquinas

Now that we have worked through some of the heavy-duty aspects of consciousness, let's take a quick detour with a lighter story.

One of the more entertaining ways to expand your consciousness is to have a real "character" come into your life; and in 1972-1973 that character came into my life in the person of Monsignor Pierre Riches (1927-2019). I was fortunate enough to be able to spend my junior undergraduate year at a university in Rome, and even more fortunate to (randomly) take a class in theological studies from Riches.

To call Riches a "character" is like calling the Titanic a boat. He was born into a wealthy Jewish family in Alexandria, Egypt; and apparently, not only had the fierce intellect of an Augustine, but also many of Augustine's earlier corporeal proclivities as well.[1] A number of Riches' early life adventures are referenced in at least two books[2] where he is described as the Jewish dandy turned Catholic priest who dined with royalty and played footsie with Robert Mapplethorpe.[3]

Like Augustine, Riches was drawn to the intellectual, metaphysics, and theology. He studied Philosophy at Cambridge and was a pupil of the great philosopher, Ludwig Wittgenstein. At the age of 23, Riches converted to the faith of the Church of Rome when, like Augustine, he was baptized in Milan; but unlike Augustine, Riches never lost his remarkable zest for living life in his own peculiar way. He interacted with America's "Beat Generation" of the 1950s, becoming close friends with writer and visual artist, William Burroughs, as well as musician, Lou Reed. He mastered many languages; and he taught in Japan, Pakistan, Uganda, the United States, and in Europe. He was an "expert" advisor to Cardinal Tisserant at the Second Vatican Council. Riches also insisted on conducting part of his ministry in less traditional ways such as working with AIDS patients in Africa; serving as an airport Chaplin at Leonardo da Vinci Airport in Rome; and (to my great benefit) teaching a class to the students at the American school in Rome even though those students were much more interested in drinking beer and ditching class to backpack around Europe rather than listening to this brilliant man wax eloquent on theological issues.

I have two distinct memories of Riches from that year. The first is simply a very mild example of why Riches was such a character. The second is the origin of the title of this chapter, and probably the original inspiration for this book more than four decades ago.

The first memory occurred during the last week of the first semester of Riches' class. We were only a few days away from the start of a four week semester break, and the only thing we students were thinking about was how we were going to travel around Europe during those four weeks rather than about the lecture. It didn't take Riches long to read the distraction and disinterest on our faces during his lecture. He stopped his lecture, commented on the mood of the room; and then added the following surprising challenge that went something like this: "None of you want to be here listening to my lecture. You would all rather be down the street at the trattoria drinking beer, listening to your music, and talking about your travel plans. If any of you had any chutzpah, you'd pick me up, throw me over your shoulder, carry me down the street to the trattoria, and buy me a beer."

At first we sat dumfounded; but fortunately, Kevin McDevitt had the chutzpah (or whatever the Irish version of chutzpah is) needed for the task. He strutted to the front of the class, hefted Riches over his shoulder, and carried him down the street with the entire class following behind in celebration of our unexpected good fortune.

The second memory occurred at the end of the second semester, and the last time any of us would see Riches again (other than for our final exam the next day). Of course, none of us had the consciousness at that time to appreciate what a gift it had been to study with Riches, and what a loss it would be for us not to be able to study (or drink or laugh) with him again.[4]

So on that day, Riches ended his lecture a bit early; and he invited us to ask him a question. It could be any question on any topic; but he was only going to answer one question, so he warned us to make it a good one.

We students then caucused, and the first obvious temptation was to ask him a very personal question about his openly far from pedestrian lifestyle. But somehow (without knowing anything about the Buddha in those days) we managed to follow the Buddha's advice that, if you have an opportunity to ask a wise man a question, make it a good one.

So one of the students asked our one question, "What is the most important thing/truth you have ever learned?" Riches thought for a moment (and you could tell he was pleased with the question); and then said, "Without exception, the most important truth I ever learned was a saying from Thomas Aquinas[5] who said:

"Quidquid recipitur ad modum receipentis recipitur."

Riches went on to state that the translation of this Latin was "a receiver receives like a receptacle receives".[6] Riches explained that this was a metaphor where the "receiver" is a person, and the "receptacle" is a person's consciousness. He stated that consciousness is like a jar. It may be a one liter jar or a two liter jar, but at any given point in time a person's consciousness has a fixed capacity just like a jar; and if you have a one liter jar, no matter how hard you try or how slowly you pour, you cannot pour two liters of liquid into that one liter jar. The excess liquid will simply spill out of the jar never to be held within. In simple terms, there is no such thing as an absolutely "objective" receiver. All information is received, processed, and acted upon (in other words "filtered") through the limited receptacle of our consciousness.

At that time, this seemed like a lame explanation, and most of us (including me) were wishing we had asked the personal question. Then at least we would have something to gossip and/or laugh about.

It was then that I raised my hand and made a comment to Riches. I no longer remember exactly what I said, but it was some challenge to Riches' claim that this was the most important truth that he had ever learned. But what I do remember, vividly, (because it really hurt my ego) was Riches responding. "David, you are a clever young man, but you're not wise. Don't take this as an insult. Cleverness is not a bad thing. It can get you quite a long way in this world, and I am sure you will go far. But you are not yet wise. Maybe someday you will be wise, or maybe you will never be wise."

Riches then went on to explain that both understanding and accepting the truth of this simple statement by Aquinas was a mandatory prerequisite for understanding yourself, for being able to really communicate with others, and for having any hope of spiritual growth. (They didn't use the term "consciousness raising" in those days, but that was what Riches was talking about.)

Unfortunately, by that time I had stopped listening. I had closed my mind (my consciousness) to nurse my ego wound. I did, however, manage to memorize at least part of this Latin phrase, which for me was quite a surprising achievement. Those who know me, know that while one of my absolute favorite activities is studying foreign languages, let's just say that I have not yet manifested the ability to easily master languages.[7] Way back in high school, the only reason I was able to pass Latin was that I played on the school hockey team; and the Latin teacher, Big Bill Sheridan, was also my hockey coach. I played left wing, which somehow magically resulted in a passing grade in Latin. Yet such is the power of the wounded ego that I was instantly able to memorize the partial Latin phrase "quidquid recipitur" probably hoping to someday prove Riches wrong.

It wasn't until years later that I realized Riches was right. This simple statement by Aquinas was indeed an important truth about life. I'm certainly not qualified to register an opinion on whether it is the "most" important truth as claimed by Riches; but I have come to understand and appreciate the many deep teachings contained within Aquinas' metaphor. There are both practical teachings for we so-called "clever" ones who hope to successfully navigate the world, as well as spiritual (consciousness raising) teachings for those who hope to someday become "wise".

You might well ask. . . if this axiom is so important, why have you never heard of it? According to the scholar, John Tomarchio, Aquinas used this axiom throughout his career, in all his major works, and throughout his metaphysics.[8] Tomarchio further states that this axiom has been readily accepted by all subsequent scholars. But as important as Aquinas, Riches, and subsequent scholars claim this axiom to be, according to Tomarchio, it has received little commentary or thematic study by subsequent scholars. Tomarchio seems to suggest that this lack of scholastic attention is not a knock on the fundamental importance of this axiom; but rather, an acceptance of this axiom "as a piece of philosophical common sense".

We've all heard someone say the following, and probably we've even said it ourselves, "I don't talk politics or religion with my friends." Why might someone say this, especially when politics and religion are such important topics? It is because we know from our common sense experience, not only how difficult it can be to change another's mind on a political or religious issue, but that even engaging in such a discussion can cause friends to enter into a stressful and sometimes hurtful argument. It's near impossible and equally frustrating to argue with a person who has a closed consciousness. . . and even more so since we now understand that our own consciousness is also closed, even though we are absolutely sure we have the correct (expanded) understanding and solution to the particular dispute.

Yes, "quidquid recipitur. . ." is essentially based on common sense. Even the most uneducated cannot dispute the fact that you cannot pour more than one liter of a liquid into a one liter jar. And even the so-called "educated" understand (at least theoretically and when you explain it to them) that a person receives information, reasons with that information, and takes action regarding that information from a consciousness receptacle that is both created and restricted through the filters of that person's genetics, culture, education, and experience. But do we really appreciate and take advantage of this fundamental truth in our daily lives?

The incredible and limiting power of the filters to each person's individual receptacle is a topic that will be fully discussed in Chapter Four of this book. But for now, there are three macro-points that we need to begin to consider.

First (from a somewhat self-serving and parochial perspective), although "quidquid recipitur" may be but a piece of common sense; if you want to be a better communicator (whether it be to your spouse, children, boss, co-worker, enemy, or friend) you had better first take into account the reality and power of this axiom. You must try as best you can through the limitations of your own receptacle to understand the other person's receptacle, and then phrase your words and take your actions accordingly. Otherwise, for example, you are doomed to argue in vain when you try to explain to your five year old child the benefits of going to bed before 9 pm. Or on a much more serious note, you will never convince the citizens of Baghdad of the claimed benefits of Western democracy while those citizens are being killed in their streets and mosques. They simply won't hear your otherwise well-reasoned arguments. Even more troubling, (whether "they" are your five year old child or citizens of Baghdad) their consciousness receptacles may too often misinterpret your intended "helpful" advice as an attack, and respond with anger or worse.

Second (and hopefully from a deeper and more altruistic perspective), expansion of consciousness allows a person to see and interact with the world and yourself in a more authentic plane of awareness and existence. You become less and less a prisoner of your genetics, culture, habits, and fears; and you begin to access a world which could be described as a lightness of being. A helpful metaphor to appreciate the vast qualitative difference between the two worlds of limited and expanded consciousness might be to consider the difference between being "set adrift" versus being "in the flow".

Drift is defined as random oscillation from a fixed position or mode of behavior.[9] Being adrift involves lack of control, being carried by currents of wind, water, social pressure, or genetics in a random direction you neither choose nor understand. One drifts apart from family, friends, and the joie de vivre (joy of living) which is too often due to lack of understanding and perceived loss of control. A limited consciousness is akin to driftwood, floating debris, flotsam… hardly a desirable state.

Flow on the other hand is defined as proceeding smoothly, gently, steadily, easily, and gracefully with an unbroken continuity as in the manner of a fluid.[10] Flow implies abundance as in the related term, overflowing. When a person feels "in the flow" (such as Michael Jordan driving the lane for his 50th points in the game) there is a seemingly effortless, satisfying, symbiotic relationship between the person and the particular life interaction(s). Such is the deeper reward of expanded consciousness.

Third, despite both the practical and deeper promises of expanded consciousness, a person must always recognize that, no matter how "expanded" your consciousness becomes, it always resides in its own limited receptacle. If you are fortunate enough to expand your own receptacle of consciousness, then that consciousness now resides in a larger receptacle, but it is still a limited receptacle nonetheless. Expanding your consciousness is a never ending phenomenon. There is always more more work to do.

---

1 Augustine of Hippo (354-430) is one of the most significant "fathers" of Christianity. Even as a youth, his intellectual brilliance and rhetorical skills were obvious to all who encountered him. However, during a time in his youth, Augustine left the church for a life devoted to hedonism. It was during this time that Augustine wrote one of the more entertaining prayers, "Lord, grant me chastity and continence, but not yet." Following his subsequent re-conversion to Christianity, Augustine not only became a profound influence on the medieval worldview, but a continuing influence on both Christian and general philosophical thought. His writings include apologetic works on the many "heresies" during the early and formative years of Christianity; commentaries on both the Old and New Testament; and treatises on concepts such as love, free will, theodicy, and time itself.

2 "The Sun at Midday: Tales of a Mediterranean Family" by Gini Alhadeff. Anchor Books, 1997 and "Our Paris: Sketches from Memory" by Edmund White. Harper Collins, 1994

3 Robert Mapplethorpe (1946-1989) was an American photographer, who's often erotic works gave rise to a national debate regarding public funding of controversial works of art.

4 In 2016, after considerable effort and investigation, I was fortunate to track down and visit with Riches one last time. By then he was quite fragile, confined to a wheelchair, and living in semi-seclusion along the Tiber River about a two hour drive from Rome. His caretaker and longtime friend prepared an expansive and tasty lunch of which Riches could only partake of a few bites. Riches insisted he remembered me from decades prior, which was wonderful to hear, but tenderly untrue. We spent the afternoon sitting together on his balcony, looking out over a tributary of the Tiber, and (at his request) singing old American songs. I shall always treasure that day. Later, I emailed photos of that day to a website shared with my classmates from 1972-73. I was not surprised by the number of warm remembrances that were posted, but I was surprised at how many classmates posted phrases such as "changed my life" with which I could strongly relate.

5 Thomas Aquinas (1225-1274) is another giant of Christianity. Many Catholic scholars have described him as the greatest theologian of the Catholic Church. After Augustine, Aquinas is the second most referenced theologian in official Catholic catechism. Thomas' most influential (yet never finished work) is "Summa Theologiae", which has influenced scholars of numerous specialties even through present day. Pertinent to our discussion of consciousness, in 2008, theoretical neuroscientist, Walter Freeman, published an article in the journal "Mind and Matter" 6(2):207-234 entitled "Nonlinear Brain Dynamics and Intention According to Aquinas" which can be found online by Googling the title.

6 This translation by Riches is not technically correct. The most commonly accepted translation is "whatever is received is received according to the mode of the receiver". This accepted translation is further supported by the manner in which Aquinas uses this axiom throughout his writings. Either translation results in the same point for purposes of this book.

7 I should probably just speak plainly and state that I suck at learning other languages. Some people can sing, and some can't. Some people can learn other languages, and some can't. But one of the very few superstitions I fall prey to is that "thoughts held in mind follow in kind". So in the hope that I might someday become fluent in another language, I prefer to phrase my linguistic challenges in a more hopeful manner.

8 Dr. John Tomarchio is a professor at St. John's College in Annapolis, and published the following abstract online: "Computer linguistics and Philosophical Interpretation" by John Tomarchio, 2006.

9 This definition and examples are largely from one of my favorite online dictionaries. . . yourdictionary.com.

10 *Id.*

CHAPTER THREE

ARE THERE RECOGNIZED "LEVELS OF CONSCIOUSNESS?
(The Psychosocial and The Transpersonal)

No problem can be solved from the same
level of consciousness that created it.
—Albert Einstein

The goal of consciousness expansion is to increase the size of our consciousness receptacle in a meaningful way. By "meaningful" I mean a quantum expansion,[1] a paradigm shift,[2] in the size/scope of our individual consciousness receptacle. In other words, expanding our consciousness to another "level" so that we actually see and relate to the world and ourselves as if from a different dimension. . . new values, new realities. . . a more authentic plain of awareness and existence.

No doubt we have all achieved what might be called "mini-bursts" of conscious awareness from time to time. A typical example of this might occur when we have unintentionally hurt a loved one. Of course, a person's consciousness may be so limited that they are oblivious to the hurt, and even less to your causing the hurt; but in most people, there will be a mini-burst of conscious awareness when we realize that our consciousness was such that we misread the situation and unintentionally hurt someone we care about. Unfortunately for me, such mini-bursts too often occur after I have already acted like a horse's ass. I suppose I could console myself by recognizing that I at least had a mini-burst after causing the problem, but wouldn't it be so much better if I could expand my consciousness receptacle to a new level so in the future I could handle such situations with more skillful means?

An often used yet excellent example of a mini-burst can be found in a story told in various iterations by many ministers and teachers. It is worth repeating.[3]

Mr. Williams was commuting home from work on the train. It had been a long and stressful day. He was tired. The Transportation Authority had recently disallowed alcoholic beverages on the train, which eliminated his customary coping mechanism. All he wanted was a quiet and peaceful commute home.

Shortly into the commute, two children approximately five or six years old began to behave loudly and obnoxiously. This not only disturbed Mr. Williams, but everyone else in the train car. The situation became further exacerbated, not only by the fact that the disturbance was increasing in intensity, but because the father of the children just sat there doing absolutely nothing about it.

Mr. Williams could feel impatience and anger welling up inside him, but his consciousness was such that he recognized this and held back taking any action. He could stand the noise if he had to. After all, he was a father himself, and knew his kids were no angels. But it was the inaction of the father of the two boys that eventually became too much for Mr. Williams to handle. How dare this man allow his children to disturb all these people on the train!

So against his better judgment and totally out of character, Mr. Williams got up and walked down the aisle to confront the father by calling him out on his failure to control his children. The father then looked up and into Mr. Williams' eyes. Instantly Mr. Williams could see and read the profound sadness on the man's face which became even more apparent when the man said, "I'm so so sorry. My wife passed away last month, and I just haven't been able to discipline my kids as I should. I'm so sorry." As you might expect, Mr. Williams' righteous indignation immediately gave way to profound guilt as he became "conscious" of what was really behind the situation. He had a mini-burst of conscious awareness. Mr. Williams was able to see and assess a situation from a different perspective than moments earlier; but there was no paradigm shifting expansion of his consciousness receptacle.

While these mini-bursts are likely a positive sign that one is a caring person, what we are really searching for and trying to achieve in consciousness expansion is more than a mini-burst. We want a quantum change, a paradigm shift, a bigger consciousness receptacle, a new "level" of consciousness. But are there such "levels" of consciousness? Are there levels that once reached establish a larger conscious receptacle? How does a person know that they have reached a new level? Once reaching a new level, can one revert back to a lower level? Can a person be on multiple levels at the same time? Is there a strict sequence of levels that each person must follow? Finally, just how difficult is it to expand one's consciousness to a new level? Let's take a look at "levels" to try and answer these questions.

After looking at the complexity of "consciousness" in Chapter One, it should not surprise you that numerous scholars and mystics as well as an even greater number of wannabe sages have proposed numerous different systems for levels of consciousness. Moreover, the term "levels of consciousness" has a number of different contexts not all related to the purpose of this book. In order to simplify our overview of levels of consciousness, I have focused and divided the major systems for levels of consciousness into six categories: Medical, Evolutionary, Altered States, Freudian, Psychosocial, and Transpersonal.

The first category of "Medical" levels of consciousness is not directly related to our investigation, and is simply mentioned here for academic completeness. "LOC" is common medical shorthand for level of consciousness. It is found in medical evaluation techniques such as the Glasgow Coma Scale which uses visual, verbal, and motor responses to determine the LOC of a patient from the level of fully awake down to the level of deep coma or death.[4]

The second category of "Evolutionary" levels of consciousness is simply an historical chronology of the major/quantum changes in the levels of consciousness as they evolved in the animal kingdom over billions of years. As discussed in Chapter One, scholars Feinberg and Mallatt postulate the first three such levels as: Mapped Exteroceptive, Introceptive, and Affective Consciousness. So called "higher" levels of Evolutionary consciousness would include "Meta-Awareness" which involves such features as awareness of being aware, thoughts about the self, and thoughts about thoughts. Meta-Awareness is the current evolutionary consciousness level of humankind. Although, as we will see later in this chapter, there are scholars, mystics, and many more wannabe sages who not only claim that the next Evolutionary level of consciousness will be a "Transpersonal" experience of cosmic oneness; but also claim to have already achieved such cosmic consciousness, at least in transient spurts.

__The third category__ of "Altered States" of consciousness is a fascinating topic which we will very briefly touch on here, revisit later in this chapter when we examine Transpersonal levels, and then revisit again in Chapter Eight when we examine the benefits of meditation. Altered States of consciousness involve an induced change in one's baseline level of consciousness through interventions such as hypnosis, alcohol intoxication, drug intoxication, meditation, and even common sleep during which processes such as dreaming occur. These altered levels of consciousness are often referred to as "states" as opposed to "levels" of consciousness since the vast majority of the time they are temporary, and the person almost always returns to their baseline "level" of consciousness after the altered state of consciousness is completed.

A number of scholars and mystics recommend "inducement" into an altered state as a tool for consciousness expansion. Altered States can provide a person with a temporary window of time through which to view the world and yourself from a different perspective while not being as trapped/filtered by forces such as our ego, our culture, or matters we are sure are "facts". While there is no doubt that an altered perspective via an altered state can become a valuable tool to increase consciousness, this does not mean that observations made in the altered state are helpful or even remotely true. For example, does the sublime experience of cosmic oneness that a number of scholars and mystics claim to have felt during advanced meditation or on an LSD trip really mean that a grain of sand, a bird, and a human being all share one consciousness? On a more mundane perspective, does the too often ignoble experience of alcohol intoxication really mean it is a good idea to leave your spouse and run off with your new found "soulmate" sitting next to you at the bar? An altered state by definition provides a different perspective on the world, but whether that altered state reveals a more authentic plain of existence, a new "level" of consciousness, is up for debate.

Altered States are still a relatively new topic of investigation in the scientific community, and for a somewhat older yet excellent summary/analysis of this topic I refer you to "States of Consciousness" by Charles T. Tart, PhD.[5] Tart argues that the term "discrete" states of consciousness should be used rather than the general term of "altered" states of consciousness to allow for the specific differences found under different types of inducements into a discrete state.[6] Tart then examines how each discrete state can alter such things as one's memory, emotional energy, the subconscious, sense of time, and personal identity[7], which are all key factors in the complex construction of consciousness.

The fourth category of "Freudian" levels of consciousness has to do with what Sigmund Freud called the three levels of awareness: conscious, preconscious, and unconscious. (While these three levels were first postulated by Freud, calling them "Freudian" levels is my label not his.) In simple/general terms: "conscious" involves current awareness of thoughts, emotions, and actions. "Preconscious" involves latent awareness that can be somewhat easily brought back into conscious awareness. One example of the preconscious is kinaesthetic awareness. As you walk down a cobblestone street, you constantly make kinaesthetic judgments/decisions on balance of which you are not aware/conscious. Yet you could easily bring such balance decisions into awareness, and will likely do so if the cobblestones become more difficult to traverse. Another preconscious example could involve a person unaware that they are biting their fingernails because they are nervous. "Unconscious" involves thoughts and emotions that cannot be brought back into conscious awareness, except perhaps by psychotherapy. (As noted in Chapter One, the term "subconscious" can further confuse these three Freudian levels when it is both used and misused as a synonym for preconscious and/or unconscious.) These three "Freudian" levels are absolutely valid phenomena, but they are not the levels of consciousness expansion we are primarily concerned with in this chapter.

The fifth category of "Psychosocial" levels of consciousness is the category where scholars agree that increasing levels of consciousness expansion definitely occur. This category has historically been both the most studied category of the scholastic community as well as the common cultural belief of Western society (predominantly Europe and the U.S.). In the scholarly literature, this category is more commonly referred to as "Cognitive" or "Developmental" levels because it involves the study of how phenomena such as personality, mental ability, and maturing brain structure develop in stages as an individual ages. But I prefer the term "Psychosocial" for this category because it more completely describes the two indivisible yin/yang parts of consciousness…the inner world of internal stimuli (psychological) and the outer world of external stimuli (social).

This category is almost exclusively the province of scholars rather than mystics. We will take a brief exploration of four of the most historically significant and compelling scholars: Sigmund Freud (1856-1939); Jean Piaget (1896-1980); Abraham Maslow (1908-1970); and Erik Erikson (1902-1994). It would not be possible (nor the purpose of this book) to discuss in detail the extensive work of each of these scholars. Rather, we will focus on particular biographic and paradigm changing aspects of each scholar. As in Chapter One, I purposely include biographic data on each scholar to demonstrate how some of our most renowned thinkers came to their beliefs; and perhaps more pertinent, how and why these paradigm shifting beliefs changed over time. Citational references are offered for your further investigation of detail.

It should be noted that the term "consciousness" is not often used in the early history of this field of study. Rather, terms like "mental-development" and "awareness" and "knowledge" are used; but since these terms are each essential aspects of the more complex phenomena of consciousness, there is still much to learn from these scholars. The same is true of the term "levels". At least initially, the original scholars in this field preferred the terms "steps" or "stages". Then Maslow (but even more so, commentators on Maslow) brought the term "levels" into the common parlance of this topic.[8] As we will see when we look at the sixth category of Transpersonal, a scholar named Ken Wilbur brilliantly but frustratingly complicated in the extreme the semantics of this area of scholastic inquiry by distinguishing among the terms: levels, states, waves, lines, structures, and phenomenal aspects on consciousness. But never fear, we will walk through this maze of jargon together and glean the macro-point teachings.

Sigmund Freud (1856-1939) was the principle pioneer in developing stages of the human psychological/social development which became known as Freud's Stages of Psychosexual Development. Many of us have heard/read that Freud postulated that the human psyche is composed of three interacting parts/forces: the id, the ego, and the super-ego. According to Freud, the id is the unconscious and instinctive component which operates impulsively to gratify largely sexual desires. (Think "reptilian" brain as discussed in Chapter One.) The ego is the personality or sense of self. While the super-ego, which is both unconscious and conscious, incorporates societal morals and mores. (Think of your super-ego as your inner parent telling you how to behave.) All act together to produce how an individual evaluates and responds to both internal and external stimuli.

Freud postulated five stages of psychosexual development:

Oral	Ages 0-1
Anal	Ages 1-3
Phallic	Ages 3-6
Latent	Ages 6-puberty
Genital	Ages puberty-death

Details about these stages can easily be found online; but the pertinent point to consciousness expansion is that Freud believed that it was critical for normal development to pass through each stage successfully and completely before a person could successfully engage the next stage. Each stage brought certain challenges (largely sexual/pleasure seeking) that needed to be overcome. If not, a "fixation" would occur stunting a person's psychological development to forces from that stage. For example, being fixated at the Oral stage would result in that adult person developing destructive oral practices such as excessive eating or drinking. And if you think this theory couldn't get any more frightening, Freud also felt strongly that this psychosexual energy essentially formed an individual's personality (consciousness) by age five.

One cannot help but take a few moments of silent compassion for those parents who for generations obsessed over the particulars of potty-training less their child develop psychotic tendencies. Fortunately, Freud's stages of psychosexual development did not withstand the challenges by subsequent scholars. In addition to criticizing Freud's overemphasis on sexual energy, the following valid criticisms were made: Freud's theory was not scientifically nor even empirically tested, much less verified. There was no controlled observation of children at different ages over time. Rather, the vast majority of Freud's data was from recollections of adult males undergoing psycho-analysis by Freud. Hardly a representative sample of the human population (although I have many female friends who could offer numerous, valid, and personal anecdotal stories to the contrary).

Nonetheless, Freud established several macro-points about the stages/levels of psychological development that have not only stood the test of time, but are essential to understand if there is any hope of consciousness expansion. These macro-points are:

1. Personality/consciousness develops in stages.

2. The components of personality/consciousness are multifactorial, and include such powerful forces as primitive drives (which we now know as reptilian), repressed beliefs/forces in the unconscious, and cultural influences.

3. An individual's personality/consciousness can become fixated, and can only be subsequently expanded with great commitment and effort.

More about these Freudian macro-points in Chapter Four.

Jean Piaget (1896-1980) developed the Four Stages of Cognitive Development:

Sensorimotor	Birth through 18-24 months
Preoperational	18-24 months through age 7
Concrete Operational	Age 7 to 12
Formal Operational	Adolescence through Adulthood

According to Piaget, each of these stages represents a significant and new cognitive development in a deeper and more complex understanding of the world...in my words, an expansion of consciousness to a new level. Piaget acknowledged that different individuals may pass through these stages at different rates, and that an individual may display characteristics of more than one stage at a given time. However, Piaget insisted that no stage may be skipped, and that all cognitive development follows this sequence of stages.

(This book won't go into detail on the specifics of Piaget's stages, because they are largely pre-adolescent; but for a readable and more detailed analysis see "Piaget's Theory of Intellectual Development" 2nd Edition by Herbert Ginsburg and Sylvia Opper,[9] which also provides insightful and succinct bibliographical data on Piaget. Many excellent summaries of Piaget's stages can also easily be found online.)

Piaget is well recognized by scholars as a seminal giant in the field of childhood cognitive development. From the 1920s well past the 1950s, Piaget was considered "the" child psychologist in the eyes of Europe and the United States. He authored more than forty books and hundreds of articles on this subject. He helped create the Center for Genetic Epistemology at Geneva University which brought together from around the world leading scholars in diverse fields of biology, psychology, mathematics, and others to share their research and insights into cognitive development. (An interesting factoid is that in the early forties, Albert Einstein specifically suggested to Piaget that Piaget investigate a child's understanding of time, velocity and movement which resulted in Piaget publishing two books on the subject.)[10]

Piaget's paradigm shifting insight was that children are not mini-adults as previously believed. Their cognitive development is not a "quantitative" process of more information being learned over time. Rather there is a profound "qualitative" process in how children in different stages of cognitive development view the world. A child simply cannot help but think differently than an adult. An example of this (only too well known by parents of two-year-olds) is that a young child can only view the world through egocentric eyes. It is only as a child moves through the sequential stages of cognitive growth that their moral compass includes social empathy.

So how did Piaget reach this paradigm-shifting insight? Of course Piaget's publications were the result of extensive scientific study, but it is fascinating how this flame was lit. . . how Piaget's consciousness was expanded. In 1920, one of Piaget's first jobs was working at the Albert Binet Laboratory in Paris evaluating results of standardized tests to measure a child's intelligence. The purpose of the test was to judge the level of intelligence by the number of correct answers. In scoring these tests, Piaget noticed that children in a particular age range tended to have the same type of wrong answers to the same questions. This caused Piaget to question whether older children were not just "brighter" than younger children; but rather, whether children of different ages just processed the world differently. Perhaps more importantly, it caused Piaget to question the very nature of intelligence. Piaget concluded that an older child with more correct answers on the test was not automatically more intelligent than a younger child with fewer correct answers. Again, the two just processed the world differently.[11]

Two of Piaget's subsequent insights are also helpful in our study of how to expand our consciousness receptacle: 1) the types of intelligence; 2) and the causes for the expansion of intelligence.

Prior to Piaget, there were few formal tests of intelligence. There was the Binet-Simon I.Q. test and a few scattered memory tests which equated intelligence with rote memory. From his work with children, Piaget rejected both these types of tests. For Piaget, there were not only stages of development in intelligence, but different types of intelligence. It's interesting to note that this second belief in different types of intelligence is currently (and correctly) all the rage in the popular understanding of intelligence. One person may be a master of rocket science yet lack the social intelligence to make a friend, while another person may have the musical intelligence to play six instruments yet lack the mathematical intelligence to understand square roots. Search online "types of intelligence", and you'll find types of intelligence such as: musical, visual-spatial, verbal-linguistic, logical-mathematical, body-kinesthetic, interpersonal, and intrapersonal. When we stop to think about the many kinds of intelligence, we realize that our own empirical observations confirm this truth. Yet to this day (and even though there are now many scholarly books on multiple types of intelligence), the vast number of our schools do not consider this reality in formulating their curriculum. Most schools are one size fits all.

Piaget was one of the first to recognize this truth about multiple types of intelligence. He also presented new metaphors for describing a particular intelligence. For Piaget, intelligence is equated with intellectual "competence" in a particular aspect of life. He taught that each type of intelligence was an "instrument" to interact within a particular aspect of the world. (Later in this chapter will learn that each of these "instruments" is better referred to as a "line" of consciousness.) This to me is a macro-point in understanding the most fundamental function of consciousness. I would simply restate it as: Consciousness is an instrument to more authentically interact with both yourself and the world.

Piaget's understanding on the causes of how intelligence (consciousness) evolves is also instructive. With his Ph.D. in natural sciences, Piaget certainly acknowledged that individual intelligence was a function of brain anatomy and genetics. He also acknowledged the importance of social factors such as parental and peer interaction. These two primary/major causes come as no surprise to us, but it came as an intriguing surprise to me that Piaget was adamant that a third critical factor must be included: activity.

Piaget focused on both mental and physical activity. For Piaget, knowledge is not automatically given to the passive observer. Knowledge of reality (consciousness) must be discovered and constructed by the "activity" of the child.[12] The child sees others standing and walking, and then actively experiments until she can do the same, all the while developing the kinetic knowledge of balance, motion and strength. This genetic compulsion for a child to learn by trying to copy other children, especially older siblings, is well known to observing parents and grandparents.

Piaget also wrote about the role of emotion in the development of intelligence. Although Piaget did not spend much time investigating emotion, he often stated that "no act of intelligence is complete without emotions". For Piaget, emotion is the energetic or motivational aspect of intellectual activity[13]. We will further explore the inexorable tie between emotions and consciousness expansion in the next chapter.

Let's complete our brief overview of Piaget with his optimistic teaching that the expansion of intelligence does not have to abate nor even deteriorate with old age. In 1968 Piaget wrote how intellectual functioning can improve even in old age as a direct result of proper use of intellectual skills and practices.[14] We will examine more current thinking on this topic in Chapter Five "The Promise of Brain Plasticity".

Abraham Maslow (1908-1970) is still the scholar best known to the current public regarding "levels" of consciousness. In his "Hierarchy of Needs Theory",[15] Maslow postulates that a human being is a "perpetually wanting animal" motivated by five sets (levels) of basic needs: Physiological Needs; Safety Needs; Belonging Needs; Esteem Needs; and the ultimate needs of Self-Actualization. These sets/levels of needs have been arranged by subsequent scholars and lay commentators in a hierarchy (pyramid) in order of their "biological urgency".

SELF-ACTUALIZATION NEEDS
"peak" experiences,
self-fulfillment, openness,
lack of prejudice, creativity

ESTEEM NEEDS
recognition of importance,
self-respect, respect from others, ego

BELONGING NEEDS
hunger for affection,
welcome place in a group,
friends, family, sexual intimacy, community

SAFETY NEEDS
freedom from fear and chaos
organized world or religious view
financial resources, job security, safe neighborhood, property

PHYSIOLOGICAL NEEDS
homeostasis of the body
oxygen, water, food, sleep, pain avoidance, sex (without love),
waste elimination[16]

Biological urgency means a lower level need is "more clamorous in its motivation, and takes motivational priority" over higher level needs. Maslow terms this phenomenon "prepotency" of needs which means that expression of a higher level need "presupposes that [lower] needs [that have] greater prepotency have been, at least for a time, satisfied". It is important to note that this human "motivation" is not synonymous with human "behavior". A person does not automatically act upon any given need no matter the strength of the prepotency. Human free will does exist, although that free will is highly influenced by needs.

Maslow also states that "the fact that higher [level] needs do not appear to be universally pursued, does not mean such needs are secondary or derivative. Rather, it only means fewer people have been able to satisfy the lower, more proponent needs."[17] This allows us to understand why Maslow's theory is almost always displayed in pyramid form.

At least in his initial/seminal publications, it seems Maslow never wrote about "levels of human consciousness" per se, (at least as far as I have been able to find). Rather, he wrote about human motivation as being activated by hierarchical sets of human "needs"; but an argument can be made that Maslow's writings directly apply to levels (or expanding, yet still limited, receptacles) of human consciousness. In describing human motivation, Maslow specifically states the mental process of biological urgency "will monopolize consciousness and will tend of itself to organize the recruitment of the various capacities of the organism".[18] For example, when discussing the very basic psychological need of hunger, Maslow states:

> It is then fair to characterize the whole organism by saying simply that it is hungry, for consciousness is almost completely preempted by hunger. All capacities are put into the service of hunger-satisfaction. . . almost entirely determined by the one purpose of satisfying hunger. The receptors and effectors, the intelligence, memory, habits, all may now be defined as hunger-gratifying tools.[19]

In other words, these "needs" are not consciousness per se, but these needs have such a powerful and sometimes overwhelming influence on consciousness that a person's consciousness is kept at the "level" of those needs until those needs are met.

Consistent with this book's emphasis in Chapter Four that there are "filters" to our consciousness, it is also interesting to note the comments of Richard J. Lowry, one of the foremost scholars on the writings of Maslow. Lowry writes that, for Maslow, observing "the effects of need deficiency motivation is like looking at the world through a clouded lens, and removing those effects is like replacing the clouded lenses with a clear one".[20]

This is a critical macro-point in the understanding of the dynamics of conscious expansion. These levels of needs contain an almost overwhelming influence on a person's consciousness. The influence/force of these needs is both psychological (through emotions such as love, anger, depression, excitement) and corporeal (such as hunger, rapid pulse, insomnia, temperature changes). Moreover, Maslow adds another macro-point: that, in the average person, these needs are more often unconscious (which we now know as non-conscious) rather than conscious. This is consistent with what we learned from Dennett and others in Chapter One.

Both the psychological and corporeal power of these needs, along with the reality that these needs are often not consciously appreciated, are fundamental reasons why both scholars and mystics stress the difficulty of moving up and out of a given consciousness level. There will be much more discussion of this in the next chapter; but for now consider the following "escalating" examples of the incredible and compelling power of needs in human consciousness and conduct:

1. An obese person on a strict diet will still eat a candy bar.

2. People who belong to a certain country club would never support a Democrat publically (and vice versa) even if they believe the Democrat to be the better candidate.

3. People in abusive relationships don't leave that continuously destructive relationship.

4. In certain cultures, people whose family honor has been questioned because a female member of that family fell in love with a person of another religion will actually kill that family member in the name of family honor!

These needs, these clouded lenses, can help create a consciousness receptacle that compels a person to commit the relatively innocent act of breaking a diet with a candy bar to the horrendous act of taking the life of a family member. These needs have a potentially overwhelming power, even more so if a person is unaware of them. An almost infinite number of examples of "clouded lenses" reinforced by the filters to our consciousness exist. Overcoming the collection of needs in each level is hard work. Not many make it to the top of the pyramid.

Earlier in this chapter we learned that Maslow was not the first to write about sequential levels of mental/personality/consciousness development. Yet it is fair to include Maslow as a "paradigm shifter" on this topic. There are at least three primary reasons to support this claim. First, Maslow helped change the prevailing academic orthodoxy away from the dark psychology of Freud and the rigid psychology of Behaviorism to what became known as the Humanistic School of Psychology. Second, (for good or bad) Maslow helped change the prevailing cultural orthodoxy of institutional authoritarianism into "me first" individualism. Finally, Maslow helped bring Eastern philosophy into Western culture.

Maslow helped change Western psychology. . . We've touched very briefly on the somewhat dark Freudian understanding of levels of consciousness. Let's now take a quick look at Behaviorism. The psychology of Behaviorism was in vogue in the late 1940s when Maslow began to write. While there were many different schools of Behaviorism that developed in the early 20th century, Behaviorism in general saw psychology as a science that can and should be measured and understood through empirical observation of how a person interacts with their environment. It essentially took the extreme position that all consciousness is learned. Both humans and animals are born with a mind/consciousness that is a blank slate. Therefore, human psychology/consciousness could be studied and tested by studying the behavior of animals; i.e. Pavlov's dog salivating at the sound of a bell. It could be argued that Behaviorism was darker than Freudianism because it postulated a robotic understanding of both human consciousness and free will.

Maslow has been called "the father of the Humanistic School of Psychology" which essentially rose up as a counter-response to both Freud's Psychoanalysis and Behaviorism. Humanism considered each person as individual, and focused as the subjective experiences of the individual (qualia) with an emphasis on free will as opposed to predetermined Behaviorism. For example, a person can learn and obtain the conscious strength to recognize and leave an abusive relationship. Humanism is often described as "the third force" in the historic development of psychology following (Freudian/Jungian) Psychoanalysis and Behaviorism.

Maslow helped change Western social norms. . . Some of us are old enough to remember the culture of the 50s. Although it was an exciting time of promise following the end of World War Two, the cultural structures were still rigid and authoritarian. Those of you not old enough to remember may have caught a glimpse of this by watching the popular television series "Mad Men". Most families went to church on Sundays (or synagogue on the Sabbath). The word "atheist" was probably never read nor even heard. The president, judges, and policemen were respected. The father was the king of "his" castle. Mom cooked, cleaned house, and took care of the kids (and dad). If dad was lucky enough to have an administrative job, he always wore the cultural uniform of a white shirt, tie, and a hat to work. Our institutions were held in high regard. When the nightly news anchorman (always a man) came into "the" living room television (families only had one tv) and told you something (particularly if it was Walter Cronkite) you believed every word he said. Then came the 60s. . . individuality, self-centeredness, drug experimentation, sexual experimentation (and damn good music).

Given the "me first" ethic of the 60s, it is probably no coincidence that, even though Maslow first published his theory in 1943, it was not until the 60s that his theory took off in popular Western culture. Maslow's theory allowed for the ego appeal of great individual potential. Both the fact that Maslow uses the term "hierarchy" and the fact that his needs theory was often placed in a pyramid form surely contributed to the competitive ego appeal of Maslow's theory. With my college know-it-all ego in full bloom, it was actually one of my first "wow" moments when I studied Maslow as a college freshman in 1970. Surely I was on my way to Self- Actualization! (Unfortunately, almost half a century later, I'm still waiting. . .)

Maslow helped change Western philosophy. . . Finally, Maslow was one of the first to bring Eastern philosophy into psychology. He was familiar with both Hindu and Buddhist teachings, and incorporated them into his understanding of the human condition. In particular, Maslow helped change, or at least question, the long standing Christian paradigm that mankind is born inherently bad. Specifically, mankind (always "mankind" never "humankind") is born with original sin, is therefore inherently sinful (bad), and can only be "saved" through the death and resurrection of our Savior, Jesus Christ. Maslow took the complete opposite position of foundational Christianity by starting with the premise that a person is born inherently good, and that salvation/happiness/personal development occurs when there is knowledge and an opportunity to expand consciousness. This is classic Buddhist thought; and, while there were many causative factors other than Maslow, it is fascinating to observe how Buddhist philosophy has so rapidly spread through Western culture and psychology practices since Maslow.

Maslow has a number of detractors, both from the Academy (learned institutional/university commentators) and more often from short (often superficial) commentaries in magazines or online. The primary criticisms of Maslow's theory which are pertinent to our discussion on consciousness expansion are as follows: 1) Maslow fails to use scientific methodology in establishing his theory. 2) Maslow cannot reduce complex human motivation/consciousness to five simple levels. 3) Maslow's levels are too Eurocentric and culturally dependent.

As to the first criticism. . . It does seem to be correct that Maslow's research was not as academically rigorous as many of his peers. Much of his writings seem more sociological or philosophical than scientifically conducted research. This seems to be especially true when Maslow explores the top level of Self-Actualization. Not finding a significantly large dataset of self-actualized humans, Maslow was forced to speculate about the psyches of famous historical individuals. Maslow acknowledges this limitation in his "Personal Foreword" to his book "Motivation and Personality".[21]

> The study to be reported in this chapter is unusual in various ways. It was not planned as an ordinary research. . . I chose only to convince and teach myself rather than to prove.[22]

As to the remaining two criticisms. . . Yes, without a doubt, as we have been learning, human motivation/consciousness is much more complex than five levels. Yet numerous scholars using peer-reviewed scientific methods have confirmed that human cognitive development (consciousness) almost universally progresses in sequences. As we will see when we look at the work of Ken Wilber, this seems to be true not only cross-culturally, but throughout history. Although there are different cultural and historical "expressions" of human cognitive development, the very general stages/levels are essentially the same, even though these stages may be numbered and described differently by different scholars. Moreover, when we explore Wilber, we will see how much of this criticism of levels vanishes when Wilber explains multiple "lines" of cognitive development occurring within each level.[23]

Erik Erikson (1902-1994) was a Danish born American, and the first major psychologist to develop a series of detailed sequential stages of development across the entire lifespan of a person. Maslow's theory was not age dependent, was not as academically rigorous as Erikson's, and did not focus on the progression of levels over time. Freud and Piaget's theories theoretically covered the entire human lifespan, but their work was almost completely focused on early childhood. Erikson was much influenced by Freud, but (like most modern scholars) rejected Freud's over-focus on pleasure seeking primitive drives as the *sine qua non* of personality/consciousness development. Rather, Erikson believed one's sense of self, which Erikson called "ego identity", arose over time in "psychosocial stages" as an individual psychologically responded to social interaction.

Initially, Erikson postulated seven, later eight (and as we will see finally nine) such psychosocial stages:

1. HOPE (infancy). . . basic trust vs. basic mistrust
2. WILL (early childhood). . . autonomy vs. shame
3. PURPOSE (play age). . . initiative vs. guilt
4. COMPETENCE (school age). . . industry vs. inferiority
5. FIDELITY (adolescence). . . identity vs. identity confusion
6. LOVE (young adulthood). . . intimacy vs. isolation
7. CARE (adulthood). . . generativity vs. stagnation
8. WISDOM (old age). . . integrity vs. despair[24]

At each stage, a person is faced with a psychological crisis/challenge which involves the process of integrating two seemingly opposite poles of that person's current level of consciousness. For example, as you can see in the first stage of infancy above, the conflict is between basic trust and basic mistrust. The data point for resolving this conflict is most often whether the infant's mother meets the infant's basic needs. If an infant resolves this conflict and develops basic trust, that infant then develops the psychosocial strength of "Hope" and moves onto the next stage. If not, the negative experiences occurring during the development of basic mistrust will dominate the consciousness of that person's life. Such an "identity crisis" may be mild to severe depending on the intensity of the related experiences during that stage.

Erikson's analysis of each psychosocial stage provides important insights into the nature of consciousness. While much of Erikson's writing is technical and in an older writing style, the internet is replete with excellent summaries on the important aspects of each stage. Without making a judgment on whether Erikson's particular theories on psychology are up to snuff with the most current and "in" psychological theories, it is an interesting and often valuable exercise to review these stages and compare one's own experiences in each stage, as well as to anticipate the challenges in the stages yet to come. To quote Erikson's wife and longstanding collaborator, Joan Erikson (1903-1997):

> How difficult it is to recognize and have perspective for just where one is presently in one's own life cycle. Today is just like yesterday until you sit back and take stock.[25]

It is interesting to discover that Erikson's lifelong study (and his own consciousness expansion) regarding personal identity rose from his own youthful identity crisis. In fact, Erikson was the scholar who invented the term "identity crisis". In recounting his youth, Erikson wrote "my identity confusion [was at times on] the borderline between neurosis and adolescent psychosis".[26]

It is not difficult to understand why Erikson developed personal identity issues. Erik's mother, Karla Abrahamsen, a member of a prominent

Jewish family in Denmark, gave birth to Erik while estranged from her husband, Valdemar Salomonsen, a prominent Jewish stockbroker. Erik's mother moved to Germany shortly after giving birth, and three years later married Erik's Jewish pediatrician, Theodor Homberger. Erik's surname was then changed from Salomonsen to Homberger. The name of Erikson's biological father was never revealed; but Erikson's tall, blond, blue-eyed, Scandinavian features belied any pretense that his father was ethnically Jewish.[27] In public school, Erik was teased for being Jewish; and in temple school, he suffered equivalent peer hazing for his looks, often being called "goy". (A Yiddish term meaning gentile, but which can also be used as a derogatory slur.) After graduation from gymnasium (high school), Erik attended art school in Munich; but soon dropped out and spent years wandering, somewhat aimlessly, around Germany and Italy "adopting the tentative identity of a wondering artist".[28]

At the age of 25, at the urging of his oldest friend, Erik became a tutor in Vienna at a small private school for children of wealthy parents. As fate would have it, these children were undergoing psychoanalysis by Anna Freud, the daughter of Sigmund Freud. Anna Freud noticed Erik's sensitivity to the children, and convinced Erik to enroll in the Vienna Psychoanalytic Institute where Erik specialized in child analysis; and a brilliant career was launched. Erik and his wife, Joan, left Europe in the 30s due to the rise of fascism. They became naturalized American citizens, (again) changed their name, this time to Erikson, and taught at Harvard and Yale before settling in for many years at Berkeley. The Eriksons' writings on psychosocial stages continued to influence both scholars and the public even today.

The final (and at my age the most relevant) contribution by Erikson to the scholarly literature on levels of consciousness occurred in 1997 with the publication of the book "The Life Cycle Completed Extended Version with New Chapters on the Ninth Stage of Development".[29] Erickson's previous "final" 8th stage was believed to occur from retirement (around age 65) until death. As the Eriksons personally lived through their 80s and early 90s, they realized a 9th stage was needed for what they termed "very old age" of 80s and 90s. They named this 9th stage "Gerotranscendence".[30]

In simplified terms, the previous final (8th) stage of "Wisdom" involved resolving the psychological crisis of Integrity vs. Despair. At around age 65, most people (originally mostly men) retired from their work/profession. If they had raised a family, their children were now out on their own. One's previous ego-identity/consciousness which had been tied up in being a doctor, plumber, father or mother, was now disappearing. The Eriksons observed that this could lead to despair, especially as a person realized more and more that death was around the corner. The Eriksons argued that successfully navigating this stage depended on whether a person was able to look back on their life and see that they had lived a worthwhile life of integrity. If so, they could more easily appreciate the dignity of the end of the life cycle even in the face of death. If not, (the consciousness of) such persons would be subject to despair and fear of death.

As the Eriksons lived longer, they not only "intellectually" realized, but actually "experienced" that life is very different at 85 than it was at 65 or even 75. The principle reason being that more and more body parts just didn't work like they did before. Now you might wonder why smart people like the Eriksons didn't realize this sooner? I can only answer from what I learned from my own dad who once gave me the good news/bad news that:

> Every decade of my life got better and better. My 50s were better than my 40s. 60s better than 50s. Even 70s better than 60s. I guess I expected my life to continue to get better and better; but when you get into your 80s, it can get surprisingly depressing because more and more body parts just don't work like they used to.

In describing the 9th stage, (I suppose the real bad news is) the Eriksons didn't just see one major psychological crisis/challenge as they did in each of the previous eight stages. Rather, they warn that "all" the major psychological challenges that you previously overcame reappear! For example, the infancy crisis of basic trust vs. basic mistrust re-raises its ugly head as elders are forced to mistrust their own capabilities, or entirely trust others. The crisis from the 2nd stage of early childhood of autonomy vs. shame re-occurs for the same reason.[31] (I'd go on, but this is getting a bit depressing since I'm well into my late 60s; and I'm sure you get the point.)

The Eriksons offer a two-part solution (my terminology not theirs) to meet these challenges; warning that even under the best of circumstances despair is always lurking to some degree, and the challenges of the prior eight stages will likely keep re-occurring.

First, you must accept and develop a sense of humility. As noted in the Introduction to this book, humility is always a fundamental pre-requisite to consciousness expansion; but humility becomes even more essential to your emotional survival when your kids take away your car keys or when someone has to feed you.

Second, develop and enjoy an attitude of "transcendence". But wait. . .doesn't transcendence mean experiences or even existence beyond the physical world? Doesn't this drag us back to Cartesian Dualism? Well, yes and no. That is indeed a definition of transcendence (beyond the physical realm); and as we will see when we get to the sixth category of levels in this chapter "Transpersonal", there are those who believe there can be an actual transcendent/metaphysical change in consciousness. However, the Eriksons are using transcendence as a "metaphor" of a transcendental perspective/ attitude (transcendental or transcendent-like consciousness) rather than actual metaphysical transcendence.[32][33]

The Eriksons' acknowledge that their 9th stage of Gerotranscendence is based extensively on the work of Lars Tornstam (1943-) who suggests that the challenges of old age can (almost by genetic design) bring about a paradigm shift in meta-perspective from a materialistic and rational view to a more transcendental perspective.

> . . . the very process of living into old age, encompasses a general potential towards gerotranscendence. Simply put, gerotranscendence is a shift in meta perspective, from a mate-rialistic and rational vision to a more cosmic and transcendent one, normally followed by an increase in life satisfaction. . . . It defines a reality somewhat different from the normal mid-life

reality. . . the gerotranscendent individual experiences. . .a redefinition of time, space, life and death, and a redefinition of self.[34]

While this claimed natural glide into a transcendental consciousness as one ages long past retirement may seem unlikely to traditional Western thinking, such a change has long seemed obvious in much of so-called Eastern thinking. For example, in ancient Hindu texts, the four stages of life are set forth as: Brahmacharya (student), Grihastha (householder), Vanaprastha (retired), and Sannyasa (renunciation). It is during this fourth stage when ideally a person's life obligations and consciousness are such that the person can devote their time/consciousness to spiritual/reflective matters, which involves a humble, open-hearted acceptance of life as it really is.

Now that I understand the Erikson's 9th stage (at least intellectually), I also realize that I have often observed such a transcendental attitude in many elders, but certainly not in most. At least in my experience, such fortunate so-called transcendental elders seem to laugh easily (often at their own mistakes), read a lot, almost never talk about their own successes, and are authentically happy to interact with people they have not met before. I suspect that the success in achieving such a transcendental consciousness depends to a very large degree on just how difficult your physical and emotional life is when you are in the 9th stage. Are you in pain? Are you mobile? Are you financially secure? Are there people around you who love and support you? But one of the macro-points of this book is that you will have a greater chance to expand into transcendental consciousness if you are aware of its existence and you possess the humility and courage to attempt to seek this next level of consciousness. (An active and loving relationship with grandchildren doesn't hurt either.) The good news, at least according to Tornstam and the Eriksons, is that elders with a transcendental consciousness are both happier and healthier than those without such consciousness.[35]

The sixth category of "Transpersonal" Levels of Consciousness got its name when a small group of "out of the box" thinkers got together in Menlo Park, California in 1967 to discuss what they perceived as limitations on the growing Humanistic School of Psychology.

That working group included two of the founders of Humanistic Psychology, Abraham Maslow and Anthony Sutich. Also in this group was Stanislav Grof who has written a fascinating, succinct, and "insider" history of the founding of Transpersonal Psychology entitled "A Brief History of Transpersonal Psychology".[36] As you will recall, Humanistic Psychology arose as "the third force" in opposition to Psychoanalysis and Behaviorism. Transpersonal Psychology saw itself as the "fourth force". This first Transpersonal group believed that Humanism, although becoming more and more popular, especially with the public, had missed out on a critical and fundamental element of the human psyche. That element was "spirituality" (a term which is fast becoming more and more co-opted, especially by younger generations as the emotional utility of organized religion fades).

By "spirituality", this group did not mean organized religion. For this group, spirituality was the mystical and beyond the ordinary physical world experience of reality. . . a whole new level of consciousness. In many ways it was a return to Dualism because it essentially argued for a transcendent (non-physical) mystic connection to the godhead (although different groups gave that godhead different names). On the other hand, Transpersonal wasn't pure Dualism because it didn't postulate two distinct and separate worlds of material and non-material as believed by Descartes. Rather this Transpersonal world of the seemingly material and non-material was all one interrelated/interbeing world.

Transpersonal represents the far end of the spectrum for understanding/defining consciousness. All of existence, all of reality, is One. This includes the inanimate such as a grain of sand; all animate beings including plants, animals, and humans; and the Godhead itself most often referred to by current mystics as "Spirit". This is not Dualism. It is a form of Monism, and it is only through a Transpersonal level of consciousness that one can sense and understand this mystical Oneness.

This group believed that Transpersonal Psychology should include Eastern philosophies; mystical traditions of the great world religions such as Kabbalah from Judaism, Sufi from Islam; spiritual experiences from Christian mystics such as Catherine of Siena, Teresa of Avila, and Bernard of Clairvaux; aboriginal and ancient mystical traditions from ages past; as well as the experiences from psychedelic experimentation (especially with LSD) exploding during the 60s. The founders of Transpersonal Psychology felt that such mystical (transcendent/non-physical) experience had been wrongfully written off by the psychology profession, including the manner in which the Humanistic School was developing.[37] Accordingly, these founders launched the Association of Transpersonal Psychology and started the Journal of Transpersonal Psychology.[38]

It was the mystical experiences that put the "trans" in Transpersonal Psychology. These early founders believed that such mystical practices, which included induced Altered States, allowed the practitioner to experience, at least for a brief time, new levels of consciousness that transcended (above and beyond) the previously accepted limited realm of physical reality. Grof labels such mystical experiences "holotropic" because he believed such states reveal a cosmic wholeness or oneness with "no boundaries" between or among things or concepts. Time, space, people, hamsters, pain, color are all one. Boundaries between such things are an illusion.[39]

Grof observed that these Altered States of past mystics and current psychedelic experimenters seem to occur in two forms. The first he called "immanent divine".

> A person having this form of spiritual experience sees people, animals, plants, and inanimate objects in the environment of radiant manifestations of a unified field of cosmic creative energy. . . and realizes that the boundaries between objects are illusory and unreal.

The second he called "transcendent divine".

> . . . manifestation of archetypal beings and realms of reality that are ordinarily transphenomenal, that is unavailable to everyday state of consciousness.[40]

It's not an overstatement to suggest that Grof and other Transpersonal adherents were in awe of such reported mystical experiences. Grof describes them as "healing", "transformative", and (pertinent to our overview) "evolutionary" in the sense that such Altered States are not only a glimpse but claimed "proof" of the next Evolutionary level of consciousness. . . above and beyond the current Meta-Awareness level of common human consciousness.[41]

Grof readily acknowledges that over the centuries established science not only looked upon these experiences with incredulity, but with outright derision. He chronicles how established Western psychiatric literature has historically described such experiences as pathological. Grof points out that: St. John of the Cross was labeled a "hereditary degenerate". St. Teresa of Avila was dismissed as a severe hysterical psychotic. Mohammed's mystical experiences were attributed to epilepsy. Buddhist meditation was described as "artificial catatonia".[42]

To his credit, Grof readily and fearlessly admits that "the issue of critical importance is, of course, the ontological nature of the spiritual experiences."[43] In plain words, are these experiences illusions generated by the human brain, or are they actually a window into a new and Evolutionary level of consciousness. . . a completely different understanding of reality? Unfortunately, in spite of his bold admission that proof of the ontological existence of such Transpersonal experiences is critical to believing in such elevated levels of consciousness, Grof just offers the same incomplete proofs as most all Transpersonal adherents. These "proofs" tend to fall into four types.

The first type of "proof". . . is one we have already explored in detail in Chapter One. . . that quantum physics demonstrates the emptiness of all boundaries in matter, and that traditional academic science has been unable to explain this.[44] As discussed in Chapter One, the above statement is absolutely true. Science cannot "yet" explain quantum entanglement or wave-function collapse. But that (current) inability is simply not "proof" that Altered States are ontologically independent realms of advanced consciousness above and beyond Meta-Awareness.

The second category of "proof". . . is that during the past millennia when the greatest minds of the so-called West developed advanced science, the greatest minds of the so-called East were developing advanced states of consciousness through techniques such as meditation. I have great respect for the teachings of the East, and have spent decades studying and practicing such teachings. Chapters Eight and Ten of this book offer such teachings as tried and true techniques for expanding consciousness, but only expansion within the known level/realm of Meta-Awareness. Eastern teaching is to be respected and learned from, but it is not (yet) "proof" of higher realms.

The third type of "proof". . . is the claimed consensual validation of those who have experienced Transpersonal realms of consciousness.[45] This third claim can be (somewhat cynically) divided into three sub-proofs:

A. The described Transpersonal experiences of practitioners have been consistent both historically and cross-culturally.

B. The described Transpersonal experiences are more accurate than everyday perception.

C. Some of these practitioners have been able to accomplish Transpersonal phenomena such as remembering past lives or bending spoons with their minds.

None of the above sub-proofs withstand even the most empirical investigation.

A. As to the first sub-proof, that claimed Transpersonal experiences share common themes both historically and cross-culturally, Grof is "generally" correct. (This is confirmed by scholars such as Ken Wilbur as we will see later in this chapter.) Yet, is this some amazing revelatory insight or proof of Transpersonal consciousness? If a person induces an Altered State, whether through psychedelics, alcohol, or other means, is it surprising that the human brain yields similar general experiences in different cultures over time? In each of those separate situations, the human brain of the actor is essentially the same anatomically. This shared expression of common themes is not proof of a new Transpersonal consciousness. It is only proof that cross-culturally and across history human brains have similar reactions to Altered

States. Moreover, if you read Grof's foundational book "The Cosmic Game: Explorations of the Frontiers of Human Consciousness"[46] you will find this first sub-proof is disproved by Grof's own examples. Grof's book describes the particulars of hundreds of claimed Transpersonal experiences (many under hallucinogenics and many conducted by Grof himself) to which Grof must go to intellectual acrobatics or unsubstantiated claims to find other than general similarities.

B. As to the second sub-proof, that Transpersonal vision is more accurate than everyday perception, I can only cite to you my own youthful (drug and alcohol induced) Altered States where I would have bet the farm that the light rays coming off the lava lamp revealed the true nature of the universe. Your experience with psychedelics may be as limited as mine was, or more likely non-existent; but let's look at alcohol intoxication, an Altered State many of us have engaged in. Many of us can (perhaps unfortunately) remember being so drunk that we truly believed the guy on the bar stool next to us was our new best friend; that the gal or guy at the end of the bar was the most beautiful/desirable person in the world; or that together with our co-imbibers we had now solved several of the major problems in the world. Were any of these passionately held beliefs "more accurate than everyday perception"?

C. As to the final sub-proof, that there exists demonstrations beyond the accepted ordinary physical realm, I also rely on my own research, investigation, and experience. I do this not because I am a confirmed skeptic. In fact, my motivation is the exact opposite. I want there to be proof of a Transpersonal world! Therefore, I have from time to time taken days/weeks to investigate and track down such claims that I have read about in New Age writings. The vast number of times, it traces back to such limited extent information that the claim can neither be proved nor disproved. All other times, the proof is that the claim was unequivocally false.[47]

Just one such mini-example of disproved Transpersonal/mystical claims involved my time spent studying with a highly regarded "Tulku" in Nepal. Under the Tibetan Buddhist tradition, a Tulku is a recognized reincarnate (such as the Dalai Lama). During one day of teaching, the Tulku not only described the Transpersonal "proof" of "rainbow bodies" (although he did not call it Transpersonal nor a proof), but provided specific descriptional detail on how he "personally" observed a rainbow body. According to the rainbow body phenomenon, when a highly evolved person dies, the body does not decay. Rather it becomes smaller and smaller while exuding beautiful fragrances instead of the putrid odors of decomposition until it dissolves into five radiant lights like a rainbow. After the teaching, I had the opportunity to question the Tulku in a somewhat persistent manner that this wise and loving man was no doubt not used to; but the validity of the claim of rainbow bodies was so obviously such an amazing "proof" if true that I broke tradition and pressed on. I wanted rainbow bodies to be true! Unfortunately, to my disappointment, after close questioning I learned that the Tulku, contrary to his express teaching just moments earlier, had not personally seen a rainbow body as claimed, but had only heard about it from a friend, who in turn had heard it from a friend, etc., etc. Now perhaps this enlightened man simply recognized me as unworthy to engage with him on such a deep ground, and simply acquiesced to my pre-existing disbelief of rainbow bodies; or more likely maybe rainbow bodies are simply only a beautiful teaching myth and not an ontological reality. Who knows for sure?

Ironically, as I was struggling through the writing of this section of Chapter Three, I was informed of what could be considered a quasi-transpersonal experience such as all of us have probably had from time to time. I was enjoying the fatherly pleasure of having breakfast with my adult daughter who is a highly successful life coach and counselor for teens and parents of teens. My daughter told me about an unexplainable event that occurred during a recent teen retreat. Out of a large window, they observed a deer that strayed into the yard. My daughter told the teens that her mother (my wife) often thought of her own deceased mother whenever she saw a deer because her mother loved deer so much. In a playful manner, my daughter then asked the teens, "What should we name the deer?" Then to my daughter's surprise, one kid yelled out "Phillis" which is certainly not a common name, and was remarkably the name of my wife's mother! Coincidence or cosmic connection? Who knows for sure?

The fourth type of "proof"... is to make the naked claim that highly acclaimed scholars have done the scholarly work to establish the existence Transpersonal realms. The scholars most often named by proponents of Transpersonal consciousness (and many New Age wannabe sages) are: Carl Jung and his work on archetypal domains and the collective unconsciousness; Dr. Robert Lanza and his work on quantum theory (which we examined in Chapter One); and Ken Wilber and his work on the Integral Model of consciousness (which we will address next in this chapter). (I should add here that there is no doubt each of these impressive scholars would be rightly horrified to be described as "New Age".) I have the greatest respect for each of these three amazing scholars, yet I fail to see how their personal experiences/beliefs/writings are proof of Transpersonal consciousness.

Ironically (months after I thought I was finished writing and editing this chapter), I was reading what has been called "Jung's Autobiography" in which Jung describes the first time he got drunk after he went off to college, and so I added Jung's remembrance of that event here:

> I found the various little glasses so inspiring that I was wafted into an entirely new and unexpected state of consciousness. There was no longer any inside or outside, no longer an "I"... the earth and sky, the universe and everything in it that creeps and flies, revolves, rises, or falls, had all become one. I was shamefully, gloriously, triumphantly drunk.[48]

Not only is this not proof of Transpersonal consciousness, but at least to me (admittedly neither a trained nor untrained psychologist) indicates Jung's psychological predisposition to believe in Transpersonal phenomena. We know that both prior to and especially subsequent to this first college drinking experience, Jung not only believed in his own clairvoyance, but also in: poltergeists; alchemy; clocks stopping at the exact time of their owner's death; ghosts; and many other occult practices, beliefs, and events which in his own words "overstepped the limited categories of space, time, and causality".[49] Maybe such a predisposition was a rare and valuable gift which allowed Jung to go on to develop his deep and important insights into analytical psychology and the role of the therapist? At the very least it represents a consciousness that allowed Jung to think outside the boxes of cultural and scholastic conformity. But it's not proof of Transpersonal levels.

The New Age market place is awash with scholars, mystics, and many more wannabe sages expounding on levels of Transpersonal consciousness. Just search online "levels of consciousness", and you will literally find hundreds of examples such as: The Three Levels of Consciousness by Philip Holder; The Four Tiers of Extrasensory Awareness by Robert Gibson; The Five Ascending Levels of Awareness of Community with God by Moshe Miller; The Six Levels of Higher Consciousness by Mary O'Malley; The Seven Shamanic Levels of Consciousness by Dirk Gillabel; The Eight Circuit Model of Consciousness by Dr. Timothy Leary (yes, that's the same Timothy Leary of psychedelic fame); The Nine Levels of Consciousness by Soka Gakkai International; The Ten Levels of Consciousness by Dreamcatcher Reality; The 12 Levels of Consciousness of Mankind by Archangel Metatron; and the Hawkins' Consciousness Scale with 0-1000 Levels of Consciousness by David R. Hawkins, M.D., Ph.D. (who is a cottage industry unto himself, and who has published dozens of books in multiple languages around the world).

Just like our study in Chapter One of the "Way Out There" category of consciousness, one is tempted to dismiss these Transpersonal teachings as crazy stuff; or at least as a last-gasp pull of Cartesian gravity to replace the increasingly less satisfying promises of an "afterlife" by organized religion. But for at least two reasons, this would be an arrogant mistake. First, because it assumes our own (judgmental) consciousness receptacles are vast enough to "know" that any Transpersonal teaching is crazy stuff. Second, because we would be making a decision to ignore so-called "Eastern" teachings on consciousness which Grof and others correctly point out have been developed by brilliant and dedicated minds over millennia.

Grof points out that the contemporary Western scholar who most skillfully explains and defends Transpersonal psychology is Ken Wilber, and this may indeed be so; but more pertinent to our overview is Wilber's exceptionally sophisticated understanding of levels of consciousness.[50] So let's keep our consciousness receptacles open should any more convincing evidence of the Transpersonal arise.

Ken Wilber (1949-) is one of the foremost current scholars to study, analyze, and explain levels/states of consciousness. Wilber may in fact be the most prolific author on the subject of the "spectrum of consciousness" having published more than two dozen scholarly books about consciousness which have been translated into over thirty languages. Wilber was an intellectual prodigy; but dropped out of the Duke University Doctoral Program in Biology to pursue extreme self-study of both Eastern and Western spirituality/religion/mysticism and psychology. Although he is essentially self-taught, few if any (including his critics) question his brilliance. Wilber initially described himself as a "pundit" (before this word took on the pejorative context of "talking heads" on cable news) meaning that he was someone who could both thoroughly learn and then explain (to us regular folk) a complex topic like consciousness. He now describes himself online as an author and theorist, but he is known to other scholars and readers as the founder of "Integral Psychology" which includes his "Integral Model of Consciousness". Wilber is well aware of the vast complexity of consciousness, and so chose the word "Integral" in furtherance of his "endeavor to honor and embrace every legitimate aspect of human consciousness".[51] Wilber finds truth from the practices of the paleolithic shaman to the discoveries of cutting edge neuroscience.

It is perhaps ironic that Wilber is often described as "the smartest man you've never heard of". I suspect that many scholars in the field of consciousness may not have heard of Wilber because his fundamental understanding of consciousness arises largely out of the Eastern tradition of one cosmic consciousness. Moreover, almost all of his initial publications were published by a smaller (yet excellent) Buddhist publishing house, Shambhala Publications, Inc. Yet to miss out on Wilber is to miss out on a brilliant paradigm shifter. That being said, at least for me, there have been three great difficulties in studying Wilber. Although, the struggle to try and overcome the difficulties has been well worth it.

The first difficulty is that Wilber's works are heavily jargon-laden, and his explanation of levels of consciousness is exceptionally multifaceted when compared to other great theorists. For example, he doesn't just write about "levels" of consciousness; but rather distinguishes among levels, states, types, lines, structures, four quadrants of perspective, and phenomenal aspects of consciousness just to name a few of Wilber's definitional concepts. This can present quite a challenge to the reader, because you must first learn/memorize each distinction in order to proceed further with Wilber's theories. Is this difficult? I think so. Is this a bad thing? I think not. We've already taken a look at the complex nature of consciousness; and if you are going to really explore such complexity, you must begin with agreement on terminology and then go deep.[52]

The second difficulty with Wilber's work is that he has from time to time modified his theories over the 40 plus years he has been writing. At first, this can be a discouraging and frustrating problem, especially when you have put considerable effort into mastering the terminology and concepts. Is this a bad thing? Again, frustrating, but not bad. Not only should you admire a person for being willing to change his views about consciousness; but from what we've explored in this book so far, if you are not willing to change your views about consciousness, it is a certainty that you will not expand your consciousness. You will be still stuck in your same conscious receptacle, no matter how impressive that receptacle may appear to the world.

The third difficulty is perhaps only applicable to me personally. Wilber's work is so thoroughly researched, impressively written, and deeply explorative of new areas of thought that it embarrasses and discourages me as a writer. But that's my problem. . .

Wilber is on the extreme end of the Monism spectrum that sees only one "Kosmic Consciousness".[53] For Wilber, everything in the universe is part of this one consciousness from matter to the Godhead, which Wilber often calls Spirit. Within that consciousness are many and continuous levels or dimensions of consciousness. These levels range from nonconscious matter to the super consciousness of the Oneness or Spirit. Everything in the universe is the manifestation of one singular consciousness.

Wilber argues that individual human consciousness can evolve through the hierarchy of these levels to become one (again) with Spirit itself. This is an almost universal ontological theme in Transpersonal and many so-called New Age philosophies. It should be noted however that this "New" Age motif actually dates back at least to the Upanishads (religious texts from India c. 800-200 BCE). In simple terms, this "Oneness" belief, although expressed in many different ways, is as old as recorded history. Such myths/traditions presuppose an original and eternal existence of God, Godhead, Brahman, or Spirit, etc.; then some type of "fall" or transition (or Big Bang) of Spirit creating the material cosmos we think we know; then a return to Spirit via salvation, or Gnosticism (esoteric, mystical knowledge at first known only to a select few), or grace, etc.; and then finally. . .stir and repeat the process eternally.

One of my favorite and most poetic such myths comes from "A Course in Miracles", first published in 1975 by the Foundation for Inner Peace, which is a 600 plus page book of supposedly channeled "inner dictation" from Jesus to two psychology professors in New York. This definitely qualifies under the Way Out There banner. Yet there are thousands of adherents, including a dear and close minister friend of mine who I love and highly respect. While I don't ascribe to the claimed source of "A Course in Miracles", the book contains numerous poetic and beautiful thoughts on life, including the following "Christianized" Transpersonal myth of the reason for the fall from Godhead resulting in the creation of the material cosmos:

Thus are you not the dreamer, but the dream. . .

Into eternity, where all is one, there crept a tiny, mad idea,
at which the Son of God remembered not to laugh.

In his forgetting did the thought become a serious idea,
and possible of both accomplishment and real effects.

Together, we can laugh them both away,
and understand that time cannot intrude upon eternity.
—Chapter 27 Section VIII

Although many believe that traditions and theories regarding levels within the cosmic Oneness come only from the Eastern tradition, Wilber correctly points out in his writings that this hierarchy of levels has been known about and taught about for millennia in both the Eastern and Western traditions. Wilber researched and documented more than 100 such models from both the Eastern and Western Traditions, and from premodern through postmodern times. If you wish to learn more about the massive and complex subject of the claimed history, description, benefits, as well as how to (allegedly) access these claimed Transpersonal levels of consciousness, you can do no better than Ken Wilber. A detailed examination of Wilber's Transpersonal levels (which Wilber calls "Integral" rather than "Transpersonal") is beyond the scope of this book, but we will now examine the impressive work Wilber has done in explaining "Psychosocial" levels of consciousness. Whether you believe in Transpersonal levels or not, there is much to be learned from Wilber on the proved reality of psychosocial levels.

The following are six macro-points we can learn from Wilber about Psychosocial levels of consciousness whether or not we subscribe to Transpersonal levels:

1. Levels are real. There is overwhelming cross-cultural and cross-historical evidence that many components of human consciousness are acquired/available to the individual in "levels".

2. These levels are not fixed like stairsteps or rungs on a ladder, but are fluid and more like overlapping waves or colors in a rainbow.

3. Each level contains numerous and individual "lines" of competence which can extend and exist on multiple levels of consciousness.

4. A developing line cannot skip a level.

5. Lines and levels are affected by "states" of consciousness.

6. After a person arrives at physical maturity, it is quite difficult to evolve to a so-called higher level.

So let's examine each of these macro-points of Psychosocial levels of human consciousness.

1) Levels are real. . . Wilber's extensive research has confirmed the overwhelming cross-cultural and cross-historical evidence that many components of human consciousness are acquired by the individual in what has been referred to by scholars as sequential/developmental levels or stages. According to Wilber, these include such components as: aspects of cognition, morals, psychosexuality, needs, interpersonal relations, and motor skills.[54]

Wilber studied over one hundred models of levels of consciousness from numerous cultures and throughout historical time. As expected, the particular descriptions, symbols, and manifestations of each theory of levels varied culture to culture and over time. However, Wilber and other scholars found that the "deep features" of all theories remained the same. Those deep features are very basically: The immature consciousness of a fetus/baby/child (as aptly described by Piaget), which Wilber terms "preconventional" consciousness. The variable consciousness of most so-called normal adults (as described by Erikson at least in Eurocentric/modern culture), which Wilber terms "conventional" consciousness. Finally, there is what could be called a type of altruistic consciousness (as suggested by Maslow as Self-Actualization), which Wilber terms "postconventional" consciousness (keeping in mind that Wilber includes Transpersonal levels in his postconventional). All models of consciousness arise from these three deep features or basic levels of preconventional, conventional, and postconventional no matter how many levels or different descriptions of the levels are used. Wilber terms any such model "the spectrum of consciousness".

2) Levels are waves not stairsteps. . . Another of Wilber's paradigm shifting insights into levels of consciousness is not to think of "fixed" levels as many commentators on Maslow's pyramid often do. Levels are not fixed

like stairsteps or rungs on a ladder. How could they be since so many of us have aspects of our consciousness that are obviously on different levels? Wilber offers two heuristic metaphors for better understanding levels: as overlapping waves, or as colors in a rainbow. After all, we now know that the specific descriptions of levels not only vary from culture to culture, but also from scholar to scholar even within a culture. Wilber, for example, typically uses nine sometimes ten levels in his particular spectrum of consciousness. To borrow from Dennett, levels are a "user illusion" to try and begin to comprehend the spectrum of consciousness.

3) Each level contains numerous lines of specific competences . . . For me, "lines" are one of the most critical insights by Wilbur in understanding levels of consciousness. (Please note that Wilber readily credits the work of Howard Earl Gardner, a developmental psychologist from Harvard, for Gardner's prior groundbreaking work regarding how different aspects of personality/consciousness mature along separate lines of development.) Earlier in this chapter, we learned about the paradigm shifting insight by Piaget that there are numerous kinds of intelligence which Piaget referred to as competences in particular aspects of life. . . things like interpersonal relationship competence and motor skill competence. There are numerous such potential competences, although many may be interrelated to other competences such as moral development and interpersonal relation competence. Wilber terms each of these potential competences a "line".

It is easy for us to understand how an individual can evolve more quickly in one line verses another. . . or even become pathologically fixated in a particular line as suggested by Freud. Since we now know there are numerous lines at each level, it should also be easier for us to understand how certain lines will continue through multiple levels. Take the line of communication skills as an example. You have the babbling of an infant, then the "me-me" communication of a child, then perhaps the crude and insensitive language of psychologically stunted adult, and then maybe the thoughtful and reflective higher level language of a person with an expanded consciousness. The macro-point here is that for each of us our overall consciousness receptacle will contain multiple lines at multiple levels. I'm thinking now is a perfect time to steal an apothegm from Wilber: Thus, "there is nothing linear about overall development."[55]

4) A developing line cannot skip a level. . . The enfolding/acquisition of lines of competence must proceed in sequence. Wilbur offers the metaphor of an acorn developing into an oak tree. You cannot go directly from acorn to full grown tree without pushing through the stage/level of sapling. A person can (and does) have multiple lines of competence at multiple levels, but a developing line cannot skip a level. This Wilber macro-point is somewhat easier to grasp if you first accept Wilber's contention that a subsequent level doesn't replace a preceding level. A new level is not a new stair leaving the entirety of the old stair behind. Rather, the old level completely enfolds into the new level much like the enfolding of life from atoms, to molecules, to cells, to tissues, to organs, to organ systems. As Wilbur says, you can't go from atoms to cells by skipping the level of molecules.

5) "States" of consciousness as catalyst. . . According to Wilber, there are three very general "states" of consciousness: Ordinary, Altered, and Nonordinary. Ordinary states include what is known as "the three great states" of waking, dreaming, and deep sleep. Altered States, as we saw earlier, are generally states induced by such things as alcohol, drugs, or special practices like meditation or ritual. Nonordinary states are what we now understand to be in the Transpersonal realm and the claimed phenomenological experience of "Oneness".

Wilber divides Nonordinary states into four groups: "psychic" which claims to involve the phenomenological experience of nature mysticism or being one with nature; "subtle" which claims to involve deity mysticism or being one with the ground of being; "casual" which claims to involve formless mysticism or being one with formless consciousness; and "nondual" which claims to involve integral mysticism or being one with the seeming opposites of form and emptiness. As we saw when we briefly looked at Grof, it is claimed by Transpersonal adherents (including Wilber even though he specifically states he is "Integral" not "Transpersonal") that such states reveal deep truths about consciousness that can be a catalyst in evolving up the lines/levels in the spectrum of consciousness toward return to the Oneness of Spirit/Godhead.

I understand this is a lot to try and grasp from my brief overview of states. Let me conclude with Wilber's teachings on Altered States. Altered States can each act as a catalyst for consciousness expansion. According to Wilber (and I am in agreement), these states are almost always temporary. They are available no matter your so-called level of consciousness or size of your consciousness receptacle; but almost always, the consciousness expansion benefit you obtain from the Altered State is derivative of your baseline level of consciousness. In other words, persons at different levels will almost always interpret and benefit from the Altered State at their current level of consciousness. Sometimes, however, an Altered State may act as a catalyst to guide a line to another level. Finally, although such Altered States mostly occur randomly, a person can with extensive practice have some control over the timing and experience of these Altered States through techniques such as lucid dreaming or meditation. A bit more on this in Chapter Eight.

6) Expanding your consciousness to the next level is darn hard . . . Wilber has also studied the success rate of individuals evolving to the next level. Unfortunately, his findings are more than a bit discouraging. Wilber has found that although progress is definitely being made along lines of competence, completely evolving (all lines) to the next level is a rare event. In particular, according to Wilber, after physical brain maturity, further evolving two more levels almost never occurs.[56] This difficulty is largely due to the almost overwhelming power of the filters to consciousness which will be discussed in Chapter Four.

It is interesting to discover that Wilber's findings show that most advancement along lines of competence occur from birth through physical maturity. This is not surprising because that is when your brain and body and emotions mature. At the very least, this is an important "heads-up" to conscientious parents. After physical maturity, there is a lull in expansion of consciousness during what could be described as the work and child-raising decades. Wilber understandably speculates that this lull occurs due to the often overwhelming time and energy demands during those decades.

(Of course your lines of competence in your particular area of work or in child-raising may likely expand during this time.) The only good news from Wilber seems to be that after retirement, the window opens wide again for consciousness expansion. We can observe that this seems consistent with the findings of the Eriksons, Lars Tornstam, and ancient Hindu texts on the four stages of life discussed earlier in this chapter. Section II "Transformance" of this book hopes to provide powerful and proved practices for expanding consciousness.

Macro-Points on Levels of Consciousness... So what have we discovered during our overview of levels of consciousness? We learned that there definitely are levels of consciousness which represent a distinctly larger receptacle of consciousness at each level . . . new values, new realities. . . a more authentic plain of awareness and existence. There are numerous models of such levels of consciousness from the most basic and fundamental model of preconventional/conventional/ postconventional to the Way Out There Transpersonal models with hundreds of levels. The Psychosocial models, which are largely confirmed by peer-reviewed science, are developmental models from birth to maturity; but theorists like Maslow, the Eriksons, and Wilber have provided us with highly insightful models that extend throughout adulthood.

Given the many different models which number and describe levels so differently, it seems certain that levels cannot be considered fixed as in stairsteps or rungs on a ladder. Wilber has provided us with the useful metaphors of overlapping waves and colors in the rainbow to help us understand the following macro-point: Although all the models are different, there is definitely a "spectrum" of increasing consciousness; and the various models are valid tools to help us understand the challenges, show us the way, and allow us to measure our progress along the spectrum. The essential first step in beginning a new challenge is to first try and understand that challenge the best you can, and certain models of the spectrum can be invaluable in understanding this difficult task.

Unfortunately, we have also learned that expanding one's level of consciousness along the spectrum is a much more difficult task than anyone might anticipate. It turns out Freud was correct when he postulated about the reality and power of fixation, even though he was often mistaken as to the specific causes of the fixation. Maslow was also correct that the power of needs can also keep us fixated. On the positive side, we have Wilber to thank for his model of "lines" of competence which, at least for me, seems to make the challenge of consciousness expansion a bit easier to comprehend and undertake. Perhaps I won't achieve another level of consciousness, but I can realistically hope to continue progression along critical lines of consciousness. At my age, I am also encouraged by Wilber's research that the path along the spectrum potentially becomes more accessible in the later stages of life.

While I suspect that Wilber is correct that evolving to an entirely new level of consciousness is extremely difficult, there is agreement among those we have been referring to as scholars (the academic professions) and mystics (spiritual and transcendental practitioners) that it is quite possible to bring particular lines of competence to a higher level. This of course raises the profound question: Which lines of competence should we be working on? Fortunately, we can obtain guidance on the answer to this question from both the scholars and the mystics.

The answer must begin by first deciding what your competence/consciousness raising goals are. Are your goals along the lines such as becoming a better dancer, becoming a top geologist, or becoming rich and famous? Ha! If so, you're reading the wrong book. But if you seek to further approach goals such as Maslow's Self-Actualization; the Erickson/Tornstam goal of Gerotranscendence, or even the ultimate Buddhist goal of Enlightenment, please read on.

In subsequent chapters you'll find that both scholars and mystics are not that far apart on why and what lines of competence/consciousness are best suited to further approach such goals. Lines of competence in humility, patience, and compassion are often the first that come to mind; and such lines are consistently taught by the great mystics. Yet foundational to the development of such lines are lines of competence in self-awareness and self-regulation. Self-awareness is needed because the essential first step in attempting to change something is to first try and understand how that "something" operates. That "something" not only includes the nature of consciousness, but our own self-reflective ability to recognize our own challenges and limitations of consciousness. Self-regulation is needed in order to transform your consciousness against the almost overwhelming powerful filters to that consciousness. The next chapter will explore those filters.

---

1 For an interesting and short (543 words) article on the history of using the term "quantum", go online to "The History of using 'quantum' to mean 'really big'" by Merrill Perlman; Columbia Journalism Review, 8-4-14.

2 The term "paradigm shift" was first used by the American physicist, Thomas Kuhn (1922-1996), to describe a major change in the previously accepted (essentially sacred) rules and values of a scientific doctrine such as the laws of gravity. The term has since been used to describe any new and profound change from previously accepted norms. Thomas S. Kuhn "The Structure of Scientific Revolutions" University of Chicago Press, 1962.

3 I have heard a similar story from so many people that I do not know who to credit in the footnote.

4 Other medical models use decreasing LOC such as conscious, confused, delirious, somnolent, obtunded, stuporous, and comatose. You can find online an excellent article at nursinglink.monster.com on "Altered Levels of Consciousness" for more information on what I have termed Medical levels of consciousness.

5 Charles T. Tart, PhD. "States of Consciousness" iUniverse.com, Inc. 2000. Note also that relatively recently, the Johns Hopkins University founded and opened the Johns Hopkins Center on Psychedelic and Consciousness Research which includes research into altered states.

6 Tart at p5.

7 Tart at p11-17.

8 It was interesting for me to observe that Maslow rarely used the term "levels" in his original, foundational lectures and publications. Yet subsequent commentators almost universally always use the term levels as well as the pyramid form. See page 103 of "Motivation and Personality" Second Edition, Harper & Row, Publishers, Inc., New York 1954, 1970 for a rare example of Maslow using "level" in his early works: "In the finding that living at the higher need level can sometimes become relatively independent of lower need gratification. . . we may have a solution to an age-old dilemma of the theologians." (Here and after "Ginsberg and Opper".)

9 "Piaget's Theory of Intellectual Development" Second Edition, Prentice-Hall by Herbert Ginsburg and Sylvia Opper, Englewood Cliff's, New Jersey, 1979.

10 Ginsberg and Opper at p8.

11 Ginsberg and Opper at p3.

12 Ginsberg and Opper at p6.

13 Ginsberg and Opper at p14-15.

14 "Memory and Intelligence" by Jean Piaget & Barbel Inhelder, Basic Books, Inc., New York, 1973 page 379 translated from French publication 1968).

15 A. H. Maslow "A Theory of Human Motivation" was originally published in Psychological Review, 50, 370-396 in 1943. This relatively short paper can now easily be found online. Citations in chapter will be to the 2013 publication by Martino Publishing, Mansfield Centre, Ct. Here and after "ATHM". ATHM was later developed in Maslow's book "Motivation and Personality" published in 1954 by Harper & Row, Publishers, New York.

16 This graphic is a composite of mine from various writings by Maslow. Many other such graphics can easily be found online. As I was searching for a citation to Maslow's first use of this pyramid, it was interesting for me to discover that Maslow was likely not the author of this pyramid representation nor even the word "pyramid" to describe his hierarchy of needs. See, "Who Created Maslow's Iconic Pyramid?" Scott Barry Kaufman (2019); Scientific American Blog Network, published online at https://blogs.scientificamerican.com/beautiful-minds/who-created-Maslows-iconic-pyramid/; citing a prior study: "Who Built Maslow's Pyramid? A History of the Creation of Management Studies' Most Famous Symbol and It's Implications for Management Education" by Todd Bridgman, Stephen Cummings, and John Ballard; Academy of Management Learning & Education, Vol. 18, No. 1 Essays & Dialogues (2019), which can be found online at https://doi.org/10.5465/amle.2017.0351.

17 ATHM at p1.

18 ATHM at p13.

19 ATHM at p3.

20 "Toward A Psychology of Being" Third Edition by Abraham H. Maslow, John Wiley & Sons, New York, 1999, Forward page "x".

21 Abraham H. Maslow "Motivation and Personality" Second Edition, Harper & Row, New York, 1954, 1970 at p149.

22 I would also add my own criticism that Maslow spent an inordinate amount of his lecture and writing time on the highest need level of self actualization, including describing the self actualization attributes of famous people Maslow never met nor even knew in any psychological depth. . . including a number of historical figures long dead. I speculate that this focus was actually a big part of Maslow's public popularity in the 60s. Think about the type of person who would read Maslow in the 60s? Who buys such books or reads such articles? Most likely people who are educated, searching, and highly motivated by esteem needs. . . a/k/a ego needs. And how would such a person picture themself. Without a doubt as a current (or at the least a future) member of the top of the pyramid club. . . self actualized. I offer such speculation in confidence because this is a seemingly never ending ego need battle that I have been fighting for many years as evidenced by my interaction with Monsignor Riches referenced in Chapter Two. Anyone reading this footnote want to admit to the same?

23 As somewhat of an aside. . . In researching Maslow, I was fortunate to come across ten recommendations that Maslow prepared for educators in helping each student grow into a self-actualized person. While Section Two of this book offers powerful individual practices that can help in expanding consciousness, these ten recommendations by Maslow (although perhaps too general in

scope to be a practical tool in daily practice) are "conceptually" as good as anything I have read, been taught, or practiced. They are as follows: 1) We should teach people to be *authentic*, to be aware of their inner selves and to hear their inner-feeling voices. 2) We should teach people to *transcend their cultural conditioning* and become world citizens. 3) We should help people *discover their vocation in life*, their calling, fate or destiny. This is especially focused on finding the right career and the right mate. 4) We should teach people that *life is precious*, that there is joy to be experienced in life, and if people are open to seeing the good and joyous in all kinds of situations, it makes life worth living. 5) We must *accept the person* as he or she is and help the person learn their inner nature. From real knowledge of aptitudes and limitations we can know what to build upon, what potentials are really there. 6) We must see that the person's *basic needs are satisfied*. This includes safety, belongingness, and esteem needs. 7) We should *refreshen consciousness*, teaching the person to appreciate beauty and the other good things in nature and in living. 8) We should teach people that *controls are good*, and complete abandon is bad. It takes control to improve the quality of life in all areas. 9) We should teach people to transcend the trifling problems and *grapple with the serious problems in life*. These include the problems of injustice, of pain, suffering, and death. 10) We must teach people to be *good choosers*. They must be given practice in making good choices.

24 See "The Life Cycle Completed" Erik H. Erikson Extended Version with New Chapters on the Ninth Stage of Development by Joan M. Erikson (Erik's wife 19030–1997). W.W. Norton & Company 1978 at p56–57. Here and after "TLCC".

25 TLCC at p3.

26 "In the Shadow of Fame: A Memoir by the Daughter of Erikson", by Sue Erikson Bloland, Penguin Books Ltd., London, 2005 at p62. Here and after "ISF".

27 ISF at p57–59.

28 ISF at p59–61.

29 It appears from the book written by Erikson's daughter, Sue Erikson Bloland (see FN 27) that this last book by Erikson was probably written by Erikson's talented and long-time collaborating wife, Joan M. Erikson, due to Erikson's diminishing cognitive abilities during the final several years of his life.

30 TLCC at p123.

31 TLCC at pp106–108.

32 TLCC at pp126–129.

33 It's interesting to note that online grammar sites offer an apparently little known distinction between the terms "transcendent" and "transcendental" suggesting that "transcendental" is a little less extreme than "transcendent" with "transcendental" more of a metaphor of an experience rather than representing the extreme difference between the material world and the claimed transcendent world. See for example the online site WorldReference.com under transcendent vs. transcendental.

34 TLCC at pp123–124.

35 *Id*.

36 "A Brief History of Transpersonal Psychology" can be found at www.stanislawgrof.com (Here and

after "BHTP".)

37 BHTP at pp3, 8-9.

38 BHTP at p3.

39 BHTP at p6.

40 BHTP at p7.

41 BHTP at p5.

42 BHTP at p4.

43 BHTP at p7.

44 BHTP at p8-9.

45 BHTP at p7.

46 "The Cosmic Game: Explorations of the Frontiers of Human Consciousness" by Stanislav Grof, State University of New York Press, Albany, 1998.

47 A well presented and fair critique of the "proof" of Transcendental (psi) claims, written by a proponent of Transcendental consciousness, Don Salmon, entitled "Integral Psychology, Beyond Wilber-V: Inviting Open-Minded Skepticism of the Materialist View" can be found online at www.integralworld.net.

48 "Memories, Dreams, Reflections" C.G. Jung. Recorded and edited by Aniela Jaffe. Translated from TW German by Richard and Clara Winston. Revised Edition, Vintage Books, Edition, New York (1989) at p76-77. (Here and after "Memories".)

49 Memories at p100.

50 BHTP at pp11-14.

51 "Integral Psychology: Consciousness, Spirit, Psychology, Therapy" by Ken Wilber, Shambhala Publications, Inc., Boston, 2000 at p2 (Here and after "Integral Psychology".)

52 Wilber himself recognized the difficulty of working your way through his understanding of consciousness. I suspect this is why in 1998 he published a relatively short and easy to follow book entitled "The Essential Ken Wilber: An Introductory Reader". Shambhala Publications, Inc. Boston, 1998. I would recommend beginning with this book for further investigation of his understanding of consciousness.

53 Wilber spells Cosmos with a capital K, which he claims is a reintroduction of the original Pythagorean term that not only includes the physical cosmos as we commonly know it, but all physical and transpersonal (spiritual) levels/realms of reality both manifest and not yet known. Also, Pythagoras wrote with a "k" because there was no letter "c" in Greek. "Sex, Ecology, Spirituality: The Spirit of Evolution" Shambhala Publications, Inc., Boston, 1995, 2000 at p45.

54 There are many books by Wilber that support these claims. Perhaps the most on-point would be "Integral Psychology" which includes over 65 pages of citational "Notes". Another source, although

perhaps a bit difficult for a first-time read of Wilber, is an online site created by Frank Visser at "Waves, Streams, States, and Self—A summary of My Psychological Model" at www.integralworld. net (Here and after "Visser".) This is also an online site for criticism of Wilber.

55 "The Eye of Spirit: An Integral Vision for a World Gone Slightly Mad" by Ken Wilber, Shambhala Publications, Inc., Boston, Massachusetts 2001 at p134. Not surprisingly, this phrase cannot be found in my 1997 edition of this book.

56 "Kosmic Consciousness" an audio cd lecture by Wilber published by Sounds True.

CHAPTER FOUR

ARE THERE OBSTACLES TO CONSCIOUSNESS EXPANSION?
(The Main Filters To Consciousness)

The nature of our mind is observed.
This means we build a world full of
illusion for ourselves because of the
distorted way we perceive reality. . .
Consciousness has the job of manifesting
and differentiating our perceptions [of reality, but]
our consciousness rarely touches reality. . .
We imprison ourselves in our own
distorted images of reality.
—Thich Nhat Hanh[1]

If our working definition of consciousness is correct. . . the degree to which you are aware of and knowingly responsive to your internal and external environment. . . then these words of Thich Nhat Hanh set forth an insurmountable truth. *We will never really know reality!* This is because the data coming into our consciousness is always filtered. The word "filtered" is chosen to help try and describe how numerous factors and forces alter, restrict, color, prevent, change, and even falsely create data entering and ruminating in our consciousness. These filters fundamentally and profoundly affect our thinking, feeling, and acting. . . in other words, the degree to which you are aware of and knowingly responsive to your internal and external environment.

We've already learned about a number of ways that data entering our consciousness is filtered. We learned from the Ancient Greeks that our very sense organs can and do fool us. We learned that Descartes (the otherwise brilliant and "out of the box" thinker who claimed to doubt everything) still clung to Dualism because his consciousness prevented him from questioning a faith belief in the Christian God of his time. We learned from Feinberg and Mallatt that our present day consciousness is still affected by ancient evolutionary changes that occurred millions of years ago; a key one being pejoratively described as our "reptile brain". We learned from Koch how the very neuronal correlates of our brain/consciousness not only use filters such as often incorrect rapid decision making based on past experiences, but include such things as Zombie agents of which we are not even aware until they react without conscious direction. We learned from Freud, Piaget, and Erikson not only how much our adult consciousness is affected by our early childhood, but that the expansion of our consciousness can even become fixated/arrested. We learned from Maslow how we are driven by almost overwhelmingly powerful needs that are "like looking at the world through a clouded lens". And we learned through Dennett and James that consciousness itself is likely a user illusion, or at least something that constantly changes as it flows. Understanding and accepting that there are significant filters to our consciousness is without a doubt a required first step regarding any attempt to expand your consciousness, and the fundamental/primary macro-point of Section I of this book.

There are many ways to describe the numerous filters to human consciousness. Here are six categories of filters for us to explore:

1. Ignorance,
2. Genetics;
3. Non-consciousness;
4. Culture;
5. Emotions; and
6. Circumstances of the moment.

These categories are not meant to be all inclusive. Moreover, all overlap and blend together to some degree. Admittedly, they are simply a heuristic device that will help give us a more nuanced overview of the enigmatic nature of consciousness.

1. *Ignorance. . . the root power of all filters*

Ignorance, the root and stem of every evil
—Plato

One could make a simple linguistic argument that the root impediment of all filters to consciousness is ignorance. If "level of consciousness" is commonly understood as one's "state of being aware"; and if "ignorance" is understood as one's "state of being unaware"; then by definition, ignorance is the polar opposite and the most fundamental impediment to consciousness raising.

Ignorance is not only the root power of all filters to consciousness, but there are different types of ignorance. Once again, scholars have parsed a seemingly simple word like "ignorance" into multiple types. Any online search will reveal more than 30 terms for types of ignorance.[2] For example, there are types of ignorance such as: antecedent, vincible, domain, nescience, and enlightened ignorance. But not to worry, many of these types essentially mean the same conceptual thing, and most can be boiled down into three general types: innocent, willful, and Socratic ignorance.

"Innocent" simply means the person was unaware of a pertinent fact(s) when thinking, feeling, or acting. For example, when a person quickly jumps out of a river because they mistakenly think a stick is a snake. "Willful" means a person thinks, feels, or acts with a willful intent not to learn the facts or relevant information. For example, when the accusers of Galileo refused to look into his telescope. "Socratic" involves a frank acknowledgement by a person that they never really know anything with absolute certainty. Socratic ignorance especially includes the fact that they don't know what they don't know. The concept of Socratic ignorance comes in part from words attributed to Socrates:

So I withdrew and thought to myself: 'I am wiser than this man; it is likely that neither of us knows anything worthwhile, but he thinks he knows something when he does not; whereas when I do not know, neither do I think I know; so I am wiser than he to this small extent, that I do not think I know what I do not know.[3]

Socratic ignorance requires a higher level consciousness acceptance of the filters to consciousness. It is an absolute prerequisite for any hope of meaningful consciousness expansion.

Unfortunately, a person whose consciousness receptacle operates in the realm of willful ignorance will likely have a near impossible challenge in expanding their consciousness to another level even though that willful person may demonstrate great mastery in other specific "lines" of competence. As we learned from Ken Wilbur, incompetence in one or more lines of competence due to wilfull ignorance in certain matters does not preclude expansion of other (perhaps many) "lines" of competence (for example in sports, handicrafts, or running a business). However, it is unlikely any meaningful progress will be made in. . . the degree to which such a person is aware of and knowingly responsive to their internal and external environment. This is because a pattern of willful ignorance almost always signifies cognitive rigidity. Not only is such a person's consciousness closed to new ideas, but there is frequently a "fear" of almost any social, family, religious, employment, scientific, or political change. Such a pattern of cognitive rigidity can often be seen in the political and religious spheres, especially in such groups self-labeled as "conservative". Such rigidity is almost always fear based even though the person is likely unaware of and vehemently denies such fear. This fear is often unknowingly expressed in anger and even hatred toward any group or person arguing for change based on new data. Willfully ignorant beliefs that would easily be disprovable with minimal inquiry are too often a matter of existential dogma for groups of such persons.

But before (we)[4] social liberals mount our high-horses of claimed moral superiority and evolved consciousness, be aware that so-called "progressive" individuals also have their own typical issues of willful ignorance. This often takes the form of "purity" tests, a type of elitism that not only looks down upon, but totally disregards any data from a person or group that dares to have any opinion (related or unrelated to the issue at hand) that is not "politically correct".[5] After all, how could such unevolved persons who refuse (for example) to recycle their trash or support gay rights have anything of value to say on any other topic? The mantra of "purity" progressives is: The politically incorrect have absolutely nothing worthwhile to say. There is also a "fear" basis to liberal willful ignorance, but it is not usually fear of change. It is often more "ego" based: I'm more evolved than the conservatives, and I won't hear anything to the contrary. Borrowing from Maslow, this liberal willful ignorance is driven more by the level of "Esteem" needs rather than by the level of "Belonging" needs of the conservatives. So, if you're a follower of Maslow and "progressive", you can perhaps content yourself with the illusion of being one level higher on Maslow's pyramid, but progress in consciousness expansion will still be blinded by ego needs. No matter how evolved we think we are, we are all subject to the filter of ignorance.

As we will discuss later in this chapter, persons from both conservative and liberal groups are now more than ever bonding together into segregated groups of similar believers with their own exclusive sources of news/information in order to satisfy their Maslovian needs for social acceptance and ego gratification. Moreover, because both conservatives and liberals can and do develop advanced lines of competence in areas such as politics, religion, and money making, these rigid groups have the ability to create and control businesses, schools, religious sects, political positions, cultural organizations, and news organizations which further "filter" their members from any challenge to their sacred beliefs that could arise from new information. It's not hard to see how ignorance not only creeps in, but in most cases is the root of all filters to consciousness. As well stated by Thich Nhat Hanh, as well as numerous other scholars and mystics . . . We imprison ourselves in our own distorted images of reality. Hopefully our ignorance filter is mostly innocent ignorance, but I suspect we also all have at least a touch of willful ignorance.

2. *Genetics. . . Which contributes more to human behavior, nature or nurture?*

Which contributes more to the area
of a rectangle, its length or its width?
—Donald Hebb[6]

The nature versus nurture debate involves whether human behavior is determined by genetics (nature) or by life experiences (nurture). But it's also very much about consciousness, because both genetics and life experiences filter our consciousness.

The nature versus nurture debate goes back at least as far as the Ancient Greek philosophers. In a general sense, Plato (428-348 BCE) was a "nature" advocate, while Aristotle (384-322 BCE) was more of a "nurture" advocate. Plato argued that all knowledge, forms, and concepts reside in the World of Forms; and so the nature of a person was to a large extent predetermined. Life experiences do not teach us anything new, but only remind us of what already exists. Aristotle on the other hand believed a person was born as a blank slate, and gained knowledge and behaved as the person was nurtured through the experiences of life.

The nature versus nurture debate continued through the beginnings of the Modern Age with philosophers like Descartes (1596-1650) arguing for the nature side. Their primary argument seems to have been that man (always "man" back then) was created by God and in the image of God; and accordingly, had an inherent noble nature beyond that of mere animals.

One of the few philosophers of that time taking up the nurture side of the dispute was English philosopher, John Locke (1632-1704). Locke actually coined the Latin phrase "tabula rasa" (Plato's blank slate) when he argued that a person is born as a blank slate, and that all behavioral traits are learned during life.[7]

Frankly, while we can appreciate Locke's consciousness changing challenge to the cultural Cartesian gravity of believing human behavior traits come from our God-given nature, it is difficult to understand why any sensible person would believe such an extreme "tabula rasa" theory that a person is not born with at least some genetic predispositional traits. Although "genes" were unknown in Locke's time, the practice of animal husbandry (selective animal breeding) were known for more than 1000 years before Locke. It was longstanding common knowledge in agricultural society that aspects of nature could be bred into livestock. On a lighter argument, any tabula rasa theory fails my "Observable Parent/Grandparent Test". Admittedly, this very non-scholarly test can easily be dismissed as a theory unencumbered by scientific data; but any observable parent (and even more so an observable grandparent since they are going through the child rearing process a second time and without the stress of being the actual parent) can tell you with absolute certainty that each of their children/grandchildren was born with distinct personality traits that have changed little to none over the course of that child's life. Nonetheless, the full-on nurture argument (that 100% of human nature and behavior comes from life experience) continued to flourish within many influential areas of society.

As scholars and wanna-be scholars continued to debate nature versus nurture over the next two centuries, each of these theories took a turn to the dark side. In some cases, the turn was taken to a very dark side.

In 1883, the full-on nature argument (that 100% of behavior traits come from genetics) began to take a dark detour with thought leaders like Francis Gault (1822-1911), an English sociologist, psychologist, anthropologist, and cousin of Charles Darwin. Gault not only coined the phrase "nature versus nurture", but also coined the term "eugenics" meaning "well-born". Gault argued that healthy and smart people should bear more children with the goal of improving the human race. We all are familiar with the multiple tragic paths eugenics has taken, reaching its nadir in the 1940s with the Nazi regime; but it unfortunately continues even into current times.[8]

On the opposite side of the spectrum, the full-on nurture argument (that 100% of human nature and behavior traits come from life experiences) detoured into its own darkness of Behaviorism (as discussed in Chapter Three) from around the 1920s and even up until the 1970s.

Give me a child, and I'll shape him into anything.
—B.F. Skinner[9]

Fortunately for humankind, extreme/purist positions on nature verses nurture began to fade toward the middle of the 20th century. Both scholars and the lay public increasingly accepted that nature versus nurture was a false dichotomy, and that both genetics and life experiences each play roles in the development of human behavior. The debate was no longer "which" is responsible for human nature, but "how do" genetics and life experiences work together to form human nature, human behavior, and (I would add) individual human consciousness?

A seminal time in understanding the awesome role of genetics in forming human nature occurred in 1953 when James Watson (1928-) and Francis Crick (1916-2004) discovered the double helix structure of DNA. Following this discovery, genetic research by scholars from around the world exploded into how genes control not only the physical form but also the behavior of all plants, animals, and not just humans. Let us now look at some of the key terms in genetics.

"DNA" (deoxyribonucleic acid) is the molecule that contains the genetic Master Code of all living organisms. The DNA Master Code determines in large part how every aspect of each living organism will look and function. All DNA, whether plant, animal, or human is made from what are called "sequences" (permutations) of only four amino acids which exist in "base pairs". These four base pairs are known as A, C, G, and T for adenine, cytosine, guanine, and thymine. Human DNA has a string of permutations of more than three billion base pairs. There are very few things in this wonder-filled world more amazing than the genetic progress of a zygote (a single diploid cell created from the fusion of sperm and egg) developing into a human being as a result of its DNA Master Code.

"Genes" are essentially pieces of the DNA Master Code. A particular gene is a snippet of a piece of base pair sequence from the DNA Master Code. Genes vary in size from a few hundred base pairs to over two million base pairs. It is estimated that a human being has between 20,000 to 25,000 genes. Genes are both the basic physical and the basic functional units of heredity. This means that genes are responsible for both the morphology (form) of the living organism and for its function. It is commonly understood that genes are responsible for such things as the color of your eyes, whether your ear lobes are attached, and whether and when you will eventually go bald. But less well known is that genes are also largely responsible for a person's personality traits, which can reasonably be defined as the enduring patterns of thoughts, feelings, and behaviors.[10] The scholars of Behavior Genetics define the genetic characteristics of an organism as its "genotype", and define its observed behavior as its "phenotype". A macro-point of this subsection is that genes not only influence human form, but also influence functions such as: cognition, emotion, learning, memory, perception, and neuroplasticity. (This last function will be discussed in detail in Chapter Five.) With power like that, how can genetics be anything but a filter to our consciousness?

Yet perhaps an even more seminal moment into nature versus nurture filtering consciousness occurred in 1956, shortly after the discovery of DNA when British developmental biologist, Conrad Waddington (1905-1975), published a paper in the journal "Evolution" which some scholars call the origin of "epigenics".[11] Epigenics is Greek in derivation, and essentially means "above" or "on top of" the gene. Think of epigenics as an extra layer of instructions as to how genes "express" themselves.[12]

"Epigenetics" is the study of how genes function. . . how a gene turns on, turns up, turns down, turns off. As noted above, scholars call this process "gene expression". Genes are fixed. They need to be activated by an outside signal. It will come as no surprise that gene expression can be triggered by factors from the endogenous (inside the body) biological world of hormones and metabolic needs. But most profoundly in the last 20 years, advancements in epigenetics have resulted in nothing short of a paradigm shift in the understanding of gene expression. It is now well accepted that exogenous (outside the body) factors such as stress, sleep, exercise, diet, weather, psychological counselling, and meditation activate gene expression up, down, on, and off. This environmental activation is much more influential than prior scholars ever anticipated.

> It has now been proven beyond doubt that although
> our genes are fixed, their expression is highly dependent
> on what our environment throws at us.[13]

Epigenics answers the why, when, and how genes affect their coding instructions involving all physical and functional aspects of a human being. It is not overreaching to suggest that epigenics is the current tip of the spear for research on the creation, function, and development of the human condition. . . including consciousness. As we will learn, the most salient aspect of epigenics for our investigation into filters of consciousness is that life experiences/nurture (what scholars are now calling "environmental factors") play an inseparable role in the expression of our genes. Genes need environmental factors for expression. Nature and nurture are in a yin/yang relationship. Nature provides the gene, but nurture influences expression of that gene. Moreover, as we will see (especially in the next chapter on brain plasticity), an individual is potentially in a position to intentionally affect/alter certain types of gene expression through changes and practices in their environment.

Having now looked at the key vocabulary and processes of genetics, let us now look at the seminal research on epigenetics; specifically, the yin/yang interaction of nature and nurture in contributing to an individual's personality/consciousness.

Scholarly research into the roles of nature and nurture have historically focused on twins, with a special focus on the scientifically optimal setting of monozygotic twins raised apart. This is because monozygotic twins, commonly known as "identical" twins, are derived from a single and then split fertilized ovum (a mature female reproductive cell. . . a/k/a egg). Their genotypes are identical. Then when genetically identical twins are subsequently raised apart, there is supposedly a controlled environment to measure the effects of nurture on one genotype. If the phenotypes (personality traits) of the identical twins are different, then such differences must be due to nurture, or what scholars now call environmental factors.

The first seminal study involving monozygotic twins raised apart was a multi-decade study completed in the late 1980s by members of the Department of Psychology and the Institute of Human Genetics at the University of Minnesota, which instantly became well known, both in scholarly fields and lay publications as "The Minnesota Study".[14] The Minnesota Study found that 70% of personality traits such as IQ, temperament, occupation, leisure-time interests, and social attitudes were due to genetics. The New York Times then ran with the hyperbole that these 70% "findings shatter a widespread belief among experts and laymen alike in the primacy of family influence.[15] The "nature" argument was again dominant.

But the newly revived pre-eminence of nature over nurture did not last long. In 2015, the first meta-analysis on the roles of nature and nurture was completed at the University of Zagreb.[16] This appears to have been the first "meta-analysis" to systemically analyze all relevant research on the genetics of personality. (A meta-analysis is scientifically significant because it reviews, analyzes, and statistically combines all leading prior studies on a topic.) This Zagreb study found a much more modest yet still significant role for genetics, finding the average affect of genetics on personality was only about 40% with 60% being due to "environmental influences". The study also found no difference in these percentages between males and females.[17]

These Zagreb percentage findings were confirmed in 2017 in a supplemental study by essentially the same Zagreb team entitled "Heritability of Personality.[18] This supplemental study also found that genetic effects on individual aspects of phenotype were due to small influences from many genes, perhaps thousands.[19] There is no single personality gene. As with many aspects of genetics, multiple genes contribute to genetic action/results.

The above studies, as well as other scholarly research into the roles of nature and nurture, have provided us with further interesting insights into the roles of nature and nurture with regard to personality. Various scholars have identified numerous and different personality traits. "Traits" can be understood as general, observable, and largely enduring behavioral patterns.

Each of us has numerous traits. For example, American psychologist Gordon Allport (1897-1967), considered one of the most eminent psychologists of the 20th century and a founder of "trait theory", once put together a list of over 4000 such traits. However, most scholars agree that there are "The Big Five" personality traits. These are often referred to as "OCEAN" for: Openness to new experiences; Conscientiousness in task/goal performance; Extroversion; Agreeableness; and Neuroticism. All other traits are often considered subcategories of The Big Five.

An individual's degree/display of each of these five personality traits is found on a bell curve throughout the world population. Some few individuals are at the extreme ends of the bell curve (for example with personality traits of extreme extroversion or introversion), but most are in the middle. These Big Five traits are expressed without regard to culture, although the specific form of expression varies among different cultures. But more pertinent to our investigation is that scholars have found that these broad traits are quite powerful, and seem to be difficult to change even over a lifetime. This difficulty is consistent with Ken Wilbur's belief that it is quite difficult to move one's consciousness up an entire level, and likely impossible to move up two levels.

So what are the macro-points we have learned about the filter of genetics? We've learned that genetics (our particular genotype) has a strong affect/push not only on our personality (our particular phenotype); but also on our cognition, emotions, learning, memory, perception, and even the way our brain changes (brain plasticity). That's a darn big chunk of our ability to be aware of and knowingly responsive to our internal and external environment. It certainly seems like quite a powerful filter, especially when we also learned the significant difficulty involved in changing the fundamental Big Five traits of our personality. The good news is that current scholarly research has confirmed that environmental factors, some of which we have control over, can affect "expression" of certain genetic personality traits. This makes it possible for an individual to change/weaken less desirable genetic tendencies and/or change/strengthen desirable genetic tendencies. In Chapter Five we will explore the science of brain plasticity to investigate how we can rewire our genetic tendencies.

3. *Non-Consciousness. . . and its powerful habit energy*

Most of what is real within ourselves is not conscious,
and most of what is conscious is not real.
—Erich Fromm[20]

We now know there are at least three general subsets to the collective term we have been using. . . "non-conscious".

1. There are the zombie agents, essentially reflex reactions that occur without our conscious awareness.

2. There are the habit energy of thoughts, emotions, and actions that occur without reflection or even in error due to the evolutionary design that causes our brains to rapidly respond based on the habits of past experiences.

3. Finally, there are the psychological repressed memories which Freud called the "unconscious".[21]

As to zombie agents, by their very definition, there is not much we can do about them other than be aware of their general existence. They are reflexes. Many are not even initiated from the brain, but rather from the CNS outside of the brain. Nor would we necessarily want to be aware of them before they occur. Don't know about you, but I want my hand to immediately jerk away when I touch a hot stove.

As to habit energy. . . All scholars agree that the power of habit is both omnipresent and often overwhelming. As we learned in Chapter One, we are essentially pattern seeking beings. The evolutionary design and initial function of our brain is based on the habits of prior experience. Not only are the "outgoing" thoughts, emotions, and actions filtered through habits, but so too is our evaluation of "incoming" data. Our brains rush to find a pattern/narrative to evaluate, sort, and store incoming experience. More often than not, without awareness of or reflection about, perception is filtered downward into mere habit. Emotions become habit. Actions become habit. If we wish to expand our consciousness, we cannot forget the macro-point that the brain is a bias producing machine almost exclusively based on habit. This leads to filtering of our consciousness, which can produce a non-conscious bias on essentially all matters of cognition, emotion, and action.

The current scholarly term for this non-conscious bias is "cognitive bias".[22] This is actually an umbrella term since (not surprisingly) scholars have now isolated and confirmed literally hundreds of subtypes of such biases/effects. (Simply search online for "list of cognitive biases".) Each of these subtypes essentially involves the same phenomenon: the brain's fundamental tendency to filter our conscious awareness, emotions, and conduct.[23]

Some of these subtypes of cognitive bias can be a bit humorous at times (less so when you discover a subtype applies to you personally). "Spotlight Effect" involves the tendency of a person to believe they are being noticed much more than they actually are. For example, believing that everyone in church is noticing that one of your earrings has a chip in it, or that your tie has a spot on it. "Fundamental Attribution Error" involves the tendency to believe that what a person is observed doing is actually indicative of who they are in the rest of their life. For example, believing that the person who cut in front of your car must be a real jerk in all aspects of life. "Dunning-Kruger Effect" ("DKE") involves believing that you are way smarter and more capable than you really are. You might think DKE would more often be found in smart people with big egos; but surprisingly, it is much more commonly found in persons with quite limited knowledge and a lack of consciousness about their own limitations. Due to the powerful filter of DKE, persons suffering from DKE often respond with anger when confronted with data conflicting with their understanding of a matter/topic. This aggressive response is motivated by fear, the most powerful motivator of consciousness (as discussed in the next subsection on the "unconscious").

A potentially more serious and destructive subtype of cognitive bias is "Othering". It involves dehumanizing a person, class, race, or nation. It can be as seemingly innocent as yelling at the television during football season that, "All Greenbay Packer fans suck!" (A clear exaggeration, but fully justified when Greenbay is trouncing your home team.) On a much more tragic note, Othering can be used by political leaders to justify ethnic cleansing. Massive atrocities such as slavery, the Holocaust, and the current wars in Syria and Yemen are obviously horrendous and unjustifiable. Yet when these now almost unimaginable atrocities occurred, they were supported by hundreds of thousands of citizens who otherwise would be considered "normal" psychologically. The power of Othering on the consciousness of people is frightfully and tragically powerful.

Of course, no person who takes the time to read a book like this is racist, sexist, or biased in any way against others. Ha! I invite you to take the Harvard "Implicit Association Test" at implicit.harvard.edu. We are all biased to some degree.

As to the (Freudian) unconscious. . . Numerous scholars, both brilliant and not so much, have written tomes on the nature and function of what Freud called the unconscious. Over the decades, many such scholarly theories on the unconscious have gone from scholarly and lay dogma into virtual disrepute (Freud's overemphasis on sexual motivation for example). Although interesting and educational, such psychological theories of the unconscious are beyond the focus of this book. What is important to again reference, however, is the very real danger of becoming "fixated" in a pathological (or even less than pathological) unconscious state that can and will prevent consciousness expansion along certain critical lines of development, as discussed in Chapter Three.

There is another macro-point on the Freudian unconscious that should also be addressed. It is recognizing the fundamental and awesome power of fear. Fear is the most powerful motivator to consciousness. Maslow describes levels/needs of biological urgency that are so powerful that they monopolize the entire organism. But what underlies, what compels those needs? It's fear. Just look at the ascending levels of Maslow's pyramid. Fear underlies and motivates them all: Physiological needs, Safety needs, Belonging needs, and Esteem needs. (Perhaps you can make an argument that fear does not motivate Self-actualization needs. I'm in no position to know because my consciousness is nowhere near that level; but I suspect that at least initially the motivation involves fear of a wasted life, although mystics seem to be in agreement that reaching that level of consciousness involves releasing all fear.)

You don't have to be a disciple of Maslow to appreciate the power of fear. Study any scholar on levels of consciousness. For example, go back to Chapter Three, and take a look at Erikson's nine psychological stages. See how easy it is to understand the underlying role of fear in each stage. Fear is the most powerful motivator, not only on what we have been calling the Freudian unconscious, but on all filters. The opposite of love is not hate. It's fear.

4. *Culture. . . the creator of our identity*

We are not biologically different from one another; but we easily
get suspicious, judgmental, and defensive, misunderstanding others'
opinions, struggles, and needs. When our fears of the "other"
are stirred by ambitious politicians or corporate interests, we let ourselves
be used for others' agenda and greed. We think we are informed,
without actually seeking the raw truth. We like our information
sugar-coated with our favorite flavors. So we judge on taste
instead of content. We are pawns in larger games.
We are being played; but sadly, we too play our parts in the games.
—Philippe Lajaunie[24]

It comes as no surprise that, in addition to a personal consciousness/ unconscious, there is also a "social" consciousness/unconscious.[25] Each society determines which thoughts, emotions, and actions will be allowed to surface into awareness, and which must remain suppressed in the social unconscious.[26] This social repression is not just censorship per se. It is not just blocking the internet, or prohibiting certain protest actions. It is much deeper. It is much more insidious. It includes repressing any conscious awareness of so-called antisocial thoughts deep into the unconscious of the members of that society so that even secret/personal thoughts contrary to the values of that society never even occur to an individual!

The intensity, scope, and success of this societal repression varies from society to society. It is designed and titrated by the elites of the society; but if it is to be successful, it must also be enforced by the non-elite members/pawns of that society.

The first and most visible tools of repression are obviously information control and prohibition of certain acts such as protest marching, protest publications, and blocking access to any information deemed antisocial. Action is easier to prohibit than thinking. Prohibiting protest/information does not prevent antisocial thoughts in the consciousness of the protesters, but it does keep the consciousness of the non-protesters from becoming aware of ideas contrary to the enforced social consciousness. Ignorance is bliss.

The more pernicious tools of repression include techniques such as disinformation, intense nationalism, and "Othering" as discussed earlier in this chapter. These cancerous tools play off the Maslovian-type needs of that society. For example, control/manipulation of the Physiological needs of food, water, and sleep in North Korea; or the Safety needs of religious reward and punishment in Saudi Arabia; or the Belonging needs in more democratic countries such as the United States. Yes, even the United States represses certain so-called non-patriotic thoughts. You don't believe me? Simply go online to find current surveys by reputable researchers such as the Pew Research Group which show the large percentages of Americans who not only still believe the USA is the "Greatest Country in the World", but who would have no conscious inkling that this "Greatest Country in the World" ranks:

15th in equality of human rights;

15th in quality of life;

20th in educational systems;

27th in healthcare; and

45th in business opportunity even though we are the "Land of Opportunity" and the "American Dream".[27]

Yet most Americans believe we are Number One in all these categories, and will become upset/angered by you if you challenge their patriotic beliefs. (Thankfully, this is increasingly less so with young people who aren't afraid of internet research.) These false beliefs may be due in part to "innocent" ignorance, but "willful" ignorance is more likely the cause. This ranking information is out there, easily found online; but it is repressed into the social unconsciousness of many, largely because it is "un-American" to think or investigate otherwise.

Fortunately, the United States and many other democratic countries are in one critical/salvational way unlike North Korea, Russia, or China. True democratic countries have a plethora of distinct camps of elites each pushing their own social consciousness. Any group or person who wants to disagree that we have the greatest healthcare system in the world is free to argue, protest, publish, and otherwise advocate for an alternative healthcare system. But be warned! A powerful new obstruction to advocating new information is on the rise: getting the other side(s) to even hear your alternative point of view.

In 2008, social commentator, Bill Bishop, published the eye opening book "The Big Sort"[28] , which provided detailed scholarly research supporting his well written/explained argument demonstrating that American society is deeply divided into closed silos of beliefs and information exchange. Bishop explained why it was so divided and why it was getting worse. More frightening is that Bishop's book was not merely a harbinger of a "potential" extreme and angry divide. It was more of an "emperor has no clothes" wake up call of the already existing reality that was happening right in front of our eyes.

Bishop catalogues the now well known division promoting forces such as congressional gerrymandering which allows for extremist politicians to be elected and re-elected in safe districts; as well as the rise of partisan "talk radio", Fox News, and MSNBC which allows/causes each camp to get their "news" from only one side. But much more insightful is Bishop's argument that this increasing divide is just as much a bottom-up movement by citizens as it is a top-down movement led by venal politicians.[29]

Bishop helps us understand that it is not just a paucity of new or different ideas in each camp that contributes to the divide. It is the social enforcement of the mores of each camp by the non-elite members of each camp that causes the cultural division to accelerate and calcify. In the quest to satisfy social belonging and ego needs, those individuals who both support their in-group and attack the "other" most voraciously are held in higher regard.[30] Even powerful politicians, previously and correctly thought of as "good and decent" by both sides, stand silent in the face of behavior previously held to be beyond indecent by all sides. Compromise is socially loathed. Conformity is socially enforced.

Even more horrifying is that disputes are no longer solely about the actual issues. Rather, the true essence/motivation of the disputes is the non-conscious "us versus them" dispute, now well known as "identity politics".[31] How easy it is for our individual consciousness to become trapped in this non-conscious social energy.

Being trapped in group consciousness is also all about fear. There is the obvious and easily understandable fear of group ostracism. There is the less obvious but more compelling fear of change. This fear of change often manifests in arguments over so-called "moral" issues such as abortion, premarital sex, gay rights, and how you support the military. These are the emotional issues more easily inflamed. Finally, underlying all these fears is the (perhaps ultimate) fear that your very identity is under threat. If your consciousness is aligned with group think, it is likely you non-consciously sense that your inner identity is also under attack. Any perceived threat to your group is seen as an existential threat to your own very identity! Quite a powerful filter to individual consciousness.

5. *Emotions. . . the "energy" filter of consciousness*

> . . . emotion is central to understanding
> the important qualities of being human. . .
> —Richard Davidson[32]

No understanding of the complex nature of consciousness is complete without an understanding of the role of emotions in filtering and energizing our consciousness. Recall Piaget's statement from Chapter Three that "no act of intelligence is complete without emotions". But what do we mean by "emotions"? While scholars (both historically and currently) are in hot dispute about the nature and etiology of emotions, let us agree at least on a superficial understanding of emotions as. . . perceptible feelings seemingly directed to a situation, object, or person(s) often accompanied by physical bodily changes.[33] The potential power of emotions has long been appreciated by scholars if not completely understood. Emotions can be mild or intense; fleeting or life-long. Emotions can bring great joy to life's experiences, but can also bring crippling despair. For better or worse, at least for humans, emotions give our lives meaning by energizing our consciousness by placing color/value/energy on our thoughts and actions through the power of psychological feelings and associated physical responses.

Scholarly opinions on the nature and etiology of emotions have existed since at least the beginning of written records. It is fascinating to observe how the historical understanding of emotions so closely follows the evolving pathway of the historical understanding of the nature and etiology of consciousness. Until very recent times, Dualism and Cartesian gravity have played predominate roles in shaping both the scholarly and lay understanding of emotions. As you will recall, both Dualism and Cartesian gravity seem to be motivated by an almost existential need to believe in a transcendent aspect to human life.

In Ancient Greek times (c. 600-300 BCE), the emotions were actually known as "the passions". . . forces beyond our control that "happened to" a person rather than being created or controlled by that person. This was consistent with the dualistic distinction between the higher, gods-given, extramundane capacity for rational thought verses the lower, animal-like, material passions of the body. Descartes (1596-1650) may have replaced the "gods" with "God", but he still believed in the dualistic distinction between the transcendent God-given nature of mankind and the animal-like, material passions. Even paradigm shifting philosophers of the Enlightenment such as Immanuel Kant (1724-1804), who viewed the world/truth as more secular and "scientific" stated:

> . . . passions are illnesses of mind that
> shut out the sovereignty of reason. . .[34]

Somewhat surprisingly, this dualistic distinction between animal passions and rational thought continued for another two centuries. Not many scholars took up the challenge of trying to understand the nature and etiology of emotions. Emotions just weren't viewed by scholars as worthy of scholarly inquiry. Dualistic concepts of the emotions such as. . . rational thinking good vs. emotional responses bad. . . continued to rule the day. Both the scholarly and lay understanding of emotions really didn't change much over two thousand years. Emotions were not perceived as being consciously generated. Uncontrolled emotions "happened to" a person much like an illness. This dualistic thinking was used by states, religions, and many other societal organizations to generate and enforce both secular and moral laws/codes. In particular, out of this ignorance, women and even entire races were discriminated against for variations of the argument that they were not able to control their emotions.

It was not until the late 20th century that the scholarly and societal understanding of emotions began to change. This change was largely brought about by the advent of brain imaging technology; advances in understanding the neurocorrelates of consciousness (as discussed in Chapter One); epigenetics (as discussed earlier in this Chapter Four); and brain plasticity (as will be discussed in Chapter Five). Lay accessible yet scholarly books on the nature and etiology of emotions exploded.[35] Yet there still remains a key dispute that has more than a tinge of Dualism.

The current scholarly dispute regarding the nature and etiology of emotions involves scholars in the "Naturalistic-Universalist" camp ("N-U") versus scholars in the "Social-Constructionist" camp ("S-C").[36] The differences in the two scholarly camps are surprisingly stark.[37]

The N-U camp essentially views emotions as they have been seen for the past two millennia. Although they no longer view cognition/rationality as transcendent or bestowed by the gods or God, the N-U camp continues to argue for a dualistic distinction between cognition/rationality and emotions. While there are significant variations in the intensity of scholarly positions held within the N-U camp,[38] it is a fair generalization that the N-U camp views emotions dualistically as: a vestige of evolution still hardened into the human brain; reflexive in nature; shared by all humanity despite race or culture; manifesting in distinct and measurable physical patterns; and essentially animalistic in nature arising out of the limbic system (reptilian brain), although most N-U proponents now include at least the amygdala as another source of emotions.

In contradiction, the S-C camp essentially sees no dualistic distinction between cognition/rationality and emotions. The S-C camp sees emotions "emerging" in the same manner and (more critical to our investigation) with the same limitations/filters as consciousness emerges. Emotions are not hard-wired, nor are they solely generated from distinct areas of the brain such as the limbic system or the amygdala. Emotions are not equally shared by all cultures, and do not manifest in distinct and measurable physical patterns. Emotions are not random. They do not "happen to" us. Each individual generates their own unique emotional (both feeling and physical) response to a situation, object, or person(s). Emotions are "built" not "built in".

One of the leading proponent scholars of the S-C position is American neuroscientist, psychologist, and author, Lisa Feldman Barrett. In her scholarly yet lay accessible book, "How Emotions Are Made"[39] Barrett states:

> Emotions are not reactions to the world. You are not a passive receiver of sensors input but an active constructor of your

emotions. From sensory input and past experience, your brain constructs meaning and prescribes action.[40]

The latest science behind the S-C position appears to be quite strong. It is supported by the latest brain imaging technology, facial recognition software, and multiple peer-reviewed meta-analyses.[41] Emotions emerge in the same manner and with the same limitations/filters as consciousness. A situation, object, or person(s) is encountered. The neurocorrelates of our brain then seek to understand the new encounter by searching past experiences stored in the brain. When a pattern is recalled/recognized or a new pattern created, we respond with thought, emotion, and perhaps action. Our (seemingly) rational thought, emotional response, and (potential or real) action are each filtered and expressed in the same manner as with our consciousness.[42]

So what is the difference then between emotions and consciousness if they both emerge in the same manner? Admittedly, since consciousness and emotions are both enigmatic, it's difficult to describe the difference. As we will see when we explore neuroplasticity in the next chapter, both arise in the same neuroanatomic manner. The main difference is that emotions always involve feelings, and are often accompanied by physical bodily changes such as a quickened heart rate, perspiration, or release of hormones. As such, emotions give motivation to our thoughts and actions. As we learned from Piaget in Chapter Three, emotion is the energetic/motivational aspect to cognitive activity. As stated by Richard Davidson at the beginning of this chapter, emotion is central to understanding the important qualities of being human. Emotions are why humans, but not animals, sit in silent awe of a beautiful sunset. Emotions are a powerful filter.

6. *Circumstances of the moment.*

But Mouse, you are not alone, in proving that foresight may be in vain.
The best-laid plans of mice and men often go astray;
And leave us nothing but grief and pain, instead of promised joy!
—Robert Burns[43]

Many of us are familiar with the saying, "The best laid plans of mice and men often go astray." But we're likely not as familiar with the saying that immediately follows, "And leave us nothing but grief and pain, instead of promised joy!" The backstory behind the Robert Burns' poem helps explain why these two sayings go together, and also why the circumstances of the moment (which we will call "t-com" for convenience) can act as a filter to our consciousness.[44]

Burns' poem was essentially both an apology and a commiseration by Burns to a mouse. It seems the momma mouse had spent considerable effort building a nest in which she intended to eventually have and raise her babies. Unfortunately, Burns somewhat inadvertently destroyed the finished nest while plowing his field. Burns was appropriately apologetic for so violently and totally dispossessing the terrified mouse; but more insightful was how Burns waxed poetically about the shared reality of how planning and hard work often end in grief and pain instead of the promised joy of accomplishment.

None of us are immune from t-com. T-com can be as deadly serious as a cancer diagnosis, or as mundane as unexpectedly having to drive your kid to a soccer game an hour away when you had planned a lazy afternoon lying on the couch watching baseball. T-com comes out of the blue and disrupts, or even totally destroys, your best laid plans.

You may ask, but why is t-com a filter to consciousness? There are essentially two reasons. First, as we learned from multiple scholars in Chapter Three, t-com (which includes a seemingly infinite number of family, work, and biological obligations) too often just sucks all time out of a day, week, or even months. There simply is no time nor personal energy for the awareness, reflection, and disciplined action required for expansion of consciousness. (Recall from Chapter Three, Ken Wilber's admonishment that meaningful consciousness expansion is difficult to impossible during the hectic child-raising/working years.) Second, t-com almost always results in an emotional response, and we've just learned in this chapter how emotion can filter consciousness. The emotional response to t-com can be as minor as temporary irritation due to time wasted, or as grave as chronic depression. Emotional responses along this continuum will affect your consciousness in proportion to the degree of the emotional response.

Let's do a thought experiment to help us understand how t-com emotionally affects our consciousness; in particular, how open we are in dialoguing with others. In situation one, your favorite sports team just lost a close game. In situation two, you just lost your job. In each situation your teenage daughter then comes to you to complain that you are "treating her like a child", and that she should not have any weekend curfew. Think about how would you respond in each situation? How patient would you be? How open would your consciousness be so that you could really hear your daughter, and respond in a skillful manner to maximize your daughter actually hearing you? It's not hard to visualize how your t-com might filter you differently in these two distinct situations.

So what have we learned in this chapter about filters to consciousness? We've learned, without doubt, that there are many powerful filters that affect our thoughts, emotions, and actions. These filters cause us to see and interpret reality as if through a glass darkly. Our needs, motivations, emotions, thoughts, and actions are too often fear based due to this semi-blindness of our consciousness. Simply recognizing the existence and power of these and other filters is an essential first step in clearing our lense to reality. "Recognition" is itself an expansion of consciousness, keeping in mind that there is always more to recognize about how these filters specifically affect us.

In the next chapter, we will learn not only how our brains change in response to forces such as recognition, but how such changes can support further expansion of consciousness.

---

1 Thich Nhat Hanh (1926-) is a Vietnamese Buddhist monk, a brilliant scholar, and a prolific author. Martin Luther King nominated him for the Nobel Peace Prize for his work in trying to end the Vietnam War. He was awarded the first Gandhi Mandela Peace Medal for his teachings on "Mindfulness [which] have changed the lives of millions of people world wide." I proudly acknowledge "Thay" as one of my primary teachers throughout most of my adult life.

2 The following is a partial list of names given to types of ignorance: absolute, antecedent, arrogant, conditional, constitutional, cosmic, domain, egoistic, enlightened, factual, higher, innocent, invincible, learned, objectual, ordinary, original practical, primary, nescience, psychological, recognized,

self-ignorance, Socratic, structured uncertainty, technical, temporal, unknowing, unstructured, vincible, and willful.

3 Plato's Apology 2ld.

4 Yes, I'm not only a social liberal, but I also continue to struggle through the same filter challenges of this group.

5 It is interesting/important/discouraging to note that the term "political correctness" has now to some extent been coopted by conservatives. The term was originally intended to refer to words or acts that might bring offense or harm to certain protected groups. Yet, according to some scholars, the term is now more often used by conservatives as a claimed violation of their right to free speech; but in reality their reaction is more of a cry for regressivism. See, "Has political correctness gone too far?" by Julia Symons, the Open Society: Essay competition winner in the Sept. 10, 2018 issue of The Economist, which can easily be found online.

6 This quote has been attributed to the Canadian psychologist, Donald Hebb (1904-1985). When Hebb was asked which contributes more to personality, nature or nurture, he supposedly answered with what is known as the "rectangle analogy". See, "Where did the 'rectangle analogy' come from and how compelling is it?" By J.P. Smith which is easily found online.

7 The term "tabula rosa" (Latin for "blank slate") was made famous by Locke in his essay "Essay Concerning Human Understanding". It is interesting to note that at the time of Aristotle, writing tablets were made of wax that could be melted and scraped in order to begin anew with a blank/clean slate.

8 For more information on eugenics, see online the University of Virginia Historical Collections At the Claude Moore Health Science Library "Origins of Eugenics: From Sir Francis Galton to Virginia's Racial Integrity Act of 1924" 2004.

9 B.F. Skinner (1904-1990) is perhaps the most well known proponent of Behaviorism in the 20th century. This quote is frequently attributed to Skinner, but an online search will reveal scholarly posts disputing this attribution. Nonetheless, the quote does seem to be a fair representation of extreme Behaviorism. It is interesting to note that one of the benefits of Skinner living long into the 20th century is that video interviews with Skinner can easily be found on YouTube, which are quite fascinating.

10 It will by now come as no surprise to readers of this book that scholars cannot agree on a set definition of "personality", but my overly simplified definition should serve our purpose of achieving a meaningful overview of Behavior Genetics.

11 See "Conrad Waddington and the origin of epigenics" by Denis Noble, Journal of Experimental Biology 2015, 218:816-818; doi:10.1242/jeb.120071.

12 "Gene Expression" is a biochemical process in which the code/instructions from a particular gene is converted into a "functional product". The functional products with which our investigation is most concerned are proteins. The vast and highly varied role of proteins is impressive. Proteins not only have structural and tissue building functions, but proteins are critical for gene expression. Proteins are, in fact, the chief actor within a cell, instructing a cell as to its genetic function. Proteins also act as enzymes to carry out the numerous chemical reactions involved in metabolism.

13 "Invited Address: 'The Times They Are A-Changin' Gene Expression, Neuroplasticity, and Developmental Research" by Ronald L. Simons and Erik T. Klopack, Journal of Youth and Adolescence, March 2015, Volume 44, Issue 3, pp573-580 at p5 citing Nature 2012 p143. (Here and after "Simons".)

14 "Sources of Human Psychological Differences: The Minnesota Study of Twins Reared Apart" by Thomas J. Bouchard, Jr., David T. Lykken, Matthew McGue, Nancy L. Segal, and Auke Tellegen October 1990, Science, Vol 250 pp223-228. (Here and after "The Minnesota Study".)

15 "Major Personality Study Finds That Traits Are Mostly Inherited" by Daniel Coleman, The New York Times published December 2, 1986. Yes, it appears the NYT had the story years before the study was formally published???

16 "Heritability of Personality: A Meta-Analysis of Behavior Genetic Studies" by Tena Vukasovic and Denis Bratko, Psychological Bulletin 2015 Vol 141 No.4, 769-785. (Here and after "Vukasovic".)

17 Vukasovic at p779.

18 "Heritability of Personality" by Denis Bratko, Ana Butkovic, Tena Vukasovic Hlupic, Psychological Topics, 26 (2017), 1, 1-24. (Here and after "Bratko".)

19 Bratko at pp13-14.

20 Erich Fromm summarizing Freud in "Beyond the Chains of Illusion, My Encounter with Marx and Freud" Simon and Schuster, Inc. 1962. Bloomsbury Revelations edition, 2017 p64. (Here and after "Fromm".)

21 To read Freud's own words on the "unconscious" search online at www.sas.upenn.edu>pdf-library>Freud-Unconscious.

22 The concept of "cognitive" bias was introduced into scholarly literature in 1972 by Israeli psychologists, Amos Tvrsky and Daniel Kahneman.

23 Seminal scholarly publications on cognitive bias intended for the Academy began in the 1960's, but fascinating and lay accessible books have been readily available in recent years. See for example, "Blindspot Hidden Biases on Good People" by Mahzarin R. Banaji and Anthony G. Greenwald, Delacorte Press, New York (2013). "THE HIDDEN BRAIN How Our Unconscious Minds Elect Presidents, Control Makets, Wage Wars, and Save Our Lives" by Shankar Vedantam, Spiegel & Grau, New York (2010).

24 Philippe Lajaunie is a French-born American entrepreneur, business consultant, wonderful writer, raconteur, and a lifelong friend.

25 An older, yet still one of the most enlightening scholars on the topic of the social unconscious is Erich Fromm. See "Fromm" at pp63-95.

26 The "social unconscious" also applies to corporations. See "Why Companies Fail" by Megan McArdle, published in The Atlantic 28 March 2012. You can also search online topics such as "GM (or Ford Motor Company) makes the same mistakes over and over" for similar articles.

27 These rankings change overtime; and, of course, vary depending on the biases of the organization putting out the rankings. These figures were from a 2020 online post by US News and World Report,

but many others can easily be found online.

28 "The "Big Sort" by Bill Bishop, Houghton Mifflin Company, New York (2008). (Here and after "Big Sort".)

29 Big Sort at p28-35.

30 Consider the fact that on February 4, 2020, Rush Limbaugh was awarded the Presidential Medal of Freedom before a joint session of Congress and the Supreme Court by "He-Who-Must-Not-Be-Named". (This is the appellation given to Voldemort, Harry Potter's evil nemesis in the Harry Potter series of books.) I swore as I was writing this book that I would not mention "He-Who-Must-Not-Be-Named", the 45th president of the United States. But it is precisely the power of identity politics that allows otherwise good people to vote for such a damaged human being who in many respects has since been acting in diametric opposition to the economic and safety interests of his own voters.)

31 There are now many informative books on "identity politics: "Tribes" by Seth Godin, Penguin Group (2008); "The Righteous Mind" by Jonathan Haidt, Random House (2012); "Wiser-Getting Beyond Group Think to Make Groups Smarter" by Cass R. Sunstein and Reid Hastie, Harvard Business Review Press (2015); and (most succinctly regarding identity politics) "Why We're Polarized" by Ezra Klein, Avid Reader Press (2020).

32 Richard J. Davidson, Ph.D. is the William James and Vilas Professor of Psychology and Psychiatry at the University of Wisconsin in Madison (UWM). Davidson is also the founder of the Center for Healthy Minds at UWM which includes the website centerforhealthyminds.org which supports a vision of a "kinder, wiser, more compassionate world" through a better understanding of how the human mind works. This website is well worth visiting. Davidson's scholarly yet lay-accessible work has been supported by his close friend and collaborator, the Dalai Lama. In 2006, Davidson was recognized by Time Magazine as one of the 100 most influential people in the world. For what it is worth, Davidson is also one of my personal deep-thinking heroes. In addition to his groundbreaking work on emotions, Davidson has been a paradigm shifting scholar on meditation; and we will visit his work again in Chapter Seven.

33 See "The Emotional Life of Your Brain" by Richard J. Davidson, Ph.D. with Sharon Begley, Penguin Random House, New York (2012) for a scholarly analysis of different aspects of emotion such as emotional states, moods, traits, style, and personality. (Here and after "Emotional Life".)

34 See Kant's Empirical Psychology at p228; "The Psychology of Passions" by Immanuel Kant at 7:251.

35 Leading scholarly yet lay-accessible books include: "The Emotional Life of Your Brain" by Richard J. Davidson, Ph.D.; Avery Publications, New York (2012). "How Emotions are Made" by Lisa Feldman Barrett; Mariner Books, Boston and New York (2017). (Here and after "Barrett".)

36 There are other names that are used in the literature for these two camps, but the names used here are descriptively accurate.

37 An older, academically dense, but educational paper describing and contrasting these two camps is "A Social Constructionist Critique of Naturalistic Theories of Emotion" by American psychologist, Carl Ratner from the Journal of Mind and Behavior, 1989, 10, 211-230 which can easily be found online. (Here and after "Ratner".)

38 J ust as we learned about the distinctions between the "Old" verses the "New" Mysterians in Chapter One, there are scholarly distinctions within the N-U camp where certain scholars are not as dualistic in their understanding of emotions.

39 See Barrett footnote 35.

40 Barrett at p31.

41 Barrett at pp7, 14.

42 Also see Barrett Chapters 6-9.

43 This quote is my attempt at a modern translation of the eighth stanza of the 1706 poem "To A Mouse, On Turning Her Up In Her Nest With A Plough" by Scottish poet, Robert Burns (1759-1796). The original "old" Scottish version is mildly hard to follow, and can easily be found online.

44 The current vernacular for circumstances of the moment in "sh*t happens".

CHAPTER FIVE

CAN THE BRAIN SUPPORT CONSCIOUSNESS EXPANSION?
(The Promise of Brain Plasticity: Hope or Hype?)

> A man could, if he were so inclined,
> be the sculptor of his own brain.
> —Santiago Ramon y Cajal[1]

Brain plasticity is essentially a very general term used to describe the ability of the brain to reorganize itself, most remarkably through the creation of new and/or strengthened neural pathways. Brain plasticity should more appropriately be known as "neuroplasticity" since it involves the entire central nervous system and not just the brain. Neuroplasticity offers the exciting potential of our being able to "intentionally" change/improve the physiology of the human brain. More pertinent to the purpose of this book, neuroplasticity may allow an individual to purposely alter neuropathways to support expansion of consciousness. But is this promise of neuroplasticity hope or hype? As we will learn through this chapter, the simple answer is: It's both.

Since you're now five chapters into this book, it should come as no surprise to you that there is no agreed upon definition of neuroplasticity. This has caused scholars like British psychologist, Vaughan Bell, to call neuroplasticity a "dirty word" because:

> Neuroplasticity sounds very technical, but there is no accepted definition for the term and, in a broader sense, it means

nothing more than "something in the brain has changed". As your brain is always changing the term is empty on its own.[2]

Moreover, "plasticity" means different things to different subspecialties within the many diverse scholarly fields such as botany, psychology, and neuroanatomy.[3] Even Santiago Ramon y Cajal (1852-1934), who is considered one of the founders of modern neuroanatomy and neuroscience as well as one of the first scholars to use the term "plasticity" regarding changes in the brain, subsequently began to avoid using the term "plasticity" because other scholars expanded its meaning to include pathological/destructive brain changes rather than only positive/growth changes.[4]

Understanding the complex phenomena of neuroplasticity has recently become even more confusing due to unscientifically supported claims of wannabe sages and corporate hucksters. If you go online to amazon.com and type in "brain plasticity" you will see book titles that suggest/promise that there are brain plasticity practices and techniques that will allow you to: improve overall cognitive function; increase your memory; accelerate your athletic ability; recover from brain damage; and avoid the ravages of age-related dementia. While there is some truth in many of these claims, it is not surprising that the market place often grossly exaggerates the promise of such claims.

Exaggerated claims regarding the exciting promise of neuroplasticity have not gone unnoticed by the United States government. In 2016, the Federal Trade Commission filed suit against Lumos Labs, Inc. d/b/a Lumosity (one of the leading online purveyors of computer brain-training techniques) for claiming Lumosity's brain-training would:

1. improve performance on everyday tasks, including school, work, and athletics;

2. delay age-related cognitive decline and protect against mild cognitive impairment, dementia, and Alzheimer's disease; and

3. reduce cognitive impairment associated with health conditions, including: stroke, traumatic brain injury, PTSD, ADHD, the side effects of chemotherapy, and Turner syndrome.

The federal judge hearing the evidence for and against Lumosity's claims entered an order prohibiting such claims unless and until there is competent scientific evidence to substantiate such claims:

> Defendants are permanently restrained and enjoined from making any representation, expressly or by implication, that using such Covered Product: A. improves performance in school, at work, or in athletics; B. delays or protects against age-related decline in memory or other cognitive function, including mild cognitive impairment, dementia, or Alzheimer's disease. . . unless Defendants possess and rely upon competent and reliable scientific evidence to substantiate that the claim is true. . .
>
> Judgment in the amount of Fifty Million Dollars ($50,000,000.00) is entered in favor of the Commission and against Corporate Defendant. . .[5]

Unsurprisingly, the popular press has added to the hyped claims of neuroplasticity. As an example, in the late 1990s, public attention was aroused by press coverage which concluded that "stress kills neurons". (Neurons are commonly known by the lay-term "brain cells" although a more appropriate term would be "nerve cells". More on neurons later in this chapter.) This is a scary message to say the least, because who among us has not been under stress? A post-mortem brain study had been done after a number of wild vervet monkeys housed in a primate center in Kenya had suddenly died. Findings revealed dead neurons in the hippocampus suggesting the neurons had died from stress, and the press ran with this startling conclusion. Later it was discovered that too much time had passed between the sudden death of the monkeys and the brain autopsies to support such a conclusion. Subsequent chronic stress experiments done under controlled conditions showed that stress does not kill neurons, but of course the public never heard that later discovery.[6]

So let's slow down and take a more scholarly and reasoned look at neuroplasticity. We will explore together the following five topics which hopefully will provide an understanding of the complex nature of neuroplasticity sufficient for our purpose of providing an overview of how neuroplasticity relates to the enigmatic nature of consciousness.

1.   Contrary to many claims, the discovery of neuroplasticity is not new. Yet it is only in recent years that science has confirmed that neuroplasticity is a fundamental property of all species with nervous systems.

2.   Although scientists do not yet know all the detailed specifics of the multiple complex processes of neuroplasticity, enough is now known to aid us in our overview of the interactive relationship between neuroplasticity and consciousness expansion.

3.   The vast majority of neuroplasticity occurs early in life when the brain is developing. While this may not aid us in our quest for adult consciousness expansion, it has profound implications for child rearing.

4.   Not all neuroplasticity is a positive development for consciousness expansion. Brain changes can retard or even reverse the capacity for consciousness expansion.

5.   There do appear to be practices which generate improved overall brain health as well as neuroplastic changes that support consciousness expansion.

1) Contrary to many claims, the discovery of neuroplasticity is not new. Yet it is only in recent years that science has confirmed

that neuroplasticity is a fundamental property of all species with nervous systems.

Many commentators, both scholarly and in the popular press, have written that neuroplasticity is a "new" and even "revolutionary" discovery. Indeed, it does seem to be correct that up until the 1960s, it was still essentially widely held scholarly dogma that the adult human brain (or the brain of any mature mammal) was fixed and unchanging. It is also correct that it was not until 1998, when scientists confirmed the life-long ability of the human brain to generate new neurons, that the paradigm shift of completely accepting the reality of neuroplasticity was finally proved.[7] Nonetheless, for more than 200 years prior to that, a number of creative scholars (mostly botanists, anatomists, and others often known as "naturalists") ventured outside their individual consciousness receptacles to begin to challenge the incorrect scholarly dogma that the brain is unchangeable.

Developmental neurobiologist (and now freelance science writer) Moheb Costandi has written a most impressive, thorough, and lay-accessible book explaining all key aspects of neuroplasticity, aptly named "Neuroplasticity".[8] Costandi notes that, although neuroplasticity is often portrayed as a new revolutionary discovery, at least the concept of neuroplasticity (although that particular term was not yet in use) had been around for over 200 years.[9] Many of these early pioneers were ignored, at least for their suggestion that the brain changes throughout life. A few were even forgotten until present day historians rediscovered their work, and I suspect the identity of others will never be known. Let's take a brief look at a few of the key scholars in the early pioneering of neuroplasticity to get some historical perspective on how the collective consciousness of scholars began to change.

Since our overall topic is consciousness expansion, you may find it interesting to learn about long-standing and fundamental errors in the consciousness of neuroscience dogma as neuroscience made its impressive advances in understanding neuroplasticity. It is important for consciousness expansion to appreciate that even the most prestigious, confident, and beloved scholars and mystics are not always correct. Or as my dad once told me, "Remember David, at one time the smartest man in the cave was certain the sun was God." Let's take a look at what I'm calling the four major "wrong turns" of the scientific consciousness of neuroplasticity.

The earliest pioneer uncovered by historians regarding the changing brain is Piedmontese anatomist, Michele Vicenzo Malacarne (1744-1816). On or about 1783, Malacarne corresponded with Swiss lawyer and naturalist, Charles Bonnet (1720-1793), regarding Malacarne's hypothesis that mental stimulation/training results in brain growth in animals.[10] Malacarne used pairs of dogs from the same litter and birds from the same clutch of eggs, trained one dog and one bird from each pair, sacrificed the animals, dissected the brains, and discovered the cerebellums (later discovered to be part of the mammalian brain associated with the regulation of muscular activity) of the trained animals to be significantly larger. Malacarne credited this brain size differential to the fact that the trained animals had to use their brains more to learn.[11] In 1793, Malacarne's findings were published in the Journal de Physique (Paris) 43:73. Soon other scholars continued the research into whether and how mental exercise might result in observable brain growth in animals. But it didn't take long for this type of discovery to go off the rails.

The scholarly investigation of neuroscience really began to take off in the late 1700s and early 1800s. Malacarne's experimental findings of observable increased brain size in trained animals was subsequently confirmed by other scholars. The next obvious question became: If animal brains increased in size with increased mental activity, shouldn't the brains of so-called smart people be bigger in size? Scholars across the Western world (of drastically varying degrees of scholarly ability) began the search for evidence that brain size correlated with mental ability and character traits. . . the first major wrong turn in both the scientific and lay consciousness of early neuroplasticity.

So-called scholarly inquiry into human brain size went careening over the cliff with the birth of "phrenology" in the mid 1790s. Phrenology (a now discredited pseudo science) claimed to diagnose both mental abilities and character traits by measuring bumps on the skull supposedly caused by increased brain size in the particular areas of the brain then believed to be associated with such abilities and traits. In the very early 1800s, one of the initial founders of phrenology, Johann Gaspar Spurzheim (1776-1832), claimed that certain brain areas could be stimulated by mental exercise.[12] In a scholarly and entertaining online article by British science historian John van Wyhe entitled "The History of Phrenology on the Web",[13] Wyhe chronicles the borderline hysterical social adoption of phrenology in Europe and the United States. Social elites like Goethe and the King of Prussia became believers,[14] and "many employers could demand a character reference from a local phrenologist to ensure that a prospective employee was honest and hard-working".[15] The first major wrong turn of early neuroplasticity was on fire across lay consciousness, and even the consciousness of some scholars.

Charles Darwin (1809-1882), in his 1874 publication "The Descent of Man",[16] chronicles a number of the leading scholars of that time who claimed to have uncovered an evidential correlation between brain size and intellectual facility in humans. One of my favorite such references by Darwin is to the English physician and self-proclaimed "craniologist", J. Barnard Davis (1801-1881), who claimed to have found "many careful measurements that the mean internal capacity of the skull in Europeans is 92.3 cubic inches; in Americans 87.5; in Asiatics 87.1; and in Australians only 81.9 cubic inches." Yes, no surprise, Dr. Barnard was European. Even more entertaining is Darwin's reference to a contrary response by French physician, anatomist, and anthropologist, Pierre Paul Broca (1824-1880), who helped deflate this misbelief in the significance of brain size. Broca noted "that the mean capacity of the skull of the ancient Troglodytes of Lazere is greater than the modern Frenchmen".[17] Looks like Europeans couldn't have it both ways. Despite some brain size differential in trained animals, there was no correlation between brain/skull size and overall mental ability.

It is interesting to learn that brilliant scholars like Broca, who helped disprove the error of linking brain size to mental ability, likely contributed to (what I'm calling) the second major wrong turn of early neuroplasticity: localization of brain function. Localization held that the human brain is composed of separate areas that each completely/totally controls a different aspect of brain function. Prior to highly respected scholars like Broca, localization was not yet scholarly dogma. Scholars were divided whether brain function was localized or holistic. Holistic theory holds that the whole is greater than the sum of its parts, and that the whole cannot function or even be explained except as an interacting whole. So while there appeared to be areas of the brain primarily associated with particular functions, nonetheless the brain operated as a holistic organ where individual areas of the brain were influenced by multiple other areas of the brain. At this time in the development of neuroplasticity, there just wasn't enough scientific data to choose which brain function theory was correct.

Around 1861, Broca had a series of patients with speech disorders who were dying of other unrelated causes. Broca performed brain autopsies on the deceased patients, and found pronounced lesions in the frontal region of the cortex, which subsequently became known as "Broca's area". Broca concluded that speech was totally controlled by this specific area of the brain, and the highly esteemed Professor Broca published in favor of localization. With similar associative brain findings by other scholars looking into functions such as speech, hearing, and vision, localization became the conscious dogma of most neuroscience scholars.

It wasn't until more than a century later that localization was disproved. Ironically, localization was disproved by the discovery that patients (similar to Broca's) with brain damage to a particular area of the brain believed to control functions like speech, hearing, or vision later regained some or all lost function even though the location in the brain believed to control such function remained damaged. These new scholars initially speculated that there were two possibilities for those recoveries of brain function. Either there were yet undiscovered neural links between areas of the brain, or the brain had built in redundancies so that other parts of the brain could kick-in following damage to help recovery. (Both subsequently turned out to be correct.) The new dogma became known as "cross model plasticity". Yes, there are somewhat distinct areas of the brain associated with functions like speech, balance, decision making; but as we learned in Chapter One, the brain is a holistic organ. The wrong turn of localization was corrected; but soon after, the third wrong turn of early neuroplasticity took hold.

In 1838, German physician and physiologist Theodar Schwann (1810-1882) and German botanist Matthias Jakob Schleiden (1804-1881) were credited with developing "cell theory".[18] This is the fundamental and now universally accepted belief that all living organisms are made up of one or more individual units called cells.[19] This paradigm shifting discovery was possible due to continuing advances in the technology of the microscope and tissue staining techniques.

Undoubtedly, the most significant of the early pioneers of neuroplasticity was Ramon y Cajal (1852-1934), a Spanish neuroanatomist and gifted artist. During most of the 19th century, even though scholars were aware of and supportive of cell theory, scholars also believed in the "reticular theory", the third major wrong turn of early neuroplasticity. The reticular theory held that nervous tissue was distinctly different from other tissue in the body; i.e. that all nervous tissue was a "continuous" protoplasmic sheet rather than a "contiguous" network of individual and separated cells. Reticular theory misarose largely because microscopes of the day were not powerful enough to distinguish individual neural cells. In 1888, Cajal upended the reticular theory when he improved microscopic staining techniques that revealed nervous tissue cells whose axons ended in the close proximity but unattached to other such cells. Those cells of nervous tissue were soon after called "neurons" by German anatomist, Heinrich Wilhelm Gottfried von Waldeyer-Hartz (1836-1921), and the "neuron theory" replaced reticular theory. This and other discoveries by Cajal resulted in his sharing the Nobel prize for physiology in 1906, and for the distinguished moniker, Father of Neuroscience. Although it might be that his beautiful drawings of microscopic nervous tissue may also have played a role in Cajal's professional fame. (Examples of Cajal's drawings can be found at the end of Section I and online.)

It is sadly ironic that only a few years later in 1913, the brilliant Cajal who overturned reticular theory, contributed to a new and incorrect scientific dogma that nerve pathways in the brain are "fixed and immutable" once a person reaches physical maturity, the fourth and perhaps most significant wrong turn of early neuroplasticity. In his 1913 textbook, "Degeneration and Regeneration of the Nervous System", Cajal stated:

Once development was ended, the founts of growth and regeneration of the axons and dendrites dried up irrevocably. In the adult centers the nerve paths are something fixed, ended and immutable. Everything must die, nothing may be regenerated.

This mistaken dogma was a direct result of the limitations of microscopic technology. But I suspect that both Cajal's special prominence in the scholarly community as well as the (conscious or non-conscious) Cartesian gravity of thinking of the brain as unique from ordinary matter/tissue also played a role in the longstanding dominance of this false dogma. As aptly stated by Costandi, "This view quickly became one of the central dogmas of neuroscience, and scholars came to the general consensus that the brain is "not" materially affected by learning experience, or training. This false dogma persisted well into the mid-twentieth century."[20]

(This harsh and uncompromising sentence by Cajal that "Everything must die, nothing may be regenerated" is ubiquitous throughout present day scholarly and lay publications on the history of neuroplasticity. But, since Cajal is another free thinking hero of mine, I'd like to take the time to also refer you to another statement by Cajal that occurs almost immediately after his strong statement claiming the brain is unchangeable. For some unknown reason, this next sentence is almost universally ignored by all writers: "It is for science of the future to change, if possible, this harsh decree." Cajal's consciousness was open to change despite the seemingly strong evidence of the time against neuroplasticity.)

There seems to be little doubt that the following 150 plus years of fixed scholarly consciousness on the supposed lack of neuroplasticity in the human brain led to the current scholars, popular press, and wannabe sages proclaiming that neuroplasticity is a "new" and even "revolutionary" discovery.

Costandi reports that by the mid-twentieth century, scholars again began offering evidence of neuroplasticity; i.e. that brain tissue was not fixed, ended, and immutable. Several researchers reported finding new neural cells being born in the brains of mature animals (later termed "neurogenesis"), but these scholars were largely ridiculed or ignored.[21] Other consciousness expanding scholars agreed that, while a theory claiming an intrinsic relationship between mental ability and visible brain size should be abandoned, perhaps scholars should be investigating whether mental exercise results in micro-changes involving neural interconnections or chemical changes in the brain, particularly at the synaptic spaces where the neurons interact and communicate. The leading investigating team on such research came from the University of California at Berkeley beginning in 1953, and was headed up by biochemist Edward L. Bennett (?-2018).[22]

Bennett's team began their quest in 1953; and in 1964, using laboratory rats, the team published the first "evidence" that mental exercise not only modified brain chemistry but also the anatomy of the brain in mammals. Bennett's team knew that transmission of neural impulses between most neurons required a chemical mediator to cross the synaptic gap between neurons and react with a receptor site on the receiving neuron. (See the anatomic drawing of a synapse later in this chapter.) Advancing technology had isolated acetylcholine as one of the first synaptic transmitters to be studied in the nervous system. Bennett's team found, not only that the amount of acetylcholine increased when laboratory rats were given "enhanced experience" (such as toys to play with and mazes to navigate) as compared to control laboratory rats, but that there was a microscopic gain in weight and thickness in the cerebral cortex. Neuroplasticity was finally proved, at least in non-human mammals. The cerebral residuals of enhanced experience did not result in obvious bumps on the brain such as speculated by the purveyors of phrenology, but it was real nonetheless. Bennett concluded that "modifications that seem small in absolute terms may be large... in functional consciousness".[23]

Neuroplasticity was finally proved. Enhanced experience, now referred to in the Bennett study and by subsequent scholars as environmental complexity and training ("ECT"), did show a quite modest increase in brain growth; but more importantly, it showed increased chemical activity at the synaptic junctions. The synaptic connections were becoming increasingly important to understanding neuroplasticity. Costandi reports that "[t]oday, synaptic modification is widely regarded as the cellular basis of learning and memory".[24] This is a macro-point for understanding the causal relationship between neuroplasticity and consciousness expansion: The more ECT, the greater number and electrochemical strength of synaptic connections between neurons associated with the ECT. This vaulted role for synaptic modification has resulted in the generation of the following apothegm known as "Hebb's Rule" or "Hebb's Theory" which has become enshrined in both scholarly and lay publications as:

Neurons that fire together, wire together.
Neurons that fire out of sync, fail to link.[25][26]

Synaptic modification was indeed the working key to neuroplasticity, but to most scholars in the field of neuroscience it was not the "Holy Grail" of neuroplasticity. At least in the minds of many scholars and lay commentators, that Holy Grail would be the brain's ability to generate not just new or strengthened synapses, but the ability to generate new neurons after puberty/maturity and throughout life; i.e., life-long neurogenesis. After all, even though scholars know that there are multiple types of cells in the brain, neurons (nerve cells) are the ones thought of as "brain cells". Scholars speculated that the generation of new neurons after physical maturity ("adult" or "post-maturity" neurogenesis) rather than just more and/or strengthened synaptic connections between neurons, could definitely be equated with neuroplasticity. So the new Holy Grail, Ahab's new white whale, became "adult neurogenesis" (which for convenience, let's call it "ANG").

It wasn't until the very end of the 20th century, in 1998, that ANG was proved. A team from the Department of Clinical Neuroscience at the Institute of Neurology in Goteborg, Sweden discovered that "the human hippocampus retains its ability to generate neurons throughout life".[27] Both the popular press and scholarly journals could now proclaim the "new" discovery of neuroplasticity which not only existed at the synaptic junctions but by ANG (adult neurogenesis).

Despite this seminal and hailed discovery by the Swedish team, the significance of life-long human neurogenesis remains controversial. Although the majority of scholars now acknowledge the reality of ANG, there is a further dispute whether the very minimal amount of ANG found in the adult hippocampus (and to an even lesser extent in other areas of the brain) had any significant affect on brain function. The so-called "revolutionary" reality of neuroplasticity had arrived in both lay and scholarly consciousness, but there was and is so much more to learn.

2) Although scientists do not yet know all the detailed specifics of the multiple complex processes of neuroplasticity, enough is now known to aid us in our overview of the interactive relationship between neuroplasticity and consciousness expansion.

Neuroplasticity is indeed complex, and all its particular processes are beyond the scope of this book. New discoveries and an expanded scholarly consciousness regarding neuroplasticity are occurring at an increasingly rapid rate, especially in the field of epigenetics as noted in Chapter Four. Even the most sophisticated and advanced scholars do not yet claim to totally understand its many processes and influences. Accordingly, this subsection of Chapter Five will primarily focus on the processes of ANG and synaptic modification, the two most written about processes of neuroplasticity especially in lay publications. Hopefully, this will provide a general but solid introduction/overview of neuroplasticity, particularly as it relates to the expansion of consciousness. However, it is first important to appreciate that neuroplasticity involves and is influenced by numerous factors other than ANG and synaptic modification. These numerous other factors are both endogenous (inside) and exogenous (outside) the human body.[28]

Regarding endogenous factors, you might think (as I originally did) that neuroplasticity only involves neurons and their synaptic connections. After all, recall from Chapter One that the human brain has around 100 billion neurons, and each of those neurons makes on average several thousand synapses. Those are indeed big numbers, but the brain has a vast and equally complex supporting system for the neurons/synapses. This supporting system is an intricate and inseparable part of the brain; and (as we learned from Bell at the very beginning of this chapter) since the empty term "neuroplasticity" includes any change in the brain, changes in the supporting systems are also included under the umbrella rubric of neuroplasticity.

Let's look at a few key aspects of what could be called the endogenous supporting system. For example, neurons aren't the only cells involved in neuroplasticity. The principle supporting cells in the CNS (central nervous system) are called glial cells, which occur at roughly the same number as neurons. There are multiple types of glial cells within the CNS: astrocytes, oligodendrocytes, ependymal, and microglia, each with a plethora of functions (many of which scholars don't yet understand) facilitating and supporting neuroplasticity. Of course all the cells involved in neuroplasticity are in turn supported by the body's vascular system. . . healthier vascular systems, healthier CNS cells. In addition, neuroplastic changes involved in the electrochemistry of preparation, transmission, and receipt of neurochemical transmitters across neural synapses are affected by substances such as hormones, enzymes, and neurotrophic factors (proteins) which are produced both inside the brain and from other organs in the body. Finally, all of the above are in part subject to the particular genetics of the individual person. There is so much more to endogenous neuroplasticity than just neurons and their synaptic connections.

Regarding exogenous factors, at this point in the book, it should come as no surprise to you that neuroplasticity is affected by factors remote from the body that are too numerous to list. These include things like: prenatal experience, stress, friendships, disease, trauma, drugs, diet, exercise, habits, the outside environment of sensory input, and essentially any form of learning or remembering. I suppose you could call each of these exogenous factors a form of ECT (environmental complexity and training), and in a very general sense that would be correct. Yet, that could be a bit misleading since (as the Bennett study states) ECT involves some type of intentional/planned change in the subject's usual/routine social condition such as a scholarly researcher would introduce into the usual/routine social environment of lab rats. Since many (or even most) of these exogenous factors are essentially a person's usual/routine social condition, using the term ECT to include all exogenous factors doesn't seem quite right. But whether you choose to use the term ECT to include all exogenous factors, the macro-point is that each of these exogenous factors has the potential to cause some change in the central nervous system; i.e. neuroplasticity. This is a macro-point not only of this chapter, but of Section II of this book: numerous exogenous factors (including but not limited to what scholars would term ECT) have the potential to rewire our brains. The first step in consciousness expansion is to be aware of this. The second step is to take advantage of this critical information by selectively integrating positive exogenous factors into our lives, which we will explore in detail in Section II.

The scholarly field of neuroplasticity remains complex and controversial to say the least. The data is always changing due to leaps in technology and brilliant scholarly work. But for our primary purpose of exploring the nature of consciousness, let us return to and explore the two most well known processes of neuroplasticity: adult neurogenesis ("ANG") and synaptic modification.

Let's begin with ANG. One of the best (and lay-accessible) scholarly review articles on ANG is aptly captioned "Adult Neurogenesis In Humans: A Review of Basic Concepts, History, Current Research, and Clinical Applications" written by a team of scholars led by Ashutosh Kumar, MD from the All India Institute of Medical Sciences in Patina, India. (Here and after "Kumar".)[29] This article sets out the generally agreed state of ANG research sufficient for our limited purposes in our overview of consciousness.

In general and simplified terms, there is a dispute regarding whether the minimal amount of ANG generated is significant regarding neuroplasticity? In a comprehensive review of the current scholarly literature, Kumar provides the following now generally accepted concepts regarding ANG:

A. It is undisputed that the human neurogenesis (the creation of new neurons) occurs during the prenatal period and continues to a lesser degree while the brain is still developing through physical maturity; i.e., until adulthood.

B. There is strong evidence that ANG (adult neurogenesis) occurs in non-human mammals, and there are limited scholarly studies indicating that minimal ANG occurs in the adult human brain.

C. One obvious reason for the discrepancy of data between animal and human studies is the ethical challenges involved in experimenting on or even viewing the human brain.

D. While studies have shown an "association" of ANG with better brain health, none have yet proved a "causative" link.

The most robust study to date disputing the concept of adult human hippocampal neurogenesis was published in 2018 by Sorrells et al.[30] Almost all other studies support the reality of ANG. The most robust study supporting ANG was by Baldrini et al, also in 2018.[31] Both the Sorrells and the Baldrini studies employed reasonably similar immunohistological methods and included the same neurogenesis markers, yet contrasting results were observed.[32] Baldrini found ANG, and Sorrells did not. In a Solomon like manner, Kumar writes "Our results fell somewhere in between the results reported in other studies in that we found persistent but minimal hippocampal neurogenesis in adult humans."[33] My admittedly "scholarly wannabe" take on the literature is that ANG does exist, but it is quite minimal in quantity and limited in brain location. So we're onto part two of the ANG dispute: What, if anything, is the significance of this minimal ANG? Can ANG be a factor (positive or negative) in consciousness expansion?

Unfortunately, as Kumar points out, largely due to ethical restrictions, "human studies on the effects of adult neurogenesis have been inadequate to date".[34] As to animal studies, (most of which have been with laboratory rats) there has been evidence of an adverse "association" of decreased ANG on autopsy with certain psychiatric disorders and cognitive dysfunction.[35] "Association" in this context simply means that these two phenomena of decreased ANG and cognitive dysfunction are often found together on autopsy. . . a causative link can be inferred, but is not proved. Both prenatal and early-life stress seem to inhibit both the production and survival of new neurons into adulthood, which have been associated with depression, anxiety, and even schizophrenia.[36] However, since the causes of psychiatric and cognitive dysfunction are obviously always multi-factorial (for example, quality of parenting, trauma, addiction, etc.), their mere "associations" with decreased ANG do not seem to be absolute and definitive proof that ANG is needed for good psychological or cognitive health, nor that the absence of ANG directly causes psychiatric disorders or cognitive decline. More research is needed.

It is encouraging for consciousness expansion to note a positive "associative" finding in the animal studies for ANG. Kumar states that "Rehabilitative methods, such as exercise and environmental enrichment, have been shown to enhance adult neurogenesis in animal models and appear to be effective in alleviating depression and cognitive decline."[37] In laboratory rats the "exercise" largely involves robust wheel-running, and the "environmental enrichment" involves such things as toys, tunnels, greater space, and increased social interactions.[38] If true, is this positive "association" of environmental enrichment to reduced depression and cognitive decline that surprising? Not really. Social scientists have long known that environmental enrichment such as proper parenting, less stress, and a healthy lifestyle greatly increase the chances of a life without psychiatric or other health issues for both animals and humans. Whether there is a direct causative link between ANG and good brain health has yet to be definitively confirmed. After all, the brain is still a bodily organ which can only benefit from an enriched environment whether or not adult neurogenesis is playing a role.

Let's now look at synaptic modification. Synaptic modification is essentially "changes" in the way neurons interact with each other and with other bodily functions. We'll start with a review of some very basic terminology. It all evolves around the "neuron". Although there are over 10,000 different types and shapes of neurons in the human brain, it is reasonable to think of a neuron as a specialized cell for storing, receiving, and transmitting information.

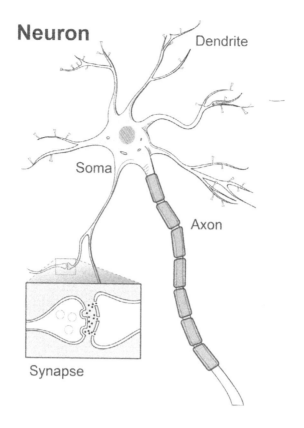

Neuron

Dendrite

Soma

Axon

Synapse

A neuron has several basic parts that each plays a role in its functions. A neuron has a cell body which is often referred to as a "soma". "Dendrites" extend from the soma in a tree-like manner. Most neurons have many dendrites, but some have only one. Dendrites themselves have many branches. The main function of dendrites is to receive information. "Axons" are also tree-like branches extending out from the soma. Most neurons have only one axon. The general role of an axon is to send information. "Synapses" are quite often described as the tiny gaps between a dendrite of one neuron and the axon of another neuron. (In a general sense, this is a functional description of synapses since the vast majority of synaptic connections are of this type. However, since there are multiple other complex types of synaptic connections, including ones with no gap, it is perhaps a bit better to think of a synapse simply as the final connection between neurons, keeping in mind that a single neuron will almost always be connected to multiple other neurons.[39])

The estimated number of synaptic connections in the human brain is staggering at potentially as many as 1000 trillion! "Neurotransmission" is the final general component of synaptic modification. An axon will not fire (transmit information) unless there is sufficient strength of signal. As further discussed in this chapter, neurotransmission involves multiple and complex metabolic processes, typically involving neurotransmitters such as acetylcholine, the one isolated by Bennett and his team referenced earlier in this chapter. Other neurotransmitters include other hormones such as dopamine and serotonin.

As previously noted, it is the current scholarly accepted belief that synaptic modification is the neural basis of both learning and memory.[40] (You will not be surprised to learn that the specific definitions of learning and memory are in scholarly dispute. However, for our purposes: "Learning" is the process of acquiring new knowledge through a number of processes such as sensory input and instruction. "Memory" is the process of retaining that knowledge over time.) You should also note that this term "synaptic modification" can be a bit misleading since the neuroplasticity of learning and memory take place at more than just new or strengthened synapses. The neuroplastic changes involved in learning and memory take place at all aspects of the neuron: soma, dendrites, axons, synapses, and neurotransmission. There are multiple distinct neuroplastic changes involved in the reformation of neural circuitry. These changes are described by scholars as both "structural" and "functional". Structural changes are essentially volumetric changes such as the formation of new synaptic pathways (more dendrites and axons). While functional changes involve metabolic processes such as frequency or strength of neurotransmission.

As you could probably surmise from Chapter One, no single neuron holds a new thought or a single memory. Rather it is groups/neighborhoods/circuits of neurons with their synaptic connections that are responsible for both learning and memory. As we learned in Chapter One, these neural networks are not strictly organized by specific categories of learning or memory. Multiple memories can be encoded in a single neighborhood/network of neurons/synapses, or a single memory can have its encoding in multiple networks. A particular thought can be triggered into consciousness by sense input (such as sight, sound, or smell), as well as by emotion, and finally by any number of non-conscious factors such as from our reptile brain or (more pertinent to consciousness expansion) from simple habits.

Each time a person "learns", neural circuits are activated and altered. Each time a person "remembers" those neural circuits are reactivated and altered. Now here is a macro-point on synaptic modification: As a general but solid rule, more frequent communication among neurons when learning or recalling will result in strengthening of those learning or memory neural pathways. Conversely, reduced communication will result in a neuroplastic diminution of such neuro connections. Neuroplasticity works both ways; creation and destruction. Hence, again the pithy saying known as "Hebb's Rule" or "Hebb's Theory":

Neurons that fire together, wire together.
Neurons that fire out of sync, fail to link.

Although Hebb's Rule is still often quoted in both the scholarly and lay literature as a generally valid rule, this saying is more of a metaphor than a hard and fast rule. For example, neurons don't actually fire "together" at the same time.[41] In addition, research has shown that neurons that are in more remote areas of the brain but with the same projection target more easily build connections than neurons adjacent to each other that don't otherwise frequently respond to the same sensory stimuli.[42] Nonetheless, Hebb's Rule does seem to generally hold true for our purpose of attempting to "rewire" our brains to aid in expansion of consciousness.

The macro-point here is that while there remains scholarly debate on the efficacy of adult neurogenesis, there is now absolutely no dispute on the reality of being able to rewire the human brain via Hebb's Rule (keeping in mind that Hebb's Rule is a metaphor that includes numerous neuroplastic processes both endogenous and exogenous to the human body). You can rewire your brain!

So how do we take advantage of Hebb's Rule to help expand our consciousness? Ha ha! We do the same as Bennett did with his laboratory rats. We select and increase ECT (environmental complexity and training) that will support consciousness expansion. We design and engage in specific practices that will help to induce synaptic modification and expand the degree to which we are aware of and knowingly responsive to our internal and external environment. This will later be discussed in more detail, but it essentially involves using specific practices (ECT) to lay down and strengthen new positive neural tracts and diminish negative tracts. Section II of this book presents powerful and proved practices to do just that. But first, let's first finish this chapter on our overview of neuroplasticity.

3) The vast majority of neuroplasticity occurs early in life when the brain is developing. While this may not aid us in our quest for adult consciousness expansion, it has profound implications for child rearing.

The type of neuroplasticity we are focusing on is synaptic modification, which continues throughout life. In fact, as you read this sentence, hopefully millions of synapses are being modified in your brain every second. This sounds like a huge number until you recall that a mature neuron can have 10,000 synaptic connections, and there are 100 billion neurons in the mature human brain. Scholars are in agreement that the dominant amount of synaptic modification occurs during the time period between early embryonic life and toward the end of the first year of life. The neuroplasticity of synaptic modification is so prolific during early life that many scholars call that process "exuberant synaptogenesis".

The embryonic/neonatal brain is actually genetically programmed to generate many more synapses than are actually needed. During the first year of life, the number of synapses not only multiplies by a factor of ten; but by age two, a toddler has around 15,000 synapses per neuron. This is 50 percent more synapses than in the adult brain, actually many more than are actually needed.

This explosion of exuberant synaptogenesis is not that surprising when you think about the almost logarithmic difference between the brain changes from an embryo to a one-year-old verses brain changes later in life; for example, from age 41 to age 42. Let's consider just a few of the things the newborn brain has to learn. Take a seemingly simple thing like crawling. For a brand new brain, this is not just getting on your hands and knees and going forward. Before you can even get up on your hands and knees (in fact before a baby can even lift up their head) corresponding spacial and motor areas of the brain must undergo tremendous neuroplasticity, especially the neuroplasticity of synaptogenesis. Multiply this by the neuroplasticity required for developing the neuroconnections for such things as hearing, seeing, vocalization, facial recognition of mom; and the even more subtle and sophisticated expanding ability to interpret social situations, and you can begin to appreciate the need for exuberant synaptogenesis.

There are two important consequences of early synaptic modification: "synaptic pruning" and the need for essentially what we've been calling ECT. These two phenomena are intertwined. Synaptic pruning is just what it sounds like: If you don't use it, you lose it. Part two Hebb's Rule again. ECT is essentially the concept of supportive environmental factors that help you "use it". Malacarne called it training. Modern day scholars like Bennett call it ECT. Appropriate ECT both in utero and during childhood are essential for optimal brain development. This essentially involves the ECT of good parenting.

Synaptic modification (essentially synaptogenesis) begins in utero. Scholars have confirmed its process as early as 12 weeks gestation, but there is every reason to believe that advancing technology will eventually find that it begins even earlier. Although different areas of the brain develop at different rates of progress, in general the peak number of synapses occurs toward the end of the first year of life.[43] This places quite a burden of responsibility on parents, babysitters, and legislators to help create ECT such as childcare, proper nutrition, and mental stimulation that would foster optimal synaptic modification. But responsibility doesn't end on the baby's first birthday.

In general, scholars agree that the human brain does not reach its full gross size until the end of puberty, around 16 years old. Moreover, the "developmental" need for ECT continues until the adult human is well into her/his 30s. Many scholars, including Costandi, report that adolescent/early adult synaptic status in the cerebral cortex is of particular concern. This is because it is now recognized by neuroscientists that synaptic formation of the cerebral cortex is not completed until a young adult is well into their 30s.[44] You will recall that the frontal cortex is involved with executive function of decision making. This is essentially the arbiter of risk versus reward decisions on subsequent actions. You don't need citations to scholarly literature to know that many teenagers and even young adults often engage in risky behavior as if their brains were nothing more than dopamine dispensing machines. Teenagers and young adults simply don't yet have the brain capacity to appreciate the consequential relationship between current emotional impulses and longer term effects. Guidance from parents, teachers, and mentors is essential for successful neuroplastic navigation of those early adult years.

4) Not all neuroplasticity is a positive development for consciousness expansion. Brain changes can retard or even reverse the capacity for consciousness expansion.

At first, one might find synaptic pruning a scary process. After all, you are losing brain circuitry. On reflection, however, synaptic pruning doesn't seem so scary because those extra synapses are not only not needed, but could actually interfere with normal brain function if not appropriately pruned. Essentially, just too many nonessential wires that could disrupt/retard brain function. Unfortunately, there are other aspects of neuroplasticity that are truly negative and concerning. These could be described by (my again somewhat arbitrary) three heuristic categories of: a) part two of Hebb's Rule; b) negative practices; and c) age-related neuropathology.

A. *Part two of Hebb's Rule. . .* is fairly obvious by its plain language. Essentially, if you don't use it, you lose it. The truth of this rule is verifiable both anecdotally and by scholarly research.

A real-life anecdotal example for me is learning a new language. Many of you have likely had the same experience. I often attempt to learn at least what I call "tourist" ability in a new language before I am scheduled to spend an extended amount of time in a new country. As I mentioned in Chapter Two, even though I don't yet seem to possess the line of intelligence/competence needed to actually master a new language, I simply love trying. After many months of struggle, I do eventually gain at least my tourist competence of the language. I can ask directions, order food, and exchange pleasantries in that new language. But as soon as I move onto other things and stop using the language: Poof! I soon lose most facility in that language. This is simply a fundamental aspect of part two of Hebb's Rule. Many of you no doubt have the genetic gift of being able to preserve unused knowledge/skills longer than I; but eventually, if we don't use it, we all lose it.

As to scholarly proof, somewhat recently scholars at MIT confirmed the common sense truth of part two of Hebb's Rule which MIT stated was a "fundamental rule of brain plasticity". Specifically, "when a synapse strengthens, its neighbors weaken".[45] So as you and your brain move on to other matters, neural circuits (including but not limited to new language neural circuits) decay. These MIT scholars reasoned that this type of destructive neuroplasticity is needed so that the brain is not overwhelmed with input. These brilliant and creative scholars were even able to isolate and identify a protein called "Arc" that modifies synaptic receptors to "maintain a balance of synaptic resources".[46] Part two of Hebb's Rule is a reality.

    B. *Negative practices.* . . involve a wide range of activities including the major categories of: addiction, bad habits, and poor health and fitness practices. The negative neuroplastic aspects of poor practices in these major categories may by now seem obvious to you. Others not so much, but all are important.

Regarding addiction, in particular drug addiction (to substances like cocaine, heroin, alcohol, amphetamines, and even seemingly less ominous drugs such as nicotine) and its cruel ability to hijack brain function is of course the most obvious. Addiction primarily does its damage by modifying the neurocircuitry of the brain's motivation and rewards systems, mainly through hormones such as dopamine (a hormone is a substance that stimulates cells/tissues into action). Dopamine functions both as a neurotransmitter and a hormone. Dopamine is mainly synthesized in the brain and kidneys, and has numerous functions. Dopamine synthesized outside the brain (of which this chapter is not concerned) helps to regulate such things as the immune system, insulin production, and blood vessel integrity. Dopamine synthesized within the brain helps facilitate movement; and more pertinent to this discussion, helps regulate one of the most fundamental cognitive functions: the motivation behind executive decision making, known in social science literature as "motivational salience". It's fair to describe motivational salience as simple common sense decision making.

Especially in lay literature, dopamine is often somewhat incorrectly referred to as the "happy hormone" because it activates neural pathways involving pleasure centers of the brain. However, it is more accurate to think of dopamine as affecting "motivation" for any action selection process. From an evolutionary perspective, dopamine motivates most animals (including humans) to choose "natural rewards" such as food, sex, exercise, and even social success. The action selected can then cause release of dopamine in the brain which stimulates pleasure centers encouraging reinforced motivation to repeat that action. This can have positive effects such as encouraging the subject to eat, procreate, and generally succeed.

The neurons that synthesize dopamine are called "dopaminergic" neurons, and are actually few in number in a relative sense: about 400,000. They are located in just a few confined areas of the brain, but their axons powerfully project to many other areas of the brain. Once dopamine enters the synapse, it binds to both dendrites and axons and increases or decreases dopamine uptake. Increased dopamine results in positive/reinforced motivation. Decreased dopamine reduces certain decisional motivation for natural rewards. This decrease can result in an extreme situation where the subject (animal or human) stops eating even though food is present and the subject is wasting away from lack of food. The danger of dopamine damaging addiction is multifarious. It causes both "structural" and "functional" maladaptations to the neural pathways. But even worse is that the amount of the drug must be increased to cause the same high. Worse yet, once the changes in the neural pathways have occurred, stopping the drug use will not eliminate the craving.

Regarding bad habits, unfortunately, you don't have to succumb to dangerous drugs to fall prey to addiction. Your brain forms strengthened and increased neural connections reinforced by hormones such as dopamine and serotonin (another neurotransmitter) from whatever you do repeatedly in your life. As a result, the "habit energy" generated by these neuroplastic processes effectively becomes an addiction, even more so if a person is unaware of the neuroplasticity of habitual behavior.

Negative neuroplasticity can result (for example) in an otherwise seemingly innocent habit such as persistently coming home from work, microwaving a quick dinner, and plopping yourself down on the couch for several hours of too often mindless television until you're ready to fall asleep. Then repeat the habit the next day. Keep this habit up long enough, and your brain will rewire to anticipate and reward this behavior. If this is the consciousness receptacle you desire, so be it. (After all, television shows like "Game of Thrones" are quite compelling.) But if you want consciousness expansion, you will need to change such habits.

Regarding poor health and fitness practices, when one appreciates that the brain is and always will be a bodily organ, the necessity of proper health practices becomes obvious. The traditional areas of major health concern are: smoking, alcohol intake, body/mass index ("BMI"), diet, and physical activity. Numerous scholarly studies (which have now existed over decades) establish beyond doubt that the brain benefits from proper health practices in each of these areas of major concern just like any other bodily organ.[47] The critical interrelationship among health practices, neuroplasticity, and consciousness will be discussed in more detail later in this chapter.

C. *Age-related neuropathology.* . . is particularly scary at my age. Although different individuals undergo age-related neuropathology at different rates, if you live long enough, the reality of age-related neuropathology is inevitable. Moreover, it begins sooner than you might suspect. As previously discussed, the human brain does not reach maturity until around the late 20s; but thereafter, age-related neuropathology begins its march of negative neuroplasticity.

In a general sense, when the brain itself begins to shrink (particularly in the frontal cortex) there is restricted somatotopic space for brain function. After about age 40, the human brain shrinks about 5% a decade. Then after age 70, this shrinkage accelerates. In a micro-sense, age-related neuropathology occurs at all the levels of neuroplasticity which we have talked about including: gene expression at the level of a single neuron; death of neurons; fewer synapses; compromised neurotransmitters and neuronal firing; compromised hormone, enzyme, and neurotrophic factor production including dopamine synthesis; and reduced blood flow. These pathologies affect all manner of brain function and cognition including memory, learning, orientation, attention, balance, and communication skills. This is depressing to say the least, but let's finish this chapter by looking at positive aspects of neuroplasticity supported by scholarly research, including hopeful practices for the aging brain.

5) There do appear to be practices which generate improved overall brain health as well as neuroplastic changes that support consciousness expansion.

We're back again to the fundamental questions raised at the beginning of this chapter: Is the promise of neuroplasticity hope or hype? Can we use some form(s) of ECT to rewire our brains to improve overall brain health/function as well as to become more aware of and knowingly responsive to our internal and external environment? The answer is a definite yes. There are scholarly confirmed studies that support both.

We should distinguish between these two potential neuroplastic goals: "improved overall brain function" and (what could be called) "directed rewiring that supports expansion of consciousness." Although there is overlap between these two neuroplastic goals, for purposes of our overview, I'm equating overall brain health with cognitive function. By that I mean treating the brain like any other bodily organ with actions such as proper diet, exercise, and rest, etc. Better brain function/health does not automatically correlate with an expanded consciousness receptacle, but a healthier brain is certainly a more optimal vehicle to achieve that goal. On the other hand, directed rewiring involves intentionally changing neural circuitry to increase awareness of and response to forces we have explored such as reptile brain, non-conscious factors, and other filters to our consciousness. Directed rewiring is building new habitual neuropathways that support expansion of our consciousness receptacle. Let's take a closer look at both improved cognitive function and directed rewiring.

Regarding improved cognitive function. . . while factors such as diet, rest, and lifestyle decisions are obviously important for the health and operation of any bodily organ including the brain, one factor that has received intense scholarly investigation is exercise.

In order to function, the brain relies heavily on both oxygen and energy substrate, both of which are delivered to the brain by vascularization (blood). While the human brain is approximately 2% of total body mass, the brain requires 15% of cardiac output and 20% of total blood glucose and oxygen.[48] In order to accommodate these high volume needs, cerebral vascular resistance in the brain is initially and ideally low. This causes the brain vasculature to be highly associated with reduced cognitive function as brain vasculature hardens with age.

Fortunately, there now exists consistent scholarly evidence that habitual aerobic exercise benefits both brain structure and cognitive function.[49] While research continues on the relationship between brain benefits and the type/ intensity of required exercise, it appears the intensity of aerobic exercise required is at least 60% of VO2 max (maximum capacity of oxygen uptake)[50] which essentially equates to a brisk walk.

Research suggests that habitual aerobic exercise not only helps preserve the structure of the brain from aging, but also enhances cognitive function. Structural changes include such things as increased cerebral blood volume and capillary densities; preservation of the structural integrity of white matter that is responsible for visuospatial function, motor control, and coordination; facilitation of the delivery of energy substrates; and reduction in the risk of microbleed.[51] As to cognitive function, a recent meta-analytic review of the effects of exercise on the brain also revealed that exercise increases BDNF (brain-derived neurotrophic factor) which is associated with better spacial recognition and verbal memory.[52] Moreover, a number of studies establish a correlation between exercise and improved cognitive function as demonstrated through the most commonly used tests such as the Mini-Mental State Examination, the Modified Mini-Mental State Examination, and the Cognitive Ability Screening Instrument.[53]

Regarding directed rewiring. . . the next steps toward consciousness expansion involve intentional/directed rewiring of the synaptic circuitry of your brain. This principally involves recognizing nonproductive habits, and then changing those habits to cultivate positive habit energy. (I'm using the term "habit energy" as a metaphor for supporting synaptic circuitry.) The power of positive habit energy will be discussed in more folsom detail in Section II of this book. But let's next look at whether there is any scholarly evidence on the degree to which a person can rewire their brain.

The most prolific as well as the most controversial neuroplastic techniques (a form of ETC) claiming to improve cognitive function are "computer based cognitive training" regimens, more commonly known as "brain games" (which for convenience let's call them "BGs"). It is well worth our time to examine the ongoing scholarly investigation of BGs. First, because BGs dominate the current marketplace of (claimed) ECT for improving brain function including synaptic modification (Hebb's Rule). Second, the marketshare power of BG producers allows them to dominate the advertising propaganda on the claimed ability to rewire the brain. Finally, although there is some questionable scholarly research being falsely promoted, there is now significant scholarly research that has and continues to be undertaken into the cognitive benefits of BGs. As we have seen, the U.S. Federal Court has already weighed in to rule that many of the claims of the purveyors of BGs are unsupported by scholarly testing. But do the scholars have anything positive to say about the benefits of BGs?

One could argue that the controversy as to what extent brain games can affect neuroplasticity came to a head in 2014 when two distinguished groups of scholars published position papers that seemingly took opposite positions on marketing claims being made by the brain training industry as to the efficacy of those claims. We can call these two papers "Consensus Statement Number One" ("CS-1") and "Consensus Statement Number Two" ("CS-2").

On October 20, 2014, Consensus Statement Number One ("CS-1") entitled "A Consensus on the Brain Training Industry from the Scientific Community" was published by the Stanford Center on Longevity in San Francisco and the Max Planck Institute for Human Development in Munich.[34] It was signed by 74 distinguished international scholars heavily credentialed and involved in such fields as neuroscience, cognitive development, and psychology. CS-1 essentially stated that the aging "baby boomer" generation was becoming increasingly anxious about potential cognitive decline, and that purveyors of BGs were making frequent, exaggerated, and misleading claims about their products. In general, this included two types of claims. First, that the skill developed in mastering a particular BG could "transfer" to other cognitive skills resulting in an increase in overall cognitive function. Second, that BGs could cure or prevent Alzheimer's disease or other forms of dementia.

CS-1 challenged the integrity of the research studies used to justify the general claim of cognitive skill "transfer", and further stated that there were "no" studies that demonstrated that playing BGs prevented or much less cured forms of dementia or Alzheimer's. CS-1 readily agreed that there was long-standing and compelling evidence that any "mentally effortful new experience" such as learning a new language or playing a BG "will produce changes in those neural systems that support the acquisition of the new skill" such as increasing the strength and number of synapses and supporting cells. In other words, if you play a particular BG long enough, you will likely become more skilled at playing that particular BG. But CS-1 insisted it was not appropriate to conclude that any cognitive benefits of BG training "transferred" beyond the BG skill to "affect broad abilities with real-world relevance". Playing a BG may result in neuroplastic changes that will make you better at playing that particular BG, but those neuroplastic changes will not "transfer" to increase overall or other cognitive skills.[55]

CS-1 also brought up an interesting and important tangential point which in general had not been previously addressed in the scholarly or lay literature. CS-1 challenged the lost "opportunity costs" of investing time and money in playing brain games instead of engaging in other activities such as reading, aerobic exercising, and/or socializing which may benefit both the cognitive and physical health of older adults.[56]

CS-1 did acknowledge the existence of "some intriguing isolated reports" that inspire additional research regarding cognitive benefits of BGs, and offered best practices type recommendations, such as using control groups and independent funding on how such future research should be conducted.[57]

Then in December of 2014, 133 equally experienced and well credentialed international scholars published what we're calling Consensus Statement Number Two ("CS-2") entitled "Cognitive Training Data Response Letter" on a website called Cognitive Training Data at www.cognitivetrainingdata.org. This site was propagated by a BG support company known as Posit Science. Posit Science was co-founded by renowned neurophysiologist, Michael Merzenich, and neuroscientist, Henry Mahncke. Posit Science definitely had a dog in this fight because it was in the BG industry, but that dog was backed by over 130 highly qualified scholars not associated with Posit Science.

A number of subsequent commentators tend to make this scholarly dispute between CS-1 and CS-2 more intense that it actually was. In actuality, CS-2 was quite respectful in its disagreements, and conceded that CS-1 had raised some valid points regarding certain exaggerated and unsupported claims of BG purveyors. Nonetheless, we now had two equally well qualified groups of scholars, looking at exactly the same data, and seemingly coming to opposite conclusions about the "efficacy of cognitive training".

This main disagreement by CS-2 was stated as follows:

> We cannot agree with the part of your statement that says "there is no compelling scientific evidence" that brain exercises "offer consumers a scientifically grounded avenue to reduce or rewire cognitive decline." We fear that most readers would take this to mean there is little or no peer-reviewed evidence that certain brain exercises have been shown to drive cognitive improvements. There is, in fact, a large and growing body of such evidence. . . Many of these studies. . . document positive changes in real-life indicts of cognitive health. . .[58]

But it was a tangential argument by CS-2 that is perhaps more interesting given what we learned earlier in this chapter about major "wrong turns" by the scholar community regarding neuroplasticity. CS-2 warned that scientific consensus statements like CS-1 needed to be careful when addressing "new" evidence/research from a new area of scientific inquiry such as BG affect on cognition.

> We need to be open, especially to evidence that may not fit our current worldview, because that is often where new discovery lies and how scientific consensus changes. That is certainly the case in the field of neuroplasticity historically, where, not long ago, a few lone voices, including some signatories to this letter, began the process of overturning the scientific consensus that brain plasticity ended with childhood – a now abandoned consensus that hold back many advances to public health.[59]

This warning essentially cautions the science community not to be stuck in their collective consciousness receptacle on scientific dogma when something new comes along. This is an excellent macro-point for consciousness expansion.[60] Nonetheless, even exciting and promising "new" discoveries need be tested by "best practices" research.

The dispute between CS-1 and CS-2 is essentially a dispute about the validity of the existing research on BGs and cognitive function. Fortunately for us, the demanding challenge of undertaking a comprehensive review of all brain-training literature from both a qualitative and quantitative review of the evidence was taken up by top scholars: Daniel J. Simmons, a cognitive scientist from the University of Illinois, and Walter R. Boot, a cognitive psychologist from Florida State University. In 2016, their 83 page comprehensive study entitled "Do Brain-Training Programs Work?" (here and after "Simons") answered many of the disputed issues about BG research.

Simons agreed with CS-2 that there were research papers on the supposed cognitive benefits of BGs, but politely suggested that the controversy between these two distinguished groups of scholars might be the result of different standards used in evaluating the evidence found in the various BG research studies. So Simons undertook to perform the first comprehensive review of all extant brain-training literature. This specifically included all studies referred to in CS-2 which CS-2 claimed were not considered by CS-1. This comprehensive review would examine the quality of such literature under a "best practices" research standard.

Simons looked exclusively for any cognitive effects gained by repeatedly performing a brain-game (cognitive task). This did not involve looking for microscopic neuroplastic changes in neuropathways or neurosubstrates. Rather, it involved looking for any "transfer" cognitive effects to other unrelated cognitive tasks or to everyday cognitive performance rather than just getting more skilled at the practiced task. After all, no one disputes the neuroplasticity that occurs when you repeat a task long enough such as shooting free throws, driving a truck, or playing a BG. Try hard enough and long enough, and you'll likely get better at that particular task, but it is "transfer" to everyday cognitive function that is promised by these BGs. "Transfer effects" could be empirically determined by the participants submitting to established cognitive tests such as the Mini-Mental State Examination and the Modified Mini-Mental State Examination which each gives a global measure of cognitive function; or tests like the Cognitive Ability Screening Instrument which indicate the presence or absence of dementia.[61]

After his comprehensive review of all the relevant research literature, Simons found:

[1] extensive evidence that brain-training interventions improve performance on the trained task;

[2] less but definite evidence that such interventions improve performance on "closely related" tasks;

[3] little evidence that training enhances performance on "distantly related" tasks or that training improves everyday cognitive performance;

[4] many of the published intervention studies had major shortcomings. . . that precluded definitive conclusions about the efficacy of training; and

[5] none of the cited studies conformed to all of the best practices.

Simmons correctly points out that many proponents of the "transfer effects" of BGs incorrectly tend to think of the brain as a muscle; i.e., the more you use it, the stronger it gets throughout the brain as a whole.[62] This is not accurate. Research studies have long held that neuroplastic changes tend to be specific to the neural substrates involved in the particular practice.[63] This is Hebb's Rule again. (In this context, Hebb's Rule also gives us a bit of neuroplastic insight as to why people develop individual "lines" of competence as we discussed in Chapter Three when we reviewed the insights of Ken Wilbur.) Repeated effort on improving one specific line of competence will likely increase competence in that specific line, and can spill over to "closely related" lines, but will not automatically "transfer" to improve competence in all lines. (Note that the validity of "transfer effects" to "closely related" practices will be relevant in Section II of this book, especially as it relates to practices such as changing perspective, meditation, and forgiveness.)

The metaphor of Hebb's Rule, supported by the scholarly research as analyzed by Simons (as well as what we have learned in the preceding chapters to this book), teaches us how to go about rewiring our brains to help support consciousness expansion:

Step One: Recognition that a vast number of our thoughts, emotions, and actions are based on non-conscious factors which this book has described as "filters" to our consciousness.

Step Two: Recognition that our brain is largely a habit machine, where thoughts, emotions, and actions are laid out in supporting neural-synaptic pathways.

Step Three: Recognition that the adventure of consciousness expansion is difficult due to the powerful filters such as the hierarchy of human needs; the powers of culture, emotions, and genetics; the demands of everyday concerns; and especially the fear of change.

Step Four: Recognition that neuroplasticity is real, and that neural pathways can be weakened or strengthened through selected ECT to support an expanded level of consciousness.

Step Five: Begin transformance with the vehicles of powerful and proved practices for expansion of consciousness.

Hopefully, Section I of this book has helped us begin to appreciate and accept the "recognition " required in Steps One through Four. In Section II, we begin our exploration of Step Five "transformance" as we continue our adventure in consciousness expansion.

---

1 Santiago Ramon y Cajal (1852-1934) (here and after "SRC") is often referred to as the Father of Neuroscience. He was a Spanish neuroanatomist and artist who specialized in neuroanatomy. In 1906, he was awarded the nobel prize in Physiology for his theory (and drawings) on what eventually came to be called the "neuron doctrine". This theory suggested that the brain as well as the entire nervous system are made up of discrete/individual units/cells known as a neural unit, now known as a neuron.

2 See mindhacks.com/2010/06/07/neuroplasticity-is-a-dirty-word. This article by Vaughan Bell notes that this quote is actually from the Introduction to the influential scientific book "Toward a Theory of Neuroplasticity" by Christopher A. Shaw and Jill C. McEachern, Psychology Press, New York, 2001.

3 For example, Google "Plasticity comparisons between plants and animals. Concepts and mechanisms" by Renee M. Borges. Plant Signal Behav. 2008 Jun; 3(6):367-375.

4 "Neuronal plasticity: historical roots and evolution of meaning"; Berlucchi G. and Berlucchi HA. at www.ncbi.nlm.nih.gov/pubmed/19002678, Nov. 2008. (Here and after "Berlucchi".)

5 See the Federal Court order of www.ftc.gov/system/files/documents/cases/160105lumoslabsstip. pdf at p5, 6, and 9. The $50 million dollar judgment was suspended after payment of $2 million dollars due to the financial condition of Lumosity. See www.ftc.gov/news-events/press-releases/2016/01/lumosity-pay.2-million-settle-ftc-deceptiveadvertising-charges at p2 of FTC's claims.

6 "Adult Neuroplasticity: More than 40 Years of Research" by Eberhard Fuchs and Gabriele Flugge; Neural Plasticity Vol 2014 Article ID541870 (2014) at p.2 which can be found online at http://dx.doi.org/10.1155/2014/541870. (Here and after "Fuchs".) An excellent, although somewhat technical article. Although the Fuchs' article specifically states that "stress *does not* kill neurons" per se both "acute and chronic stress are known to decrease hippocampal neurogenesis". See "Adult Neurogenesis in Humans: A Review of Basic Concepts, History, Current Research, and Clinical Implications", Innov Clin Neurosci. 2019; 16(5-6):30-37 at p32 by Ashutosh Kumar, MD; Vikas Pareek, Ph.D; Muneeb A. Faig, Ph.D; Sanjib K. Ghosh, MD; and Chiman Kumari, MD. (2019). (Here and after "Kumar".) Currently, the most comprehensive and lay accessible article on adult neurogenesis in humans.

7 "Neurogenesis in the adult human hippocampus" Peter S. Eriksson, Ekaterina Perfilieva, Thomas Bjork-Eriksson, Ann-Marie Alborn, Claes Nordborg, Daniel A. Peterson, and Fred H. Gage, Nature Medicine 4, 1313-1317 (1998).

8 "Neuroplasticity" by Moheb Costandi, MIT Press, Cambridge, 2016 at p13. This is one of the best books from a lay perspective to explain the history, physiology, and implications of neuroplasticity. (Here and after "Costandi".)

9 Costandi at p4.

10 Mark R. Rosenzweig, 1996 "Aspects of the search for neural mechanisms of memory" Annual Review of Psychology 47:1-32 at p5. (Here and after "Rosenzweig".)

11 Costandi at p4-5.

12 Costandi at p5.

13 See, www.historyofphrenology.org.uk/overview.htm. (Here and after "Wyhe.) The links provided in this article are also an excellent research source on the history of phrenology.

14 Wyhe at p3.

15 Wyhe at p4.

16 Charles Darwin "The Descent of Man" Volume One, 1874 as published Pacific Publishing Studio

2011. (Here and after "Descent".)

17 Descent at p37.

18 Although cell "theory" was first developed by Schwann and Schleiden, microscopic discovery of the "cell" appears to be first discovered in 1665 by English architect and natural philosopher, Robert Hooke (1635-1703).

19 It is interesting to note that viruses do not have cells. It is debated whether a virus is a living organism since a virus does not have a cell membrane, and a virus does not inherently have its own tools to reproduce itself. Rather, a virus, which has a protein coat to protect its genetic material, inserts its DNA into a host cell causing that cell to make a copy of the virus DNA creating more viruses.

20 Costandi at p10.

21 Costandi at p10.

22 For a brief but excellent summary of the mid-twentieth century investigations into neuroplasticity, see "Chemical and Anatomical Plasticity of the Brain" by Edward L. Bennett, Marian C. Diamond, David Krech, and Mark R. Rosenzweig , 1964 Science, Vol 146, 610-619. (Here and after "Bennett".)

23 Bennett at p618.

24 Costandi at p11.

25 My research has failed to uncover the author(s) of this pithy saying. All scholars credit the underlying idea to a Canadian psychologist, Donald Hebb (1904-1985), who with remarkable foresight back in his 1949 book "The Organization of Behavior" speculated that, "When an axon of cell A is near enough to excite a cell B and repeatedly or permanently takes part in firing it, some growth process or metabolic change takes place in one or both cells such that A's efficiency, as one of the cells firing B, is increased". Hebb's prediction was long before plasticity in humans was experimentally confirmed! It seems that Hebb's speculation was first reduced to an initial pithy saying "neurons wire together if they fire together" in a 1992 article by Siegrid Lowel and Wolf Singer entitled "Selection of Intrinsic Horizontal Connections in the Visual Cortex by correlated Neuronal Activity" Science, Vol 255, Issue 5041 p211 (1992). I have not uncovered who rephrased the first sentence of this saying or who added the second sentence. Please contact me if you know.

26 On a totally unrelated but fascinating matter, perform an online search for Hebb's alleged connection to unethical brain manipulation by the CIA.

27 "Neurogenesis in the adult hippocampus" Eriksson PS, Perfilieva E. Bjork-Eriksson, T. Alborn AM Nordborg C, Peterson DA. Gage FH 1998 Nat Med 1998 Nov, 4 (11):1313-7.

28 See "Brain Plasticity and Behavior" by Bryan Kolb, Robbin Gibb, and Terry E. Robinson, (2003) Current Directions in Psychological Science, Volume 18:12 issue: 1, pp1-5.

29 Innovations in Clinical Neuroscience. 2019; 16(5-6):30-37 by Ashutosh Kumar, MD; Vikas Parsek, Ph.D; Muneeb A. Faig, Ph.D; Sanjib K. Ghogh, MD; and Chiman Kumari, MD. Innov Clin Neurosci. 2019; 16(5-6):30-37. (Here and after "Kumar".)

30 Kumar at p33 citing Sorrells SF, Paredes MF, Cebrian-Silla A, et al. "Human hippocampal neuro-

genesis drops sharply in children to undetectable levels in adults". Nature 2018; 555(7696):377-381. (Here and after "Sorrells".)

31 Kumar at p33 citing Baldrini M. Fulmore CA, Tarttan, et al. "Human hippocampal neurogenesis persists throughout aging". Cell Stem Cell. 2018; 22(4):589-599.e5. (Here and after "Baldrini".)

32 Kumar at p33.

33 Kumar at p34.

34 Kumar at p34.

35 In support, Kumar cites a thorough and somewhat lay accessible article "Adult Neurogenesis and Mental Illness" by Timothy J. Schoenfeld and Heather A. Cameron. Neuropsychopharmacology volume 40, pp113-128 (2015). Schoenfeld at p5. (Here and after "Schoenfeld".) Schoenfeld also describes why rodent models are used in ANG research. Due to ethical considerations, most human research is done post mortem. Non-human primate models are too expensive. Finally, it is largely unknown if primate psychiatric models reflect conditions in humans. Schoenfeld at p13-14.

36 Schoenfeld at p3.

37 Kumar at p35.

38 Schoenfeld at p5. Kumar at p35.

39 Although our concern is how neurons transfer information to other neurons, it is interesting to note that certain neurons in the CNS also transfer information directly to muscles, glands, and even blood vessels.

40 Then again, just when we think we have the answers about synaptic modification, new research raises challenging questions. Even the mountain-top status of synaptic modification seems to be under question. In an article aptly titled, "The Demise of the Synapse As the Locus of Memory: A Looming Paradigm Shift?" Cognitive scientist, Patrick C. Trettenbrein, suggests that the true locus of learning and memory is not the synapses, but is actually sub-cellular within the DNA and RNA of the neurons. Trettenbrein states that, "The role of synaptic plasticity thus changes from providing the fundamental memory mechanism to providing. . . a bundle of mechanisms which regulate and ensure that the network and its modules perform and interact efficiently". "The Demise of the Synapse As the Locus of Memory: A Looming Paradigm Shift?" 2016 Patrick C. Trettenbrein can be found online at www.frontiersin.org/articles/10.3399/fnsys.2016.00088/full. (Here and after "Trettenbrein".)

41 See "The spike timing dependence of plasticity" by Daniel E. Feldman and Helen Wills, Neuron (2012).

42 See ScienceDaily "Neurons that fire together, don't always wire together" www.sciencedaily.com citing: "Segregated Subnetworks of Intracortical Projection Neurons in Primary Visual Cortex" by Mean-Hwon Kim, Peter Znamenskiy, Maria Florencia Lacaruso, and Thomas D. Mrsic-Flogel, Neuron (2018) Vol 100, Issue 6, 1313-1321.

43 Costandi at p41.

44 Costandi at p41-42.

45 See MIT News online at https://news.mit.edu/2018/mit.scientists-discover-fundamental-rule-of-brain-plasticity-0622 citing a study in science from the Picower Institute for Learning and Memory at MIT by Mriganka Sur et al. (Here and after "MIT News".)

46 MIT News at p1.

47 See "Cerebral hemodynamics of the aging brain: risk of Alzheimer disease and benefit of aerobic exercise" by Takashi Torumi and Rong Zhang; Frontiers in Physiology, 2014; 5:6 published online. (Here and after "Tarumi"). Also see "A meta-analytic review of the effects of exercise on brain-derived neurotrophic factor" by Kristin L. Szuhany, Matteo Bugatti, and Michael W. Otto; Journal of Psychiatric Research 2015 Jan: 60:56-64. (Here and after "Szuhany"). Also see "Neuromodulation of Aerobic Exercise—A review" by Saskia Heijen, Bernhard Hommel, Armin Kibele, and Lorenza S. Colzato; Frontiers in Psychology, Jan 2016, Volume 6, Article 1890. Also see "Physical activity and cognitive function in individuals over 60 years of age: a systematic review" by Ashley Carvalho, Irene Maeve Rea, Tanyalak Parimon, and Barry J. Cusack; Clinical Interventions in Aging, 2014; 9:661-682. (Here and after "Carvalho".)

48 Tarumi at p2.

49 Tarumi at p1. Also see, "A meta-analytic review of the effects of exercise on brain-derived neurotrophic factor" by Kristin L. Szuhany, Matteo Bugatti, and Michael W. Otto. J Psychiatr Res. 2015 Jan:60:56-64 (Here and After "Szuhany".)

50 "Neuromodulation of Aerobic Exercise – A Review" by Saskia Heijnen, Bernhard Hommel, Armin Kibele and Lorenza S. Colzato; Frontiers in Psychology Volume 6, Article 1890, January 2016. (Here and after "Heijnen".)

51 See Tarumi at p6.

52 See Szuhany at p2.

53 "Physical activity and cognitive function in individuals over 60 years of age: a systematic review" by Ashley Carvalho, Irene Maeve Rea, Tanyalak, and Barry J. Cusack; Clinical Interventions in Aging 2014; 9:661-682 at p6. (Here and after "Carvalho".)

54 "A Consensus on the Brain Training Industry from the Scientific Community" by the Stanford Center on Longevity and the Max Planck Institute for Human Development, October 14, 2014 can be found online at: http://longevity3.stanford.edu/blog/2014/10/15/theconsensus-on-the-brain-training-industry-from-the-scientific-community-2/. (Here and after "CS-1".)

55 CS-1 at p1-3.

56 CS-1 at p4.

57 CS-1 at p3.

58 CS-2 at p3.

59 CS-2 at p4.

60 It is interesting to note that Dr. Merzenich, one of the co-founders of Posit Science, was a leading pioneer in overturning the strict so-called consensus (what I called the fourth and most significant

fundamental error of early neuroscience dogma) that neuroplasticity ended at adulthood. As his co-founder, Dr. Mahncke, pointed out in "A Response to 'A Consensus on the Brain' Training Industry from the Scientific Community" also published online at www.cognitietrainingdata.org. Dr. Merzenich was pilloried for his early publications challenging the old/false consensus on adult termination of neuroplasticity. The following quote by Dr. Mahncke should be a warning to us all. "Mike Merzenich taught me as a young scientist to care more about what the right answer is than about "being right".

61 Cavalho at p6.

62 Simmons at p112.

63 Simmons at p111.

Rene Descartes
Public domain photo.

Santiago Ramon y Cajal
Public domain photo: Wikimedia Commons.

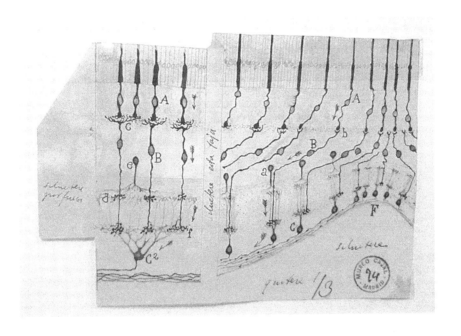

Early neural drawings by Santiago Ramon y Cajal
Public domain photo: Wikimedia Commons, Share-Alike 4.0.

William James
Public domain photo: MS AM 1092 (1185) Houghton Library,
Harvard University.

Albert Einstein
Having a little fun with reporters on his 72 birthday,
March 14, 1951.
Public domain photo.

Robert Frost
Photo by E. O. Hoppé.
Copyright E. O. Hoppé Estate Collection

Tranquility in the Snow
Photo by DJP.

The first and only meeting between H.H. Dalai Lama
and Thich Nhat Hanh.
Taken in 1993 at the Parliament of World Religions in Chicago
by my talented friend, Jessica Tampas.
Jessica gifted me the only copy of this photo many years ago.
Copyright Jessica Tampas.

Sitting and singing old American songs with Monsignor Pierre Riches on
his balcony overlooking a branch of Tiber River.
Photo by DJP.

SECTION II

TRANSFORMANCE

*Such practices almost always
involve following roads less traveled,
but then return to share
wisdom and compassion.*

CHAPTER SIX

THERAPIST, GURU, OR GOING ON YOUR OWN

The only true guru is Mr. Rogers.

—Tyler[1]

The approach of Section II "Transformance" is to introduce powerful and proved practices for expanding our consciousness into a more spacious receptacle. Although each of these practices is unique, all share a common pattern of:

1. stopping
2. looking
3. (planning)
4. practice
5. repeat.

"Stopping" involves slowing down the blistering speed at which the habit machine of the human brain is constantly producing thoughts, emotions, and actions. In particular, stopping/slowing a specific type of mental action called a "judgment". "Looking" involves focus of awareness without judgment or attachment. Just observe. Don't judge. Don't attach. You will find that stopping and looking are not governed by you as the "director", but rather by you as "witness". This can be disconcerting because it feels like you are giving up conscious control. Even more frightening can be the feeling that you are leaving your current sense of self. Hopefully, the necessity for this process has become more understandable now that we have learned about the filters and neural correlates of consciousness in Section I "Recognition". (More on this when we explore meditation in Chapter Eight.)

The third step of "planning" has been placed in parenthesis because this step is optional. You can choose to select/develop a specific practice to work on a particular line of competence needed for consciousness expansion such as: patience, egolessness, prejudice, or compassion; but the good news is that the powerful and proved practices set forth in the following chapters can bring about consciousness expansion on their own even without a specific plan or strategy.

The fourth step "practice" has many compelling facets that will soon become part of your daily life. The term "practice" reminds us that it will take continued attempts, commitment, and discipline to obtain meaningful progress. The very fact that you are continuing to practice is also a necessary recognition of your own Socratic ignorance as discussed in Chapter Four. No one has all the answers. No one is in complete control of their consciousness. No matter how spacious, consciousness is always in a limited receptacle. There is always more to discover. Practice is a commitment to that discovery.

One very positive indicator that you are well along the path of consciousness expansion is that your practice becomes more and more aligned with your consciousness. It's as if your practice becomes your window for how you are aware of and knowingly responsive to your internal and external environment. Mystics throughout history have universally taught (each in their own cultural way) that practicing internal and external awareness will inevitably result in a deeper consciousness and a natural/spontaneous generation of virtues such as humility, patience, open mindedness, and especially compassion. All of these virtues are hallmarks of expanded consciousness.

The last step is "repeat". Consciousness expansion ain't easy. Although there's never failure, just practice.[2] With each of these powerful and proved practices you will need to repeat the process of stopping, looking, practice, and repeat on a regular basis. Fortunately, as discussed in Chapter Five, we now know that skillful engagement in these practices will also generate supportive neuroplastic changes making the practice process more and more effortless to the point that you may even look forward to and enjoy the challenge of "practicing" in otherwise difficult and uncomfortable situations.

So how do we become skillful at these practices? Do we need a therapist or guru, or can we learn and advance on our own? The simple answer to these questions is: Unless a person is miraculously born as an enlightened being, we all need outside help to expand consciousness to any meaningful degree.

Why do we need help from others? After all, it's our journey! The answer to this question was a fundamental macro-point of Section I "Recognition". It is impossible to be an objective observer of your own consciousness. There are just too many powerful filters and too many habit experiences tightly interwoven into our brains for an individual to recognize and transform solely on their own. Some outside help is needed.

This chapter will explore four key avenues of outside help:

1. therapists;

2. gurus;

3. people who irritate you; and

4. sanghas.

1) Therapists. . . include psychotherapists, psychologists, psychiatrists; essentially any licensed mental health clinician. You might well be asking: Yes, I'd like to expand my consciousness, but do I really need a therapist? Perhaps not, but it may surprise you to learn about the high percentages of people who need help with psychological/mental issues. The National Institutes of Mental Health (NIH) publishes the statistics on all categories of mental health disorders at nimb.nih.gov. At the time of writing this book, approximately one out of five Americans (19.1%) suffered from a diagnosable mental illness. Approximately one out of three adult Americans (31.1%) suffered from a mental anxiety disorder at least once during their lifetime. Suicide continues to be one of the leading causes of death in our country. If you suffer from a mental health disorder, this absolutely does not mean that you can't engage in practices to expand your consciousness; but such practices are more likely to succeed with help from a therapist.

Even if you don't have a diagnosable mental health disorder, many of us have stressful challenges that can obstruct consciousness expansion such as: work pressures, intoxicants, impatience, anger issues, an unhappy marriage, long-standing and ingrained prejudices, and worries about your children. As we will see in Section II "Transformance", expansion of consciousness requires stepping away from the power of ingrained habit energies and looking closely and without judgment at our thoughts, emotions, and actions. This is not easy in the face of the seemingly unending mental stressors we all encounter daily in life. Professional counselling may be helpful.

If you're one of those rare birds with no stressful challenges, you might still consider working with a therapist to help build a deeper self-awareness. An area of related scholarly research involved the question whether therapists should be required to undergo mandatory therapy themselves in order to be licensed, even if they have no mental health issues. The research found that such therapy did tend to make therapists more empathetic and authentic to their clients.[3] More pertinent to our investigation is that at least one major paper concluded that, even without psychological issues, therapy is always valuable toward increased self-awareness:

> . . . going back to Maslow's and Roger's concept of the 'self-actualization tendency', personal development is an ongoing and lifelong process which should certainly be included and pursued during training in order to increase self-awareness.[4]

2) Gurus. . . in modern times this title/term has taken a semantic beating since its inception more than three thousand years ago. The Sanskrit word for guru is first found in the Vedas (Hindu scriptures) c. 1500-1200 BCE. There is the expected scholarly dispute as to the original meaning of the title guru; but most scholars seem to agree that the title came from the word "gu" which indicates darkness, and the word "ru" which indicates destruction. This theory derives guru to mean one who destroys the darkness of ignorance with the light of truth.

It appears the original nobility of the term guru has recently been lost for two principle reasons.[5] First, the term has been coopted and downgraded by modern commentators (especially in business) to mean a person with special expertise such as "the guru of marketing" or "the guru of derivatives".[6] Second, far too many snake oil charlatans with charismatic personalities have declared themselves gurus so that many reputable and inspiring modern day teachers (especially outside of India) hesitate to use that title anymore. Ergo, my daughter Tyler's quote regarding Mr. Rogers as the only "true" guru at the beginning of this chapter.

For our purposes, we will use the term "guru" metaphorically to mean a reputable and respected teacher who can help us move forward with consciousness expansion. Contrary to my daughter's trenchant claim, there are many such gurus,[7] even though none use that title. Most are authors, and you can learn from their books; but being in the presence of a true teacher, especially on a retreat, can be inspirational and energize your practice. (More on retreats in Chapter Seven.)

Yet the charismatic presence of such teachers can easily lead to pits of quicksand along the path of consciousness expansion. One such detour involves a type of hero worship of the guru/teacher which can devolve into an unproductive ego trip. The student non-consciously creates an elitist consciousness that deems the student "special" because of an association with a highly regarded guru/teacher. This detour can become progressively more tempting as the fame of the teacher grows. A second detour can occur when the community of the guru/teacher emphasizes "gnostic" practices reserved only for the specially initiated within the community. (Gnostic means secret knowledge which is often esoteric/mystical.) It is absolutely correct that there are deep/advanced truths about consciousness that new students may not be ready to hear because it might create confusion during early progress. Nonetheless, gnosticism should be a red flag warning for a person selecting a guru/teacher. These types of detours can too easily become reinforced by social pressure within the student community if not skillfully circumscribed by the teacher and the teacher's leadership group.

If you're on the path of committed consciousness expansion, don't underestimate these two types of detours. They are the shiny poison apples that are particularly appealing to persons on a path to "improving" themselves. Any "special", any "secret" teachings, customs, or practices should be a red flag warning that you may have veered off the path. Elitism is the diametric opposite to non-judgment, non-attachment, and consciousness expansion.

3) *People Who Irritate You.* . . are a surprising yet bountiful source of consciousness raising insights about yourself. There is a longstanding apothegm (with much debated original source attribution[8]) that states: When the student is ready, the master will appear. People who teach us some of the most important life lessons about ourselves need not be famous gurus, and in fact rarely are. If we are open and listen without judgment, we learn from parents, teachers, siblings, and (more and more as you age) our children and grandchildren. But there is another category of potential teachers who can provide us with some of the most penetrating and usually painful truths about ourselves. Those gurus are people who irritate us. . . but only if we're open to it.

For example, one of my faults is that I can be a conversation monopolizer. It's a selfish trait, and I'm ashamed to say it took me many decades to realize I even had this filter to my consciousness. During those lost decades, friends and family would from time to time hint to me about this annoying fault, but it didn't sink into my consciousness. It didn't sink in until years later after I read somewhere the insightful gem that the faults in others that annoy you the most are often your own biggest faults. I decided to experiment to see if this claim was true. When I did. . .Bam! My consciousness was opened. Conversation monopolizers really irritated me. I could finally see how irritating my bad habit was to others. More motivating to expansion of consciousness, I could now see how disrespectful it was to others. In my limited consciousness receptacle, I never wanted nor intended that. This insight was a valuable gift from a person who irritated me. I was ready, and found my guru. Now, (at times although not always) I actually appreciate running into a conversation monopolizer because it gives me the opportunity to practice.

4) *Sangha*. . . is originally a Sanskrit word that was meant to describe a community of Buddhist disciples (both ordained and lay) that live, work, learn, and practice the Dharma (Buddhist teachings) together. Since the late 20th century, the term sangha has expanded to include a more informal understanding of a community (both Buddhist and non-Buddhist) who come together on a regular basis to learn about and practice Buddhist teachings, usually with an emphasis on meditation.

Although I am not a Buddhist, I have a deep appreciation and dedication to certain Buddhist teachings (some of which will be explored in Chapter Ten). I am, however, a member of a Buddhist sangha in which I would estimate less than 20 percent of the members are actually Buddhist. We come together on Sunday evenings for an hour of silent meditation in 20 minute rounds, then a bit of social interaction with refreshments, and finally a short teaching and discussion led by different members of the sangha. Even after more than 20 years, each time I attend I'm still surprised and encouraged how this simple sangha practice centers, focuses, and energizes me.

The Buddha stressed the fundamental value of sangha by including it in his "Three Jewels" that support the heart of any practice:

> I take refuge in the Buddha,
> the one who shows me the way in this life.
>
> I take refuge in the Dharma,
> the way of understanding and love.
>
> I take refuge in the Sangha,
> the community that lives in harmony and awareness.[9]

It is not necessary that you join a sangha, become Buddhist, or even study/practice Buddhist teachings to expand your consciousness. However, it is tremendously helpful if you have the support of a sangha on your journey. Here I am using "sangha" as a metaphor for support from like-minded individuals who can energize your struggle, support your struggle, and help you free up your consciousness from the powerful filters to consciousness expansion. (Ha! It turns out our moms were correct when they warned us in our youth that, "You are who your friends are.") Your sangha need not be a formal group, although that is likely more optimal. It can be as simple as friends with whom you share and discuss meaningful books. This journey of consciousness expansion often takes the roads less traveled, which are almost always contrary (or at least different from) the socially established goals/forces of work, politics, and culture. Roads less traveled can be tough to take alone.

This chapter concludes by addressing what scholars call "The Buddha's Charter of Free Inquiry". This issue involves the false dichotomy of choosing between what a teacher says versus what you personally believe to be true. This false dichotomy arises out of inspirational quotes attributed to many of the greatest gurus/teachers including the Dalai Lama, Thich Nhat Hanh, and even the Buddha himself. Too often these purported quotes are taken out of context or even completely fake.[10] The following are typical examples of such quotes:

> Doubt everything.
> Find your own light.

> Believe nothing. . . not even if I have said it,
> unless it agrees with your own reason.

> Don't believe anything you see, read, or hear
> from religious teachers or texts.
> Find out for yourself what is true.

This type of quote involving who or what to believe allegedly originates from words ascribed to the Buddha in the Kalama Sutta.[11] Scholars have written how such quotes have been grossly taken out of context.[12] These misleading quotes are most often generated by wannabe sages, and even more frequently by purveyors of Buddhist knickknacks such as plaques containing inspirational quotes. Such quotes/teachings are disruptive to consciousness expansion because they play into the false New Age motif of "magical thinking" by implying that each of us possesses a readily accessible special consciousness allowing each individual person to "know" what teachers and what teachings can be trusted as valid. Such magical thinking is simply not true.

The Buddha's Charter of a Free Inquiry addresses this false dispute between trusting your teacher verses trusting your own belief. The Buddha teaches that each seeker should be free (and even encouraged) to question any teacher or teaching against that seeker's own experience, but always keeping in mind the limitations of that seeker's level of consciousness. This is a fine but important distinction. It arises out of an acknowledgement and acceptance of personal Socratic ignorance. Yes, test teachers and teachings. If they are substantiated by your own experience, you can then have more confidence in their teaching. If you cannot confirm a teaching, it doesn't automatically mean they're wrong and you're right. It only means more investigation is necessary.

Now let's get started on those practices. We will begin with relatively easy practices which help change "perspective".

---

1 Tyler is my adult daughter. She is a highly regarded Life Coach for teens and parents of teens. Tyler is insightful and loving, but skeptical of any scholar, mystic, and especially a dad who claims to have life's answers. When writing this chapter, I asked Tyler for some names of any gurus she held in high regard. She sarcastically responded, "The only true guru is Mr. Rogers." Fred Rogers (1928-2003) was a beloved, American, creator and host of the long running National Public Television childrens' educational show "Mister Rogers Neighborhood". As accurately stated in the website misterrogers.org, "Fred Rogers' relentless commitment to all that is good in people" led to an astonishing range of honors including the Presidential Medal of Freedom and over forty honorary degrees from colleges and universities where he was beloved by the student body. At least according to Tyler (who is rarely wrong in such matters), Fred Rogers was the only "true" guru because he lived a life of service and cared about others more than himself in all lines of consciousness.

2 I shamelessly stole the saying "There's never failure, just practice" from the grandmother of trauma therapist and author, Resmaa Menakem.

3 "Personal Therapy for Future Therapists: Reflections on a Still Debated Issue" by Maria Malikiosi-Loizos, The European Journal of Counselling Psychology, Vol 2, No 1 (2013) which can be found online. (Here and after "EJCP".)

4 EJCP at p24 online.

5 By making this argument, I do not wish to denigrate the numerous, historical Hindu and Sikh gurus who are held in high regard as saints of their respective religions. Simply search online for historical Hindu or Sikh gurus. In general, Buddhism does not use the title guru.

6 "Definition of Guru and is it GobbledyGook" by Michael Hartzell which can be found online at michaelhartzell.com/blog/definition-of-guru-and-is-it-gobbledygook.

7 There are many such teachers; too many to list. Some that I have personally found helpful are: Thich Nhat Hanh; the Dalai Lama; Lori and Jack Lawlor; John Kabat-Zinn; Pema Chodron; Norman Fischer; Sharon Salzberg; Padraig O'Tuama; Shinzen Young; Jon Stewart (yes, the comedian); Krista Tippett; Ken Wilber; James J. Walter; Al Rakowski; Alan Watts; and of course Mr. Rogers. None describe themself as a guru.

8 Various forms of this pithy saying are often used in Buddhist and New Age circles. There are scholarly disputes as to the originator of the saying that can easily be found online. For example, see "When the Student is Ready the Teacher will Appear" by Fake Buddha Quotes at https://fakebuddhaquotes.com/when-the-student-is-ready-the-teacher-will-appear. This blog impressively argues that this saying is not from the Buddha, but rather from the Theosophical Movement of the mid 19th century. I get a zen-like kick out of other related sayings such as: When the student is truly ready, the teacher will disappear. When the Tao (natural path/order of the universe) is ready, the teacher will appear.

9 This translation of the Buddha's words is from my teacher, Thich Nhat Hanh in "The Heart of the Buddha's Teaching" (1998) Broadway Books, New York at p161. (Here and after "Heart".) Heart is a scholarly yet accessible book setting out and explaining in modern terms each of the Buddha's significant teachings. Over the years, I have given this book as a gift to friends seeking a more comprehensive understanding of Buddhism.

10 See for example www.fakebuddhaquotes.com.

11 A "sutta" is sacred Buddhist literature purportedly stating the words of the Buddha. Some suttas are the purported words of other early Buddhist sages.

12 An easily accessible scholarly commentary on this is "A Look at the Kalama Sutta" by Bhikkhu Bodhi (1998), and can be found online at www.accesstoinsight.org.

CHAPTER SEVEN

CHANGING YOUR PERSPECTIVE
BY FOLLOWING ROADS LESS TRAVELED

Two roads diverged in a wood, and I—
I took the one less traveled by,
And that has made all the difference.
—Robert Frost[1]

The above quote is the last three lines of the Robert Frost poem, "The Road Not Taken". You may be surprised to learn (as I was) that this poem is the most popular and most online searched poem written by an American poet in the 20th century.[2] Even more surprising is that numerous scholars of poetry describe this poem as the most misunderstood/misinterpreted poem of the 20th century.[3]

Apparently, a few English Literature teachers, many of us regular folk, and way too many purveyors of motivational plaques and other knick-knacks misinterpret this poem as inspirational praise for lifestyle choices such as: rugged individualism; "can do" Americanism; pride in individual nonconformity; the power of self-assertion; and risking it all for potential glorious reward. Quite the contrary, however, history/poetry scholars have ascertained that Frost sent his first draft of this poem to a hiking-buddy, Edward Thomas, as a friendly joke about Thomas' frequently expressed regret after choosing between alternative hiking paths. This forced choice caused Thomas to regret missing the potential pleasantries of the hiking path not taken.[4] In other words, it is a poem about "regret" rather than about bold individualism. The poet's true intent was the exact opposite of how this poem is most frequently interpreted, and the exact opposite of why this poem (or, more likely, the last three lines of the poem) are found to be so inspirational and memorable.[5]

But this quote was not chosen to begin this chapter to encourage either regret or bold individualism. This chapter proposes a third interpretation. It proposes the practice of deliberately choosing to take a road less traveled because such a road increases the chances of being able to obtain a new "perspective". Never underestimate the potential awesome power of a simple change in perspective. Changing your perspective, even for a short period of time, allows you the opportunity and the time to experience both yourself and the world in a different way than your usual personal habits and societal preferences push you.

There are many such less traveled roads, which are perhaps better described as "practices". We will consider four such practices:

1. Nature;
2. Travel;
3. Service; and
4. Retreat.

These four practices were chosen not only because they provide a new perspective from the filters to our consciousness, but because repeated commitment to these practices will help build neuroplastic and behavioral changes supporting lines of competence crucially needed for expansion of consciousness. These are lines such as: open-mindedness, empathy, humility, compassion, and especially self-awareness and self-regulation. A final reason for selecting these practices is that they each involve "activity". Recall Piaget's insight from Chapter Three on how children learn. Knowledge is not automatically given to the passive observer. Knowledge of reality must be discovered and constructed by activity. The same is true of consciousness.

(Much of this chapter references the more advanced practice of meditation, which is also a road less travelled. Meditation is the "foundational" practice for expansion of consciousness. Meditation will be discussed in depth in the next chapter.)

The perspective changing nature of each of these practices is essentially self-evident. It's easy to see how each in their own way lifts you out of your usual routines. More helpful to our understanding of consciousness expansion will be to also look at practical guidelines to maximize the benefits of each practice, as well as red flag warnings regarding how the goals of each practice can become non-consciously corrupted.

It should go without saying that consciousness expansion is available to any person no matter their "level" of consciousness, no matter the size of their consciousness receptacle. Yet it is likely most persons working their way through a book like this are largely operating at a higher level of consciousness. As a metaphoric example (and without endorsing Maslow), it is likely most readers of this book are at least operating at or about the fourth Maslovian level of "Esteem Needs" as discussed in Chapter Three. Their consciousness is not filtered by the first level of "Physiological Needs" which is motivated by fears such as not having enough water, food, or breathable air. Nor are they operating at the second level of "Safety Needs" which is motivated by fears of threat to physical or financial safety. It is even likely most are largely free of the third level of "Belonging Needs" which is often motivated by fears such as not being accepted and readily identified as a member of a (often conservative) religious, political, or community group/tribe.

At the fourth level of Esteem Needs (speaking generally), a person's consciousness receptacle is large enough to accept without fear the reality of such things as: Socratic ignorance; global warming; institutional racism; the gender spectrum; and especially that some longstanding social and religious mores can and should evolve/change for the better. Persons at or near this level are often looking to learn and understand more about life's deeper meanings even if they are not conscious of that searching/longing. On the not so positive side, persons at this level of Esteem Needs often forget or are completely unaware of the most fundamental consciousness restricting danger/trap of this level. That danger, that trap, is ego. The compelling fear at this level is not being recognized by others (and even by your own sense of self) as somehow unique and special.

The road of consciousness expansion goes in the opposite direction of ego, narcissism, and pride. It seeks a selfless awareness and acceptance that each of us is profoundly interconnected to the world, and that each of us has the same intrinsic worth as any other person. Roads less traveled help us develop "radical humility" by building lines of competence such as: open-mindedness, empathy, humility, and compassion. (More on the critical nature of "radical humility" in Chapter Nine.)

1) The practice of nature is perhaps the simplest road less traveled. There is usually no financial cost, and nature is relatively easy to access even if you live in a city. It only takes commitment, a bit of time, and an open/observant consciousness.

There are so many deep and beautiful writings on the consciousness building attributes of nature, such as found in the timeless classic "Walden" by Henry Thoreau, that I will not attempt to compete with such insightful and poetic writers.[6] Offered instead is a short tale about my first meaningful encounter with nature back when I was a young lad.

I'm very fortunate to have had a multitude of "Maryville uncles". My dad and his four brothers (my biological uncles) were raised in Maryville Orphanage after their father (my grandfather) died and their mother (my grandmother) went to work as an in-house maid. My dad became as close to his orphan mates as he was to his biological brothers. So it was not surprising that I subsequently knew these orphan mates as "uncles" all my life. (In fact, I'm named after two of them.)

One day, when I was about eight or nine years old, my Maryville uncle, Jack, asked me if I wanted to go "hunting" in the woods several miles from our house. You can imagine how excited a young boy was at the prospect of hunting. My consciousness ran wild with ideas of guns and ferocious animals. Yet on the morning of our hunting trip, I was crushed to learn that "hunting" was just going to be a walk in the same woods I had been to several times before, but with a camera. I was so disappointed; but I loved my Uncle Jack, and so I decided to pretend that I was excited and happy to be on the so-called hunting trip.

To my wonderment, it was not long into the walk that I became just as excited as if my Uncle Jack was carrying a rifle and tracking big game. We were not on the foot-worn trail. . . the road most traveled. Instead, we were bushwhacking through the dense trees and underbrush, using every effort and newly learned skill to be as quiet as possible so that we could sneak up on our prey.

I learned what it meant to be downwind from our prey. I learned to move silently through the woods. I learned how the sun needed to be behind us to get the best photos. I saw animal tracks and animal nesting areas I never saw before. I was as excited to come upon a deer or even a squirrel as if I'd come upon a lion or a dragon. My Uncle Jack introduced me to a road less traveled, a gift that has lasted me a lifetime.

A walk in nature doesn't have to be in the Grand Canyon or by Niagara Falls to be a wonderment. Both these tourist destinations are awesome and precisely why they are well-traveled roads. All that is needed for the practice of nature is time, an open mind, and an observant manner to enjoy the silence, solitude, and amazements of a walk in the woods, a walk by a stream, or simply turning over a large rock and enjoying the micro-nature of watching tiny creatures interact. The key is that you are away from your usual routines, and willing to observe and enjoy whatever manifests.

Scholars have now determined that spending time in nature has many of the same psychological, cognitive, and physical health benefits[7] as meditation, which we will learn about in the next chapter. This should not be surprising. To really interact with nature, you practice many of the same skills and techniques as in meditation. You begin by slowing down the constant wild dancing of your thoughts and emotions. Leave your worries and projects behind. Practice self-regulation by using your non-judgmental, non-attachment awareness of whatever nature manifests before you. Nature can be an amazing gift. It is ours to enjoy when we choose this practice.

Engaging with nature helps develop humility. Nature often reveals our insignificant smallness as an individual. Despite what our species has been doing to destroy nature, nature goes on without us. The magnificent oak tree before you was there decades before you were born, and will still be there long after you are gone. The squirrels you observe gathering acorns for the winter don't care if you just got promoted or fired from your job.

The benefits of the relative "silence" and "solitude" of being in nature have been extolled for millennia by mystics, poets, and artists. All wax eloquent on how the gifts of silence and solitude generate a sense of freedom, creativity, self-awareness, and mysticism/spirituality. Why waste such gifts?[28]

There aren't any red flag warnings about a walk in nature, but there are a few guidelines: Go alone (unless you have a niece or nephew who needs an introduction to nature); don't bring your music; and after finishing your walk, don't be in a hurry to talk about your private adventure. Walk this road less traveled alone.

2) The key to the practice of travel is to distinguish between "tourist" and "traveler".

There is absolutely nothing wrong with being a tourist. Tourism can be fun, exciting, relaxing, even inspirational. Tourism at the right destination with the right activities can absolutely be a source of consciousness expansion. Yet being a "traveler" rather than a "tourist" maximizes the opportunity for consciousness expansion. As we will learn in the next chapter, this is because engaging in the practice of travel requires the same three commitments recommended for meditation: 1) on purpose; 2) in the present moment; and 3) with non-judgmental awareness. Without these three commitments, your practice can easily become superficial; or worse, a consciousness limiting ego trip.

One amusing way of knowing you're a tourist rather than a traveler is to find yourself engaged in conversations using the words "done", "did", and "do". You hear yourself saying things like: Have you done Paris yet? Well, Mary and I did Rome, Florence, and Venice; but we still need to do Sicily. Such conversations are a red flag warning that you're not practicing traveling.

"*On purpose*" begins long before you arrive at your destination. Take time before you travel to think and choose wisely. Start with "why" you are choosing a particular travel destination? Think about where you want to stay;

a tourist hotel or a more downscale place where locals stay, and where you are forced to interact with a local host. Without artificially restricting your spontaneity by over-planning, think about what you would like to do there. Do some online searching. You'd be surprised at what you can discover. For example, if you go to Taipei, Taiwan, you'll find that you can spend a morning or afternoon working with a single mom selling sweet potatoes on a street corner to help raise money to support her family. Not only are you doing a so-called good deed (and engaging in the practicing of service); but selling sweet potatoes to the locals can be a unique perspective changing interaction, especially since you probably don't speak Taiwanese Mandarin. Many such service opportunities are available in most major cities around the world. (Ha! Ironically, you can find them on "tourist" websites.) There are many other types of perspective changing activities available. You can for example take a local cooking course, or simply sit quietly in a town square and observe. Finally, learn a bit of the local language before you go; at least how to say: yes, no, hello, and thank you. Even learning the tiniest bit of local language can open windows of perspective changing opportunities.

"*In the present moment*" requires developing the skills of open-mindedness and not being afraid of spontaneity. Leave room in your travel plans to go with the flow. As the New York Yankee Zen Master, Yogi Berra, often said, "When you come to a fork in the road, take it." One way to solve Yogi's zen koan,[9] is to spend a day going on a much modified Australian "walkabout". (A once traditional rite of passage in Australian Aboriginal society was for a teenage male to leave the village, wander, and live off the land for up to six months.) You might try simply wandering for a morning, afternoon, or entire day. First, make sure you have a map and the address of your hotel written in the local language in case you get lost. Then just start walking. You'll be amazed at what you discover, or even more surprised at what discovers you.[10]

"*Non-judgmental awareness*" during travel is no different than non-judgment, non-attachment during meditation, during nature practice, or during life. The main goal of this practice of travel is to change perspective. Judgment will only get in the way. One way to optimize non-judgmental awareness is to increase your meditation time while traveling. This can be done by meditating longer or by meditating more than once a day, even if only for a few minutes. During your walkabout, you may come upon an inspirational place to meditate; a temple, a field, a lakeshore. Meditating during this time of changed perspective during travel often deepens your state of meditation as well as insights gained during meditation. Finally, one of the best ways to maximize non-judgmental awareness during travel is to travel alone. If you're already travelling with a companion, make arrangements to have a morning, afternoon, or an entire day to yourself. Ha! Don't be offended if your companion appreciates your request.

3) We receive a powerful insight from Gandhi on how the practice of service can support our quest for consciousness expansion:

> The best way to find yourself is to
> lose yourself in the service of others.

There have been reports for decades by social science scholars that volunteering brings both psychological and physical health benefits.[11] The research supporting psychological benefits is reasonably strong, but often relies on "self-reporting" questionnaires which are not as reliable as the gold standard of a double-blind study with objective measurements of health changes. Moreover, the psychological benefits fall into broad and ill-defined categories such as: life satisfaction; self-esteem; happiness; social well-being; fewer depressive symptoms; and less stress and anxiety. The research supporting physical health benefits is valid but derivative of the psychological benefits. For example, less stress results in lower blood pressure, and so fewer adverse cardiac issues. Scholars describe this derivative relationship as the "protective effects" of improved psychological health. In the words of many scholars, "good mental health leads to good physical health."

In attempting to discover how these health benefits are mediated, scholars differentiate among three categories in which an individual engages in voluntary social interactions. The first category is often called "social participation", and includes voluntary activities such as: group sports; group hobbies; or clubs such as gardening clubs. This is not a category we are looking at regarding the practice of service. The second category has the title "obligatory role participation", and includes such volunteer activities as: working at a bake sale at your church; or rendering long or short term care to a family member. Scholars use this title because research has shown that such service is often primarily motivated by a sense of obligation due to a person's perceived role as spouse, child, or church member.[12] The third category is often described as "mattering", and includes activities one would think of as classic "volunteer" or "charitable" work such as: volunteering at a food pantry; or participating in the Big Brother Big Sisters of America. Scholars understand "mattering" as "other-oriented" in motivation without the presence of perceived role obligations.[13]

Service motivated by either obligatory role participation or mattering can each generate health benefits. Service through obligation can and often does have "othering" components. Yet scholars have concluded that other-oriented service generates measurably stronger benefits in the areas of: mental health; physical health; life satisfaction; sense of social well-being; and fewer depressive symptoms.[14] Each of these benefits factors into improved cognitive function. As we learned in Chapter Five, improved cognitive function provides a better vehicle for consciousness expansion.

Yet it is the perspective change that service provides that maximizes the opportunities for consciousness expansion. While practicing service, you are forced to shift your focus and energies to the needs and worries of someone other than yourself. This is a precious opportunity to see the world through the eyes of another. This perspective change can be increased if those you serve differ from you in categories such as: age, health, economic or social status, and culture. This different perspective of service can help to generate lines of competence and supporting neuroplastic changes in skills and habits of empathy, selflessness, patience, gratitude, and compassion.

There is a longstanding and classic temptation associated with the practice of service. It involves the seductive desire to speak with others about admittedly interesting aspects of your service. You may be tempted to justify such conversations with arguments such as: This is so interesting, or I should tell my spouse everything. In finding guidelines or red flag warnings for such temptations, we can do no better than the following advice attributed to Jesus of Nazareth:

> But when you give to someone in need,
> Don't let your left hand know
> what your right hand is doing.
> —Matthew 6:3 ESV

4) A well planned and executed retreat can not only provide perspective, but increased motivation and energy to continue on the road less travelled toward consciousness expansion. But beware! Retreats are now Big Business.

One has to question whether a retreat is still a road less traveled? There are now so many different types of retreats including: nature; corporate team building; ecological; detox; health; exercise; yoga; spa; wellness; meditation; mindfulness; religious; and spiritual. The internet is awash with websites and ads for retreats; advice on how to choose a retreat; and even multiple websites on how to maximize your profit when putting on a retreat. "Wellness Tourism" (basically an upscale retreat where you travel to beautiful locations to be pampered) is now the fastest growing segment in the tourism industry, and is predicted to generate an unbelievable $919 billion dollars in revenues in 2022.[15] Retreats have become such a significant phenomenon in society that scholars have now gotten involved with research attempting to measure the health and other impacts of retreats.[16]

Retreats are now a massive and financially successful fad. They are fast becoming roads well traveled. Yet a retreat, properly structured and run, is still one of the most promising perspective changing pathways for consciousness expansion. This is particularly true if it is a "residential meditation" retreat. Let's consider some of the potential support aspects such a retreat can provide.

With a residential meditation retreat, you are leaving your usual environment and routines behind. You will be housed and fed by others. While there are almost always free times, your day will be pre-structured so that you essentially don't even have to think about what to do next. Smartphones are not allowed. All this can make it easier to leave your worries and projects behind. Retreats are typically healthy environments. The food is nutritious; and there is no alcohol, no television, no computers. There is often a prescribed lights out, so you get plenty of sleep. Many times retreats are held in a peaceful/serene setting. Most important, you are exposed to the guidance and insights of master teachers; and even though silence is generally the rule, you feel the supporting energy of like minded searchers. A residential meditation retreat gives you both the opportunity and the energy to meditate longer and deeper, which for all kinds of reasons just never seems possible at home. It's difficult to think of a potentially better environment to gain new perspectives and insights, especially about your so-called self.

Let us conclude this chapter with a cautionary discussion regarding roads less travelled. With the exception of the practice of service, each of the less traveled roads we have looked at in this chapter involve quasi-altered states of silence and solitude. They are essentially paths we take alone. They are not quite Altered States, but they can potentially provide the same perspective altering benefits as an Altered State. The myriad benefits of silence and solitude have long been extolled by scholars, mystics, artists, and poets. Trying to say more about such benefits would sound cliché. Without doubt, silence and solitude are valuable and proved states for conscious expansion. Yet what must be understood is that silence, solitude, and walking alone on roads less traveled are only "tools" for consciousness expansion. These practices are not ends in themselves. The same caution applies to the practice of meditation, which we will look at in depth in the next chapter. As the mystic/ scholar, Thich Nhat Hanh, once said, "Meditation is not an escape from life. . .but preparation for really being in life." Thinking otherwise, you run the risk of succumbing to the siren song of fetishizing these important practices, which is a subtle but fatal trap to consciousness expansion.

There are at least three general reasons for this caution. Each leads back into prioritizing and inflating a "separate" sense of self, which can be exacerbated by solitary (but otherwise beneficial) practices. In reverse order of importance, these reasons are:

Thinking of a solitary practice as more than just a tool, plays into the "magical thinking" that you have discovered a shortcut to consciousness expansion. The temptation to look for a quick fix is almost overwhelming. This is especially tempting when we learn about the extreme difficulty of meaningful, level shifting consciousness expansion as discussed in Chapter Three.

Fetishizing a practice inflates your sense of self, not only as special, but as separate, permanent, and in total control of your consciousness. This is an ego trap that can take many forms. For example: you can non-consciously begin to think of yourself in this manner because you have studied and practiced meditation (or other solitary practice) for a long time; or because you have studied with a great master; or because you have come to believe you are a great master; or even because you actually are a great master. Sadly but predictably, there are more than a few otherwise great masters with highly evolved lines of competence in teaching and certain practices, but with stunted and fixated lines of competence most always involving ego. This may be because their sense of self, and maybe even their livelihood, are tied to being seen in the role of authority in one or more special practices.

More profoundly, the wonder of solitude as an end itself misses the ultimate goal of the process of consciousness expansion. Throughout history, every highly regarded mystic and every founder of the major religious traditions from Buddha, to Moses, to Jesus, to Muhammad, has first used the road less traveled of solitude to free themselves from the filters to consciousness in order to gain their practical and mystical insights about reality. After founding and following a sect of extreme aesthetics for six years, the Buddha sat alone under a banyan tree. Moses and Jesus went into the desert. Muhammad went into retreat in a mountain cave. As their individual consciousness expanded during their solitude, each realized in their own cultural way that they were intrinsically integrated within the world. This ultimate awareness of the inter-related nature of the world filled each with profound compassion and compelled a return to the world to teach and share their insights and interact with humanity.

1 Robert Frost (1874-1963) was an American poet. Among many other awards, Frost was awarded four Pulitzer Prizes for Poetry as well as the Congressional Gold Medal.

2 See, online, "The Most Misread Poem in America" by David Orr at theparisreview.org (2015) (Here and after "Misread Poem".)

3 Simply search online under "Frost misread" for many such scholarly commentators. One of the best is David Orr, a writer, attorney, and poet, highly regarded for his poetry reviews and commentary. See, "You're Probably Misreading Robert Frost's Most Famous Poem" at lithub.com (2016) (Here and after "Probably Misreading".)

4 Probably Misreading at p3-5.

5 Perhaps the most likely reason for misinterpretation is that most people (including me) had not actually read the poem, but only heard of the last three lines which contain the words "roads. . . less traveled". In fact, Orr informs us that many people (again including me) falsely assumed the title of the poem is "The Road Less Traveled". (See Probably Misleading at p5.) Another likely cause of misunderstanding the title may be the timeless classic and best selling book by M. Scott Peck, M.D. "The Road Less Traveled A New Psychology of Love, Traditional Values, and Spiritual Growth", Simon & Schuster, New York, NY (1978). (See Misread Poem at p4.)

6 "Walden" by Henry David Thoreau; originally published in 1854, and now in the public domain. (Here and after "Walden".)

7 Numerous scholarly articles can easily be found online by searching "scholarly articles benefits of nature". See for example, "Nature and mental health: An ecosystem service perspective by Gregory N. Bateman et al; Science Advances, 24 July 2019, which can be found online. Most of the research has focused on visual aspects of nature, but a fascinating study on all human sensory aspects of engaging with nature can be found online titled: "A Review of the Benefits of Nature Experiences: More Than Meets the Eye" by Lara S. Franco, Danielle F. Shanahan, and Richard A. Fuller; Int J Environ Res Public Health 2017 Aug; 14(8): 864 doi: 10.3390/ijerph1408064. One study, which can be found online, examined the amount of time spent in nature needed to obtain health benefits, and found a collective weekly threshold of 120 minutes. See, "Spending at least 120 minutes a week in nature is associated with good health and well being" by Mathew P. White et al; Scientific Reports 13 June 2019; doi.org/10.1038/s41598-019-44097-3. One of the leading international scholars regarding the health benefits of nature is Yoshifumi Miyazaki, the deputy director of the Chiba University Center for Environment Health and Services in Japan which supports engaging with nature to improve mental and physical health. Miyazaki was instrumental in the government of Japan developing the "Forest Bathing" project. Simply search "Miyazaki" at Google Scholar for numerous articles including "Forest Walking affects Autonomic Nervous Activity: A Population-Based Study" by Hiromitsu Kobayashi et al, which can be found online at Frontiers in Public health 01 October 2018 doi: 10.3389/fpubh.2018.00278.

8 As will be further discussed in this chapter, the states of both silence and solitude are embedded deep within the practices of roads less traveled. It is interesting to note a recent study which found that solitude can play a positive role in the self-regulation of Affective Experiences, which involves consciousness and control of thoughts, emotions, and actions. See, "Solitude as an Approach to Affective Self-Regulation" by Thuy-vy T. Nguyen, Richard M. Ryan, and Edward L. Deci; Personality

and Social Psychology Bulletin 1-15-2017 by the Society for Personality and Social Psychology, which can be found online at pspb.sagepub.com. DOI: 10.1177/0146167217733073. (Here and after "Nguyen".) An older, but beautifully written and thoughtful paper on the benefits of solitude can be found online: "Solitude: An Exploration of Benefits of Being Alone" by Christopher R. Long and James R. Averill; Journal for the Theory of Social Behavior 33:1 0021-8308 (2003). (Here and after "Long".)

9 A "koan" is a succinct, seemingly paradoxical statement, story, or question used in Zen Buddhism to help the student discover a deeper, non-literal response to the koan.

10 There are often legitimate safety and health concerns when traveling. Is it safe to walk or stay there? Can I eat at this restaurant or street stand? One way to minimize these concerns is to hire a private guide, and then let the guide know with certainty that you want to avoid "tourist" type activities. It may surprise you to learn that guides hear this type of request all the time, even from tourists who have no intention of really doing something that a tourist would never do. So you will need to make your intentions clear to your guide.

11 For numerous lay commentaries, search online for "healthcare benefits volunteering". For scholarly research, search online at Google Scholar. Two of the best scholarly papers are "Health Benefits of Volunteering in the Wisconsin Longitudinal Study" by Jane Allyn Piliavin and Erica Siegl; Journal of Health and social Behavior 2007, Vol 48 (December): 450-464; which can be found online at hsb.sagepub.com. (Here and after "Piliavin".) "Volunteering and health benefits in general adults; cumulative effects and forms" by Perf W. K. Yeung, Zhuoni Zhang, and Tae Yeun Kim; BMC Public Health 2018; 18:8; which can be found online at doi: 10.186/s12889-017-4561-8. (Here and after "Yeung".)

12 Piliavin at p451.

13 Piliavin at p452.

14 Yeung at p7. Piliavin at p460.

15 Yes, it's hard to believe that's billion with a "b". But see, Global Wellness Tourism Economy Report, which can be found online at globalwellnessinstitute.org.

16 See, "Effectiveness of traditional meditation retreats: A systematic review and meta-analysis by Bassam Khoury, PhD et al; Journal of Psychosomatic Research 17 November 2016, which can be found online at http://dx.doi.org/10.1016/jojpsychores.2016.11.006. Also see, "The health impact of residential retreats: a systematic review" by Dhevaksha Naidoo, Adrian Scheubri, and Marc Cohen; BMC Complementary and Alternative Medicine (2018) 18:8 doi 10.1186/s12906-017-2078-4.

CHAPTER EIGHT

THE FOUNDATIONAL PRACTICE OF MEDITATION

Breathe to renew the depths of consciousness.
Breathe and you dwell in the here and now.
Breathe and all you touch is new and real.
—Sister Annabel Laity[1]

Meditation is the "foundational" practice for expansion of consciousness. After what we learned in Section I, you could even argue that meditation is a "required" practice for any hope of meaningful expansion of consciousness. There simply is no better practice for:

A. slowing down and observing without judgment or attachment the habit machine of the human brain which is constantly generating "filtered" thoughts, emotions, and actions;

B. generating both behavioral and neuroplastic changes consistent with and supporting expansion of consciousness; and

C. gaining insights/wisdom about your own consciousness and the nature of reality.

This claimed power of meditation practice is not only supported by more than three millennia of "Eastern" mystics, but has now been confirmed by meta-analysis research undertaken by "Western" neuro-scholars.[2] No credible scholar now disputes that there are both neuroplastic and behavioral changes congruent with the psychological and behavioral aims of certain meditation practices.[3] Meditation can help expand consciousness!

Not surprisingly, initial scholarly support for the behavioral and neuroplastic benefits of meditation practice was skeptical at best.[4] Even in present times, there is still much more peer-reviewed research that needs to be completed, especially as to the specificity of the neural mechanisms underlying the neuroplastic and behavioral changes induced by certain meditation techniques.[5] But let's take an optimistic look at what present scholarly research does show:

1) Certain meditation practices have been shown to produce both metabolic and structural neuroplastic changes. Metabolic changes induced by meditation include such things as alterations to the chemical structure of the brain including the neurotransmitters we discussed in Chapter Five.[6] Structural changes include increases in the thickness of gray matter and in the number of synaptic connections as we also discussed in Chapter Five.[7] These neuroplastic changes have been confirmed by multiple types of neuroimaging studies such as fMRI mapping.[8]

2) These metabolic and structural neuroplastic changes occur in areas of the brain associated with self-awareness and self-regulation,[9] *the two major underlying skills required for expansion of consciousness.* Recall the discussion at the end of Chapter Three of Ken Wilber's "lines of competence" as well as the discussion of the types of lines that best facilitate expansion of consciousness. These were lines of self-awareness and self-regulation. Any person seeking to expand their consciousness must develop these two fundamental lines. A person needs to be sufficiently self-aware to recognize the limitations and filters to their own consciousness. And a person needs to have sufficient self-regulation to maximize control over their thoughts, emotions, and actions. Certain meditation practices can and do generate a biological substrate within those areas of the brain which underly the consciousness raising goals of self-awareness and self-regulation.

3) While the following would come as no surprise to Eastern mystics, Western scholars have now confirmed, not only the neuroplastic changes induced by certain types of meditation, but that those neuroplastic changes are associated with improved behavioral skills "in self-referential processes such as self-aware-ness and self-regulation." [10]

Meta-analysis studies of certain meditation practices have confirmed that both neuroimaging studies (e.g. fMRI) and psychological tests (e.g. Stroop Color and Word Tests) demonstrate evidence of the following "behavioral" developments consistent with neuroplastic changes in the brain in areas associated with such behaviors.[11] Here are several examples of "behavioral" developments directly related to self-awareness and self-regulation attributed to certain meditation practices:

A. processing self-relevant information;

B. focused problem-solving;

C. adaptive behavior (life skills);

D. interoception (sense of internal state of the body);

E. emotional regulation/control;

F. sustained attention;

G. reduced attentional blink (a type of freedom from distraction);

H. more neutral valence (ability to evaluate with less emotional involvement as first discussed in Chapter One);

I. improved meta-awareness (experiential consciousness); and

J. increased consciousness of executive function.[12]

Please go back and re-read this paragraph. Take a few moments to become fully conscious how each of these specific skills (proved by scholars to be available to you through meditation) are fundamental to the degree to which you are aware of and knowingly responsive to your internal and external environment.

4) The even better than "good" news is that this symbiotic relationship among meditation, neuroplasticity, and behavioral changes is essentially a positive feedback loop. Certain meditation practices generate neuroplastic changes; which in turn generate behavioral improvement in areas of self-awareness and self-regulation; which in turn generates more skillful meditation practice; which generates further neuroplastic changes; and on and on.

5) Certain of these neuroplastic and behavioral changes have been shown to occur in as little as seven days.[13] However. . . a warning against over-optimism. . . there are currently insufficient studies as to the lasting effects of short-term meditation. As to long-term meditation, both mystics and scholars have observed extraordinary cognitive and emotional control in skilled long-term mediators.[14]

6) These neuroplastic and behavioral changes may actually be "more robust" in elderly meditators. Ah ha! Another benefit for my team of elders.[15] Recent studies have suggested that meditation can slow age-related cognitive decline.[16] Meditation can produce metabolic changes that reduce brain inflammation,[17] as well as structural changes that may protect the amount of gray matter especially in the prefrontal cortex[18] (the area of the brain associated with executive function as we learned in Chapter One).

(An entertaining, fascinating, and admittedly speculative example of the purported benefits of such neuroplastic changes in the elderly involves the theft of Albert Einstein's brain. Within eight hours of his death at 76 years of age, pathologist, Thomas Stolz Harvey (1912-2007), removed Einstein's brain at autopsy without consent of Einstein or his family, although retroactive permission was eventually granted by the family years later. Over the next several months, Harvey cut and removed hundreds of microscopic slices/sections of the brain, and stained and mounted them on slides. Harvey kept a number of slides, and distributed the remaining slides along with the remaining brain to renowned pathologists. Subsequent scholars observed and published the results of the studies of these slides.[19] While Einstein's brain was generally of normal size, there were two exceptions pertinent to our discussion. Einstein's prefrontal cortex was expanded, and gray matter was significantly thicker than even a typical younger brain. . . two of the primary neuroplastic structural changes associated with meditation. Was Einstein a formal meditator? That is highly unlikely. Einstein did not sit and follow his breath, but there is no doubt that Einstein had an incredible capacity to engage in what he called "thought experiments". Einstein was able to slow down his continuous and random thoughts and emotions, and then intensely focus on matters that were not only complex, but were completely outside the previously known realm of human thought. Did Einstein's meditative practice of thought experiments result in these neuroplastic changes? Who knows for sure?)

So what does it mean when researchers use keep using the phrase "certain meditation practices"? One of the valid criticisms regarding research on meditation is that there are so many different types of meditation practices that the research literature is not specific enough on what exact meditative practices are being tested.[20]

Indeed, there are almost as many types/techniques of meditation as there are types/theories of the nature of consciousness that we reviewed in Chapter One. For starters, although they may not call the practice "meditation", every major religion has their own meditative practices. This includes: Buddhist; Hindu; Muslim (Sufi); Shinto (Japanese); Hebrew; Taoist (Chinese); and even many Christian religions. (Such Christian sects prefer to label their practices as: "contemplation" or "sitting in the silence" rather than as meditation.[21]) Moreover, there are multiple meditation practice techniques, such as: the silent and mindful focus of Zen meditation; the use of a repetitive mantra in transcendental meditation; control of body position and breath in yogic meditation; visualization in Vipasana/insight meditation; tapping in Qigong meditation; generation of loving kindness in Metta meditation; contemporaneous oral direction of a teacher in Guided meditation; and dancing in Sufi meditation.[22] Knowing this, perhaps we can't blame the few skeptical scholars for questioning meditation research when that research is not specific enough about the type of meditation being tested.

Yes, there could and should be more descriptive specificity on the particular meditation practice used in the research. Yet when you read through the research literature, it seems that meditation researchers are almost universally referring to the oldest and simplest type of meditation: focused, non-judgmental attention, typically on the breath.

The historical Buddha (also known as Siddhartha Gautama) (c. 500-400 BCE)[23] first described this type of meditation practice as "the full awareness of breathing"[24] when he purportedly said:

> It is like this. . . the practitioner goes into the forest or to the foot of a tree, or to any deserted place, sits stably in the lotus position holding his or her body quite straight, and practices like this. 'Breathing in, I know I am breathing in. Breathing out, I know I am breathing out.'[25]

In more contemporary times, this type of meditation practice found in most research is perhaps best described by Jon Kabat-Zinn (an American molecular biologist, and one of the most highly regarded thought leaders on the practice and benefits of meditation) as "paying attention in a particular way".[26] By this, Kabat-Zinn emphasizes that such meditation is to be practiced with a three-part core:

A. on purpose;

B. in the present moment; and with

C. non-judgmental awareness.[27]

If you choose to get started with a meditation practice, you will find that there are almost too many books, online videos, and teachers available on how to meditate.[28] This can scare off or at least confuse some beginners. Much more important is to just get started. You can begin the practice of meditation on your own with some basic guidelines and practical recommendations below. See what works for you; and as noted in Chapter Six, when you're ready, your guru for further guidance will often show up as a book, video, teacher, sangha, or your own insight on how to improve your meditation practice.[29]

We will use Kabat-Zinn's three-part core as an outline for additional guidance supplemented by some practical suggestions learned during my own experience with meditation. Although I've meditated for more than 40 years, taught meditation, and studied meditation with true masters. . . I am no mystic nor guru. I continue to struggle with the challenges of sustained meditation. When teaching meditation to beginners, I sometimes joke that this makes me an ideal teacher for beginning meditators; because I know enough to teach, yet I can still closely relate to the typical struggles of becoming an accomplished meditator. Let's begin.

On Purpose. . . Meditation needs to be a commitment. Yes, you can dabble in meditation, and you'll enjoy the same intrinsic benefits of many other relaxation techniques. But our goal here is a significant expansion of our consciousness receptacle; and as we learned in Chapter Three, that is quite a challenging task. Successful meditation toward that goal takes committed and purposeful practice. Paradoxically, this commitment does not mean a gung ho, linear logic, success oriented approach. You will discover that meditation is all about patient, non-judgmental, non-attached, open-minded awareness. Simply let meditation happen to you.

Practical first steps in fostering a purposeful state of mind begin with choosing a dedicated room, corner, cushion, or chair for sitting.[30] Attempting to meditate at the same time each day can also generate supporting habit energy, but "circumstances of the moment" (as discussed in Chapter Four) can often interfere with this "best laid" plan. If so, don't fret. Simply move back to your schedule when you can. In the beginning, it's best to meditate every day. You can start with as little as five minutes of meditation, ten would be better, and twenty is more than enough to begin. Finally, obtain respectful support from family members. Otherwise your meditation time may be interrupted by the usual clamor of daily life.[31]

The next step is optional, but beginning your meditation practice with some sort of ritual is often helpful. Ritual signals your brain that it is time for meditation. . . all else should pause/stop. Master Meditation

Teacher, Thich Nhat Hahn, recommends sounding a small bell or singing bowl as you begin meditation. Ritual can also be achieved by simply repeating (silently or out loud) with your first few (intentionally) slow breaths:

> Breathing in, I know I am breathing in.
> Breathing out, I know I am breathing out.
> Breathing in, I am at peace.
> Breathing out, I am calm.
> Breathing in, I am at home.
> Breathing out, I am home in meditation.

The final step of purpose is simply to focus solely on your breathing without changing the length or force of the breath. You will find this focus to be a bit more difficult than it sounds, especially over a sustained period of time. If you find it too difficult to simply focus on your inbreath and then your outbreath, there are two techniques that may help (and that I still need to use from time to time). First, silently count your breaths either on the inbreath or the outbreath. Alternatively, replace counting breaths with a mantra. A mantra is a repeated word or sound traditionally used in both Hindu and Buddhist meditation techniques. The two most popular mantras are the word "one" or the sound "om" (pronounced aum).[32] A mantra can be repeated on the in or the outbreath, but most practitioners prefer the outbreath. This is because an outbreath is seen as a manifestation of release, which is both physically and metaphorically appropriate since you are releasing thoughts and concerns.

Present Moment. . . Your focus on your breathing represents the present moment. Proper posture greatly helps keep this focus. While it is correct that proper posture is not essential for meditation, there is a reason why three thousand plus years of Eastern mystics have recommended a particular posture. Proper posture helps you stay awake, sit longer, and focus.

Proper sitting posture begins with a straight spinal column, including tipping your head slightly forward so that the crown of your head points upward. Perhaps even more important is to relax every muscle in your body, especially facial muscles. A natural smile is actually quite helpful to relax the face, and somehow a soft smile leads to your experiencing meditation as a more pleasant experience. If you're sitting in a chair, both feet are flat on the ground. If you're sitting on a meditation cushion, a full lotus position is optimal (if you're that limber), but a half lotus (or no lotus) is essentially just as good. I typically sit on a cushion facing a blank wall about two feet away so that no physical object distracts me. Your hands can be placed in your lap or on your knees. Traditional practitioners recommend placing your hands in a particular way called a "mudra", but this is not necessary.[33] Let your eyes become irrelevant: out of focus, even a bit closed, and gazing slightly downward. Finally, let go of all your concerns (both serious and trivial). As one of my teachers used to say, "Don't worry, your concerns will still be there when you finish your meditation."

Non-judgmental Awareness. . . Developing the skill and conscious state of non-judgmental awareness is truly the key to successful meditation. Why? It is because the primary goal of meditation is to free our consciousness as much as possible from the filters to consciousness. Mystics are in universal agreement that the best way to begin to accomplish this is to observe your thoughts, concerns, and emotions without judgment. It is critical that we understand that this plane/state of non-judgmental observation is quantumly distinct from merely looking at phenomena objectively. Scholars and mystics often describe this state of consciousness as "pure witness" or "non-attachment" or "equanimity". "Non-judgment" involves avoiding the introduction of your own values, factual beliefs, prejudices, and filters. "Non-attachment" involves avoiding personal identification with any thought, emotion, or belief that represents some aspect/part of your sense of self. In meditation, you do your best to operate in the state of "pure witness". Releasing the often non-conscious obligation/stress of judging and attaching eventually leads to a sense of "equanimity". Don't be too concerned at first about the nature or experience of this state. The more you meditate, the more you will understand and appreciate the essence and value of non-judgmental awareness.

Thoughts and emotions will arise as you meditate. This is unavoidable. Some represent serious concerns, but the vast number are random, usually meaningless flashes of thought as if in a nonsense dream.[34] It is a mistake to try and suppress these thoughts or emotions. Ironically, attempts at repression tend to emphasize and embody the thoughts or emotions with false importance, and shift focus away from the moment of your breath. The more skilled practice is to simply acknowledge the thoughts or emotions as being there, make no judgment, and let them drift away. They will drift away precisely because you do not embody them with judgment or attachment.

As you continue in your meditation practice, you will become more aware of the constant, seemingly random, churning of your mind. No doubt you understood this phenomenon in an intellectual sense before you started meditating, but it's a true consciousness opener to actually experience it during meditation. With the simple initial practice of following the breath, you begin to gain the skill of slowing this mental/emotional spinning. You begin to develop the self-regulation skills of withholding judgment and attachment. You learn how to create mental and emotional space so that you can simply witness and increase awareness. You begin to understand in a deeper sense that you are not in complete control of your consciousness. Ironically, you discover this insight (that you will never gain complete control) as you actually gain "more" control over your consciousness through the practice of meditation.

These meditation skills can eventually "transfer" to "closely related" activities other than meditation. (This involves the same neuroplastic processes that we looked at in Chapter Five with certain "brain game" skills transferring to "closely related" skills in other activities.) You find yourself becoming more patient, less judgmental, and more aware in different life situations. You may even discover a joy in accepting your Socratic ignorance because you begin to realize the infinite availability of your potential awareness of the wonders of life. If you still need motivation to begin meditating, flip back a few pages in this chapter, and look a third time and more deeply at all the meaningful and scholarly supported "behavioral" developments "a" though "j" that meditation helps create. Frankly, it's pretty darn amazing that all these consciousness raising skills arise from the simple practice of following your breath. What are you waiting for?

There are deeper states of meditation. . . . While this simple practice of "the full awareness of breathing" or "paying attention in a particular way" is absolutely enough to generate all of the benefits discussed earlier in this chapter, there are still deeper states of meditation that can be achieved. Mystics are in agreement that it is a mistake to actively seek/grasp at deeper states. This is not just a mistake because you may not be ready, but because the grasping itself can prevent achieving deeper states. After all, in developing the practice of following your breath, you have just spent committed time learning and practicing how not to grasp! One of the many wonders of meditation is that it works best if you simply allow it to happen in your natural flow of practice.

The next state of meditation practice is often referred to as "insight" meditation. (There are a number of different names and techniques for insight meditation which are beyond the scope of this book, and which can easily be found online.)[35] Insight meditation begins with using your newly developed skills of slowing down the mind and maintaining focused awareness without judgment. These new skills allow you to enter a meditative state where you can choose to focus and observe without judgment matters other than your breath. Now you can bring into your consciousness such matters as: a concern that bothers you, a future plan, a bad habit, a sour mood, forgiving someone, or any life decision. The skills you have learned in your earlier meditation practice will help you to make better and more informed decisions because your consciousness will not be as filtered as it once was. You are now more skilled and more free to recognize filters, forces, facts, and tendencies that previously colored your thoughts, emotions, and actions regarding such matters. You have expanded your consciousness in meaningful and productive ways.

As your state of meditation deepens further, you will begin to become aware of and slowly begin to accept deeper truths about reality. The most fundamental of which is recognizing and accepting that your sense of self, your consciousness, is empty of "intrinsic existence". Your sense of self, your consciousness, is an ever-changing, experiential phenomenon resulting from a composite of multiple and complex heterogeneous sources, which are each in turn empty of their own intrinsic existence. We learned this "intellectually" in Section I, but meditation brings a deeper experiential awareness and acceptance of this foundational truth. Mystics describe this as "non-self awareness". (The mystical and practical implications of non-self awareness will be more fully explored in the remaining chapters. In the next chapter, for example, we will see how a non-mystic social science scholar on forgiveness practice contributes to understanding this truth.)

Eventually, even deeper states of meditation can become an "Altered State" as discussed in Chapters One and Three. Mystics in such Altered States speak of the experience of all "boundaries" dissolving; in particular, any remaining boundary of "self". Mystics describe this as a state of "pure witness". Reality is no longer about "you". There is a type of "emptiness" where thoughts, emotions, and actions come without preference or labels. The hypocrisy and ego-idiocy of judging become obvious. Many mystics describe a deep realization of an intimate connection to all of reality, which results in a renewed and total commitment of compassion. There is an awe-filled feeling of finally being "awake" in consciousness. Others go on to speak of cosmic "Oneness" as discussed in Chapters One and Three. It is this Altered State of sensing Oneness that gives voice to the far end of the spectrum in consciousness beliefs such as "Transpersonal" levels of consciousness; One singular shared consciousness; and that this One Consciousness creates reality as claimed by Dr. Lanza in Chapter One. Any person experiencing such an Altered State must then wrestle with whether such Oneness is an ontological reality or merely a beautiful and poetic feeling.

Such Transpersonal claims can be frightening or at least disturbing because they "radically" change our understanding of the nature of reality. In wrestling with such mystical claims, it's important to know that the sense of "emptiness" often encountered in an Altered State does not mean non-existence. As Shakespeare correctly stated, "If you prick us, do we not bleed?"[36] You still need to eat, work, pay bills. Even the most extreme Transpersonal advocates recognize that we all must function (at least for awhile) within the physical/material plane. It is for this reason that Transpersonal mystics speak of two realms of reality. Although various terms are used to describe these two realms, the terms "physical reality" and "ultimate reality" suffice. (These concepts will be discussed in more detail in Chapter Ten.)

It is tempting to once again place these types of Transpersonal claims in our "Way Out There" category from Chapter One. As previously stated, I remain agnostic on such claims, even though I concede that I have personally found deep meditation can result in an Altered State which does give at least a "taste" of Oneness.[37] But what is the ontological reality/significance of such a personal experience? Have I accessed "ultimate reality", or is this experience just emerging qualia generated by the "physical reality" of the material brain as discussed way back in Chapter One? Despite this experientially real "taste" of Oneness , I can't help but suspect that such Transpersonal/ultimate reality claims are just the latest grasp of Cartesian Dualism. The primal human longing for an intrinsic, individual, and permanent existence is just so overwhelming strong. Who knows for sure?

What I am sure about are the very real consciousness raising benefits of meditation. More important than my opinion, as this chapter has established, these benefits are supported by decades of scholarly research. If you desire expanded consciousness and its benefits, meditation is the single most important practice you must undertake. Although, as we will see in the next chapter, the often more difficult/challenging practice of forgiveness comes in a very close second in importance.

---

1 These are the last three lines from a poem by Sister Annabel Laity "Breathe! You Are Alive" which can be found in the book " Breathe! You Are Alive: Sutra on the Full Awareness of Breathing" by Thich Nhat Hanh, Parallax Press, Berkeley, California, Revised Edition (1996). British born Buddhist scholar, Annabel Laity, was the first person from the West to be ordained as a monastic disciple in Thich Nhat Hanh's Buddhist lineage, The Order of Interbeing. Sister Laity was also the cofounder with Thich Nhat Hanh of the Plum Village Community of Engaged Buddhism in France.

2 "The Meditative Mind: A Comprehensive Meta-Analysis of MRI Studies" by Maddalena Boccia, Laura Piccardi, and Paola Guarglia; Biomed Research Institute published online 2015. (Here and after "Boccia".) "Functional neuroanatomy of meditation: A review and meta-analysis of 78 functional neuroimaging investigations" by Kieran C.R. Fox, Matthew L. Dixon, et al; Neuroscience Biobehavioral Reviews, vol 65, pages 208-228, June 2016. (Here and after "Fox".) "Meditation Ex-

perience Associated with Structural Neuroplasticity" by Mir Saleem and Pallavi Samudrala; Annals of International Medical and Dental Research, vol 3, issue 4, June 2017. (Here and after "Saleem".) Meditation-induced neuroplastic changes of the prefrontal network are associated with reduced valence perception in older people" by Bolton K.H. Chau, Kati Kemper, et al; Brain and Neuroscience Advances, British Neuroscience Assoc, May 8, 2018. (Here and after "Chau".) "Effects of a 7-Day Meditation Retreat on the Brain Function of Mediators and Non-Mediators During an Attention Task" by Elisa H. Kozasa, Joana B. Balartin, et al, Frontiers in Human Neuroscience, 12:222, published online June 11, 2018. (Here and after "Kozasa".) For a scholarly paper criticizing research on meditation see: "Mind the Hype: A Critical Evaluation and Perspective Agenda for Research on Mindfulness and Meditation" by Nicholas T. Van Dam, Marieke K. van Vugt, et al; Perspectives on Psychological Science, vol 13(1) 36-61, 2018. (Here and after "Van Dam".)

3 See Fox at p3.

4 Two of the scholarly pioneers regarding the benefits and neuroplastic changes associated with meditation are Richard J. Davidson and Jon Kabat-Zinn. Each has written numerous research papers and best-selling lay accessible books on meditation. Each has also written about the early days of scholarly research on the benefits of meditation. See the Introduction in Davidson's book "The Emotional Life of Your Brain" Penguin Random House LLC, New York, 2012 for his recollection of his personal path in challenging traditional scholarly dogma on meditation. (Here and after "Emotional Brain".) See also, "Some Reflections on the Origins of MSRB, skillful means, And the Trouble with Maps" by Kabat-Zinn, Contemporary Buddhism, Vol. 12, No. 1, May 2011 which can easily be found online. (Here and after "Kabat-Zinn".)

5 See Van Dam.

6 See Saleem at p1.

7 See Saleem at p1.

8 See Chau at p3-5; Boccia at p3; Kozasa at p12.

9 See Boccia at p13.

10 See Boccia at p1.

11 See Kozasa at p1 and 12.

12 See Boccia at p1-2. See Chau at p20 regarding valence.

13 See Kozasa at p14.

14 See for example, Emotional Brain Chapter Ten "The Monk in the Machine".

15 Please note that the reason scholars use the phrase "more robust" in describing the benefits of such neuroplastic changes in elderly mediators is not because elders are more effective mediators than younger mediators. Rather, it is because the elderly are more susceptible to age-related brain degeneration, and so the effects of meditation are both more observable and more profound in elders.

16 See Boccia at p2; Chau at p4, 20-22.

17 See Boccia at p2; Saleem at p2.

18 See Chau at p20.

19 See for example Saleem at p3.

20 See Van Dam.

21 A compelling, contemporary mystic/scholar on contemplation is American Trappist monk Thomas Merton (1915-1968). See Merton's book "What is Contemplation?" first published 1950; revised edition 1981, Templegate Publishers, Springfield, Illinois.

22 See for example, the online article "Types of Meditation-An Overview of 23 Meditation Techniques" by Giovanni at liveanddare.com/author/giovanni/#disqus_thread; originally published January 28, 2015, republished July 13, 2019.

23 One of the best books for a contemporary look at the life of the historical Buddha is "Old Path White Clouds" by Thich Nhat Hanh, Parallax Press, Berkeley, California, (1991). (Here and after "White Clouds".) Another is "Buddha" by Karen Armstrong, Penguin Group, New York, New York (2001). Reading every book written by Armstrong would be time well spent.

24 This was from the "Sutra on the Full Awareness of Breathing" as translated by Thich Nhat Hanh in his book "Breathe! You Are Alive", Parallax Press, Berkeley, California (1996) at p3-10. (Here and after "Breathe".)

25 Breathe at p5.

26 Kabat-Zinn at p291.

27 Kabat-Zinn at p291-292.

28 I am likely a bit prejudiced because the teachings of Thich Nhat Hanh have been my primary source of meditation instruction over the decades; but multiple YouTube videos by Thich Nhat Hanh are among the best available instruction on meditation, and are easy to follow. Other highly regarded teachers, including Kabat-Zinn, also have excellent instructional videos online.

29 This suggestion that your "guru for further guidance will show up" in some form is not some New Age "magical thinking" along the lines of the popular and unfortunate phrase, "Everything happens for a reason." I couldn't disagree more with that phrase or with the magical thinking that everything will eventually work itself out for the best. The world can be a cruel and random place. Bad things happen to good people all the time, often with non-existent or unexplainable reason. There is no magic in your guru for further guidance showing up. It shows up for two simple reasons. First, such gurus were always available. You're just now more aware of their potential existence, so you notice them. It's like when you're in the market for a car, and you now notice more details during television car commercials. Second, by taking intentional and active steps to practice meditation, you have metaphorically moved your knight to the middle of the chess board. You only had three potential moves with your knight from its initial position in the first rank; but a knight in the middle of the board has potentially eight moves. Plain old luck now comes into play, and you are more likely to encounter opportunity.

30 "Walking" meditation is a wonderful variant to sitting, and is especially recommended by Thich Nhat Hanh. Video instructions from Thich Nhat Hanh on walking meditation is easily found on YouTube. Unless injury or illness prevents sitting or walking, trying to meditate lying down almost never works. You'll just drift off to sleep.

31 I'm reminded of my first introduction to meditation back in the mid 1970s. My father had the stress filled job of Executive Director of an international trade association and seven kids. After reading the National Number One Bestseller "the Relaxation Response" by Herbert Bensen, M.D., William Morrow and Company, Inc. (1975) which began the popularization of meditation in the USA, my father took up meditation. It didn't take long thereafter for my father to implement strict rules that he was not to be interrupted by any of his kids during his 30 minutes of meditation after arriving home from work each day. To this day, I'm not sure if he was actually meditating, or just using claimed meditation as an excuse for his no doubt much needed few moments of peace and quiet.

32 There are numerous online articles on the history and so-called "true" nature of the sound om (or aum). One of the most poetic and useful explanations is that om/aum is the sound that the continuous universe makes as it unfolds.

33 A "mudra" is a symbolic hand gesture which has historically been used in Buddhist, Hindu, and yogic meditation postures. There are literally hundreds of mudras, photos of which can easily be found online. A number of more traditional mystics believe a mudra emanates some special/magic-like power, but there is zero scholarly support for such a claim. On the other hand, using a mudra could generate supportive emotional energy even though there is no magical power to a mudra. I rarely use a mudra. I typically place my hands on my knees, palms down, or in my lap, palms up. There is no magic to this. I simply find it comfortable. Feel free to discover what works best for you.

34 Something that will definitely distract you at first is wondering how much meditation time is left. An easy technique to avoid this distraction is simply to set your smartphone for the meditation time desired. Be sure and program the alarm for a gentle alarm setting, and then forget about when your meditation will end. I typically am so relaxed and centered after the alarm goes off that I stay on my cushion another ten minutes or so thinking about my upcoming day. Sometimes I conclude my meditation sitting with some inspirational reading, which can also be used before your actual meditation to cultivate your mood.

35 One of the most highly respected teachers regarding "insight" meditation is Sharon Salzberg of the Insight Meditation Society. More information/guidance from Sharon Salzberg and the Insight Meditation Society can be found online at dharma.org.

36 "The Merchant of Venice" by William Shakespeare (1605); Act III, Scene I.

37 Ken Wilber was the first contemporary scholar/mystic to beautifully use the poetic phrase "one taste". See for example, "One Taste Daily Reflections on Integral Spirituality" by Ken Wilber, Shambhala Publications, Inc. Boston (2000). (Here and after "Taste".) It should be noted that Wilber uses the term "one taste" in a slightly different manner to describe "where every single thing and event in the Kosmos, high or low, sacred or profane, has the same taste, the same flavor, and that flavor is Devine". See for example Taste at p76.

CHAPTER NINE

THE RICH COMPLEXITY OF FOREGIVENESS

Father, forgive them;
For they know not what they do.
—Jesus of Nazareth[1]

It is not possible to overstate the significance of forgiveness within the process of consciousness expansion. Otherwise hyperbolic adjectives such as powerful, fundamental, difficult, freeing, rich, and complex are each quite appropriate when describing the practice of forgiveness. Forgiveness is inexorably interwoven within the expansion of your consciousness because both processes involve your sense of self. Meaningful expansion of consciousness cannot occur without meaningful development of forgiveness, and meaningful development of forgiveness cannot occur without meaningful expansion of consciousness. The practice of forgiveness stands as a very close second only to the practice of meditation in expanding consciousness.

Let's explore the: What? Why? and How? of the rich complexity of forgiveness practice.

What is forgiveness? Forgive me for starting yet another key subsection of this book with the words "scholars cannot agree on a definition of". Yet that is the situation regarding the definition of forgiveness. This lack of agreement stems from intense, scholarly debates on questions such as: Does the nature of the offense warrant forgiveness? What type of response is necessary for true forgiveness? For example, does condoning, denying, excusing, forgetting, or pardoning rise to the level of forgiveness? Is reconciliation with the offender, or at least an attempt at reconciliation, required for there to be forgiveness? Is forgiveness a process solely within the consciousness of the offended party, or is it a process also involving the consciousness of the offender? Does a person have "standing" to forgive if the offense isn't directly against that person. Moreover, scholars speak of numerous types of forgiveness including: Arrested; Authentic Process; Collusive; Conditional; Decisional; Emotional; Exceptional; Lawful Exceptional; Pseudo; Repetitious; Restitutional; and Revengeful just to name a few.[2] Fortunately, for our purposes of consciousness expansion, we don't need to dive into these academic quarrels.

Another reason for lack of definitial consensus is that scientific research into forgiveness is still relatively new. American psychologist, Michael E. McCullough, was a pioneer and continues to be a leading scholar on the evolutionary, cognitive, behavioral, and psychological components of forgiveness. His ground breaking book, aptly named "Forgiveness", begins with a history of the initial research into the psychological nature of forgiveness.[3] Somewhat surprisingly, those historic scholars we think of as the brilliant stars in the galaxy of psychology wrote very little or absolutely nothing about forgiveness. This includes many of the scholars previously referenced in this book: Freud, Jung, James, Allport, Piaget,[4] and Frankl. Until recently, forgiveness was generally considered the province of God and the ministers of pastoral care. It didn't occur to scholars that forgiveness practice could be harnessed for cognitive and behavioral advances.

Prior to the 1980s, scholarly attention to forgiveness was piecemeal and unsustained. Not until the end of the 20th century did studies regarding the conceptual links between mental health and forgiveness begin to appear.[5] In 1989, Robert Enright published the first empirically-based study in which there was an explicit focus on person-to-person forgiveness.[6] Not until the late 1990s was "forgiveness" finally recognized as an established and significant reality in the fields of both clinical and research psychology.

Despite this recent explosion of scholarly acceptance, research, and clinical application of forgiveness, there is still no agreed upon definition of forgiveness. McCullough refers to this lack of consensus as "one of the most pernicious problems in the field today".[7] (Ha! No doubt McCullough knew that the term "hard problem" was already taken.) There is, however, a growing consensus (at least in the social sciences) as to what forgiveness is "not". Forgiveness is not merely: condoning (justifying the offense); denying (refusing to look into Galileo's telescope); excusing (validating the offense); forgetting (letting the offense slip out of consciousness); or pardoning (an unrelated legal term).[8]

Leading social scientists such as McCullough, Enright, as well as a third leading scholar on forgiveness, Everett Worthington,[9] have begun to offer definitions regarding the essence of forgiveness. We can use these as a jump-off point to develop our "working understanding" for purposes of consciousness expansion. According to these scholars, the essence of forgiveness is:

> a willingness to abandon one's right to resentment, negative judgment, and indifferent behavior toward one who unjustly hurt us, while fostering the undeserved qualities of compassion, generosity, and even love toward him or her
> —Enright et al[10]

> prosocial changes in one's motivations toward an offending relationship partner
> —McCullough et al[11]

> the emotional juxtaposition of positive other-oriented emotions against negative unforgiveness, which eventually results in neutralization or replacement of all or part of those negative emotions with positive emotions.
> —Worthington et al[12]

As you can see, these definitions appear reasonable yet somewhat vague as well as jargon laden. Perhaps we can further focus our working understanding of forgiveness by realizing that what we're really doing in forgiveness practice involves two processes. The need for forgiveness arises with an offense that causes an emotional response within the offended party who perceives the offense as unjustified. The offended must then work through two processes:

1. resolving their own emotions; and
2. resolving future interaction with the offender.

The offended has multiple options for working through these processes. The oldest of which could be called the "caveman" option, where the offended seeks retribution through physical punishment. There is the "ostrich" option of condoning, denying, excusing, or forgetting the offense. Another poor choice is the "martyr" option where the offended does nothing but wallow in their own emotional disruption. Perhaps the approach most often chosen, although usually non-consciously, is the "ego justification" option where the offended chooses to hold a grudge until the insult to the offended's ego is assuaged either through apology or lapse of time. Choosing an approach to resolve these two processes depends on your ultimate goal. Our goal is expansion of consciousness, which leads to the option of "forgiveness". Resolving these two processes through forgiveness can be challenging, but is the most optimal and effective practice for achieving that goal.

To help understand how these two processes inter-relate with expansion of consciousness, let's look at what both social science and neuroscience are saying about the psychological and neuro aspects of forgiveness:

A. Forgiveness has evolutionary roots in the limbic (reptilian) system of the brain, but encephalization (evolution of brain complexity) has brought much of the neuro-forgiveness processes into the cortex (the area of meta-awareness as discussed in Chapter One).

B. Forgiveness has a genetic basis, but its expression can be influenced by ECT (environmental complexity and training as discussed in Chapter Five).

C. Forgiveness is primarily about resolving powerful emotions that can imprison and even reduce our consciousness.

D. The primary focus in forgiveness arises out of our sense of self, and the primary work of forgiveness is essentially narcissism versus humility.

A) Forgiveness has evolutionary roots in the limbic (reptilian) system of the brain, but encephalization (evolution of brain complexity) has brought much of the neuro-forgiveness processes into the cortex (the area of meta-awareness as discussed in Chapter One). Social science has developed what has become known as the "evolutionary theory of forgiveness". McCullough states that, while forgiveness presupposes injury, there are three substrates to the cognitive ability to perceive injury:

1. a sense of self;

2. ability to evaluate the injury; and

3. memory to link the injury to the offender.[13]

McCullough suggests that these three cognitive abilities initially evolved/emerged in our hominid ancestors at the time of the Australopithecine period (c. 4.4 mya) when the hominid brain evolved to develop the capacity for abstraction and reification (the complex capacity to understand immaterial concepts such as relationships, evil, and happiness as phenomena that exist in reality).[14]

The most primitive "motivation" to respond to a real or perceived injury was self-preservation, and the most primitive "response" was physical revenge/punishment. Our ancient ancestors were much more violent than is commonly believed. The archeological record is replete with evidence that our hominid predecessors (including early homo sapiens) regularly used violence as revenge and punishment.[15] This is more understandable when we learn that primitive brain structure had "rich interconnections with the limbic systems, the (reptilian) part of the brain primarily involved with the modulation of emotion".[16] As we learned in Chapter Four, emotion empowers (and too often overpowers) consciousness in both thought and action.

It's fascinating to learn from McCullough how the progressive emergence of self-awareness, particularly the emergence of the "ego", became the next powerful force in the evolution of forgiveness. It is because of the ego that our perception of self is often much grander than reality would warrant. It is because our perception of self is inextricably tied to our emotions that the ego became increasingly more energized in all life/social perceptions and decisions. This not only includes an outsized sense of self, but too often an exaggerated perception of any injury by an offender.[17]

The personal and societal problems created by the ego contributed to an increasing spiral of violence between the offended and the offender. The offended takes revenge; then the original offender takes revenge for the offended's revenge; then the offended takes more revenge, etc., with this mutually destructive exchange continuing until one or both parties are too injured to respond or dead. It's the Hatfields and McCoys. At some point, neither party even remembers how the feud started. At the very least, an otherwise potentially beneficial relationship between the parties has been destroyed. Revenge as a goal is not productive for the emotional, physical, or mercantile health of a community.

Fortunately for humanity, the option of forgiveness began to evolve to allow civilization to flourish. You could call this initial type of forgiveness "justice".[18] This "justice" occurred in various forms in different cultures, with perhaps the most well-known being the biblical "eye for an eye". Social science has identified two broad factors that seem to have been used for the so-called "justice" type of response to calculate the balance between punishment and forgiveness.[19]

The first factor is assessment of the "relationship value" of the offender. For example, is the offender in our societal group or an "other"? What are the social or mercantile benefits of a future relationship with the offender (or the offender's family/clan)? The second factor evaluates "risk of responding with punishment". For example, what are the risks of attacking another (perhaps stronger) tribe after they steal your best cattle?[20]

As societies and humanity continued to evolve in social consciousness, moral values such as empathy began to influence the forgiveness option and the application of justice. At first the motivation for an empathetic/forgiving response was largely religious. Later, these moral values enjoyed more secular motivation as societies and individuals learned to walk in another person's shoes.

Contemporary social scientists have performed wonders in developing analyses and models of how forgiveness operates psychologically and how forgiveness can provide very real health benefits, which we will examine later in this chapter. However, social scientists have not addressed what could be called the "neural correlates of forgiveness", which for convenience we will call "NCF".

Neuroscience scholars on the other hand have begun to study the brain activation patterns of the offended party in the forgiveness process. Studies on brain activation patterns in the offending and forgiven party have been done, but are even more sparse and very preliminary.[21] Neuroscience primarily uses brain imaging techniques such as fMRI to determine which areas of the brain "light up" during forgiveness and can therefore be associated with the forgiveness process. Other "lesion studies" use volunteers with known damaged brain areas for similar testing. In this early phase of such research, there are, unfortunately, so many variables regarding the type of offense and type of forgiving investigated in the various studies that only general observations can be made.

Neuroimaging studies have suggested that during the forgiveness process the area of the brain known as the striatum is typically activated. This is an area of the brain associated with reward motivation processes such as being sure to eat and moving toward success goals as we studied in Chapter Five when we looked at dopamine. The striatum is an area of the brain involved in the disbursal of dopamine. Neurological responses during the forgiveness process also involve the anterior insula, the brain region associated with multiple emotions, particularly negative emotions such as anger, disgust, and other negative responses to perceived unfair treatment. This involvement of the anterior insula suggests that the forgiveness process does not just involve a rewards motivation process. Forgiveness is thoroughly impacted with emotional involvement.[22]

Perhaps the most intriguing areas of brain activation in the forgiveness process are multiple brain areas associated with more highly evolved neuro processes. The function of these brain areas is sometimes described by scholars as "theory-of-mind" or "mentalizing" ability, or what we have been referring to as meta-awareness. These more highly evolved brain areas principally involve the temporal-parietal junction, although multiple other brain areas are also somewhat less involved.[23]

We can conclude from these imaging studies that the NCF of forgiving involves reward motivation; powerful often negative emotions; and highly evolved evaluation of multiple complex matters involving concepts such as morality, fairness, and evaluation of the situation from the offender's perspective.

B) Forgiveness has a genetic basis, but its expression can be influenced by ECT (environmental complexity and training).
There is no scholarly doubt that forgiveness has a genetic basis because forgiveness practices are found across all modern cultures, even when such practices are expressed with cultural differences. So far, little is known about the specific genetic basis of forgiveness. This is largely because forgiveness is a complex and nonspecific package of emotions that is difficult to isolate genetically. Fortunately, scholars have been able to genetically isolate certain key polymorphisms (multiple aspects/forms of a gene) of emotions with strong psychological and behavioral correlation to forgiveness. Those main emotions are anger, which has a strong "negative" correlation, and empathy, which has a strong "positive" correlation. Both anger and empathy have been extensively studied, measured, and tested by scholars; and both have been linked to specific genetic polymorphisms.[24]

Scholars use the terms: "trait forgiveness" ("TF") and "state forgiveness" ("SF") in their writings. Think of TF as similar to the concept of "phenotype" which we explored in Chapter Five. Phenotype is the observable personality characteristics/behaviors of an individual resulting from the interaction of both genes and the environment. TF is a more limited phenotype of an individual specifically regarding a person's forgiveness personality so to speak. SF on the other hand is how an individual behaves/responds during a singular insult/forgiveness process. It is a temporary behavioral manifestation. A tremendous amount of scholarly research and creativity has now been accomplished on: the nature of TF and SF; measuring TF and SF; and the benefits of improved TF and SF.[25]

The benefits of increased TF and SF will be discussed when we get to the "Why?" section of this chapter. For now, let's answer whether it is possible to improve one's TF or SF? On the downside, scholars believe that temperamental traits such as anger and empathy are strongly genetic in their influence, and so difficult to change.[26] On the positive side, and a macro-point for expansion of consciousness, there is no doubt that various programs and practices of ECT specifically directed toward forgiveness practice can improve your TF and SF tendencies and skills.

C) Forgiveness is primarily about resolving powerful emotions that can imprison and even reduce our consciousness. Scholars have researched and warned us about the potentially heavy and even life-crippling burdens of "not" forgiving. These potential burdens include not only physical and psychological health issues, but damage to family, social, and work relationships.[27] These burdens are generated by emotions.

Let's briefly review key aspects about emotions from Chapter Four. Emotions are central to understanding the important qualities of being human. Emotions can be mild or intense, fleeting or life-long. Emotions can bring great joy or crippling despair. But most critically, emotions are a prime filter to our consciousness. They give life meaning through the process of energizing our consciousness by placing color/value/motivation on our thoughts and actions through the power of psychological feelings and associated physical responses.

Any attack on our sense of self, whether it be as de minimis as someone forgetting your name or as serious as your spouse leaving you for another lover, generates emotions along with the psychological and physical consequences those emotions bring. Refusing to engage in forgiveness can allow those emotions and consequences to linger, churn, and fester. The emotional and physical damage you do to yourself by "not" forgiving can soon outweigh the severity of the original offense. The old adage eventually becomes correct: "You are only hurting yourself."

As we learned in Chapter Four, in addition to the physical and psychological consequences, such emotions "filter" our consciousness, which in turn filters our thoughts and actions. Carrying a grudge (or worse several grudges) can not only blind but shrink your consciousness receptacle. The negative emotions that can be generated by refusing to forgive can thicken and expand the emotional filter to your consciousness in ever expanding circles. For example, refusing to forgive your boss for passing you over for promotion can further degenerate into anger at all bosses, or a refusal to see anything beneficial about your workplace. Unfortunately, it is a common and destructive reality that when you refuse to forgive a boss, coworker, friend, or family member, it won't be long until more and more aspects/behaviors of that person will irritate you. This only serves to exacerbate the downward spiral. Why swirl down that drain?

D) The primary focus in forgiveness arises out of our sense of self, and the primary work of forgiveness is essentially narcissism versus humility. McCullough and others have written insightfully regarding how this perceived attack on our sense of self is essentially about narcissism versus humility.[28] There are many personality traits and emotions involved with both forgiveness and non-forgiveness. Empathy and anger are often the first two that came to mind, and the two most studied by scholars; but McCullough describes only one trait. . . narcissism. . . as the "master personality trait" and "the superordinate organizing construct that assumes most all other forgiveness traits".[29]

Narcissism hinders forgiveness. This is an absolute, and the logic is clear. If you shroud your sense of self (your consciousness) in a garment of inflated importance, it will be much more difficult to forgive an attack/insult to that self. This is precisely why forgiveness practice and consciousness raising are inexorably intertwined because both involve releasing a false sense of self.

Narcissism is simply antithetical to consciousness expansion . . . full stop. Recall the two most fundamental lines of competence that need to be developed to attain higher levels of consciousness: self-awareness and self-regulation. It is exceptionally difficult to be self-aware if narcissism filters your consciousness receptacle. It is equally difficult to self-regulate your practice toward consciousness expansion when every thought, every perceived need, and every action is filtered by your narcissistic need for your own protection and aggrandizement of sense of self.

To illustrate this in admittedly minor ways, recall the red flag warnings listed for several of the "roads less travelled" practices discussed in Chapter Seven. In the practice of "Travel", narcissism may lead you to choose a more elite travel destination instead of a destination with more potential to experience a true change in perspective. If you engage in the practice of "Retreat", narcissism may influence you to select a retreat program with the most famous guru because this will make you feel more important/special. Consider also that such poor practice choices are often made without conscious awareness. Narcissism is not only the most powerful, but too often the most non-conscious yet active filter to consciousness.

(It's interesting to note that narcissism/pride is the first sin in Christian tradition. No, it was not Adam and Eve munching on the apple. It was the Archangel Lucifer choosing hell over heaven due to the sin of pride.[30] Even more dramatic/shocking was that at least one third of the angels followed Lucifer into hell due to pride!)

But wait. . . Isn't narcissism a psychological disorder? Isn't narcissism defined as an excessive interest/admiration of oneself? Many may protest that they are not narcissists! Yet, apparently, at least some small degree of narcissism is so prevalent in the human population that narcissism can be considered a common and even a normal personality trait.[31] Unless you are an enlightened being (and unnecessarily reading this book), there is some degree of narcissism found in each person's personality, sense of self, phenotype, FT, and ST. Narcissism occurs in the human population in a spectrum ranging from minimal narcissism which often goes unnoticed to the pathologic diagnosis of Narcissistic Personality Disorder.[32]

On the opposite end of that spectrum is humility. At first, one is tempted to think of humility as meekness or even weakness; but McCullough correctly points out that "humility is the disposition to view oneself as basically equal with any other human being even if there are objective differences in physical beauty, wealth, social skills, intelligence, or other resources."[33] To be humble is to have a sense of self as essentially and intrinsically equal, neither better nor worse than any other human being; one of the ultimate goals in consciousness raising.

It's easy to see how forgiveness is a powerful practice for expanding consciousness. When you practice avoiding narcissism by forgiving someone. . .especially when they don't deserve it. . . you are practicing expansion of consciousness. Both forgiveness and consciousness expansion require releasing the filter of an inflated/false sense of self. But let's go quite a bit deeper. Let's look briefly at what scholars and mystics describe as the almost impossible challenge of expanding consciousness, not only to a totally new level, but to the ultimate level. Maslow calls this ultimate level "self-actualization". Buddhists refer to this as "enlightenment". While I am an agnostic as to whether such ultimate levels even exist, taking a look at how the great mystics view the relationship between narcissism and the ultimate level/ state of consciousness provides us with further insights on how to expand consciousness even if our consciousness never reaches the so-called level of enlightenment.

In order to accomplish this, we need to artificially break narcissism down into two forms. The two are interrelated; both are fear based; but there is a deep, almost existential difference between these two types of narcissism. There is what we will call "common" narcissism, which exists on the human population spectrum we just spoke about. Also existing throughout the human population (even though the vast, vast majority are not conscious of it), is what we will call "primal" narcissism. Primal narcissism is not so much involved in the "vanity" of the ego as it is centered in the "primal" ego fear of recognizing and accepting that our sense of self (our consciousness) is both temporary and empty of intrinsic existence. As discussed throughout this book, this involves the terrifying, existential reality that our so-called self is an experiential fiction resulting from a composite of multiple and complex heterogeneous sources, which are each in turn empty of their own intrinsic existence.

According to the great mystics, in order to attain enlightenment, a person must develop what we can call "radical humility" to completely free themself of primal narcissism. This is an extremely advanced and difficult task, likely not possible for anyone reading (or writing) this book. Nonetheless, it is a task we must strive for if we hope to attain meaningful expansion of consciousness. Primal narcissism filters our consciousness, even if we are not aware of it. While we might not be able to completely free ourselves from primal narcissism, we can certainly begin to reduce its affects on our consciousness by the knowledge gained from Section I of this book, and through the practices described in Section II. These practices begin by reducing our "common" narcissism. One of the best practices for this is forgiveness, which helps us recognize and then transform our common narcissistic tendencies.

Recognition begins with determining where you land on the common narcissism-humility spectrum. This provides you with life-essential data about your sense of self, FT, and FS, which in turn gives you a revealing picture of whether you will have significant challenges in forgiveness practice. If you discover that you have significant narcissistic traits, then you have quite challenging work ahead of you. If you can't eventually learn to release the common narcissistic understanding of self in order to forgive, you will not be ready to develop the "radical humility" necessary to reduce (much less overcome) primal narcissism.

Discovering what common narcissistic indices to look for is shockingly easy and almost comical. Just search online for "signs of narcissism", and you'll immediately find sites such as: 5 Signs You're Working With A Narcissist; 6 Signs of Narcissism You May Not Know About; 11 Signs You're Dating a Narcissist; 15 Signs of a Narcissist: Traits, Behavior & More; and 18 Ways to Spot a Narcissist. Apparently, the internet is obsessed with narcissism.

Of course, I'm somewhat poking fun at the topic of narcissism. Excessive common narcissism can be a serious psychological disorder. Yet fostering a sense of humor, especially about your own challenges, is always a helpful aid as well as a solid humility practice in expansion of consciousness. Another somewhat comical question is whether a narcissist can even recognize their own narcissistic tendencies? Apparently, scholars have concluded that they can.[34] The macro-point here is that even modest narcissism or lack of humility is without doubt an impediment to both forgiveness practice and consciousness expansion. We all need transformational work in these areas.

Why should we engage in forgiveness practice? We should seek to understand and engage in the process of forgiveness for three major reasons:

A. the practical and undisputed psychological, physical, social, and economic benefits;

B. the associated neuroplastic benefits; and

C. because forgiveness supports expansion of consciousness.

A) The psychological, physical, social, and economic benefits for engaging in forgiveness practice are a "no-brainer" reason. Johns Hopkins, the University of California at Berkeley, the Mayo Clinic, and likely most major medical centers now have blogs warning of the psychological and physical health threats of failing to forgive.[35] Physical health dangers include such conditions as: elevated heart rate and blood pressure; compromised immune system; reduced ability to produce needed hormones; and somehow even periodontal disease. Psychological dangers include: anxiety; stress; depression; problems with family, social, and work relationships; lack of self-confidence; and even an inability to feel happiness or to enjoy the present moment.[36] If those don't concern you, let me finish (more than a bit tongue and cheek) with the statement that failing to forgive can make you fat![37] Apparently, a condition that evokes an even greater fear than poor health or limited consciousness.

You don't have to be on a quest for consciousness expansion to seek these benefits of forgiveness and avoid the consequences of unforgiveness.

It's simply makes Machiavellian practical sense to take advantage of the practice of forgiveness.

B) The associated neuroplastic benefits are an additional plus for reasons discussed in Chapter Five. This is simply part one of Hebb's Rule on positive synaptic modification: Neurons that fire together, wire together. When you practice forgiveness, your brain will generate neuroplastic changes that eventually cause such practices to become your "new normal" FT (forgiveness trait) and your "new normal" FS (forgiveness state). The default mode of the habit machine also known as your brain will become more and more consistent with the virtues (lines of competence) associated with forgiveness. These are virtues such as humility, patience, open mindedness, equanimity, and compassion.

Let us not forget part two of Hebb's Rule: Neurons that fire out of sinc, fail to link. This is an equally important neuroplastic benefit because it means that synaptic support for unforgiving habits will be reduced or even eliminated.

More good news involves the "transfer effects" from new practice habits that we looked at in Chapter Five with BGs (brain games). That research confirmed that "closely related" skills can and do transfer with enough practice. We can understand then how habitual virtues (lines of competence) developed during forgiveness practice and reinforced by Hebb's Rule can transfer/emerge in "closely related" activities to forgiveness. For example, the humility, patience, open-mindedness, equanimity, and compassion developed in forgiveness practice may appear (transfer) in other areas of internal and external social interaction. These virtues tend to transfer because the newly acquired virtue/skill is essentially the same ("closely related") even though the type of activity changes. Allow me to offer an admittedly small, personal example.

Literally for decades, I had a problem with patience (or more accurately impatience) while driving a car in dense "rush-hour" traffic on the highway. It was obviously puerile, but I just (almost neurotically) needed to be in the fastest moving lane during congested traffic on the highway. I became one of those highway jerks who keeps cutting in and out of lanes always attempting to be in the fastest lane (although, in my defense, I always used my turn signal). To my somewhat credit, I did realize I had this problem; but I just couldn't shake it.

Serendipitously, after many months of engaging in forgiveness practice in other seemingly unrelated situations, I was surprised to discover that I was no longer as concerned about rush-hour traffic as I had been for so long. I wondered what had changed? It wasn't as if I had been insightful enough to use rush-hour traffic as a practice opportunity. Then it struck me that this new found patience while driving must be a transfer effect of the patience I had been learning and developing in my forgiveness practice; a truly unearned benefit of neuroplasticity.

C) Developing Forgiveness skills fosters expansion of consciousness. Let's test this claim by undertaking a thought experiment by considering two categories of inquiry. First, think about what virtues (lines of competence) it takes to forgive someone? At the very least, it takes humility, compassion, and self-regulation to control your negative emotions. This is especially so if the offense is egregious and seemingly unjustified. Second, think about the elevated consciousness level it takes to have the self-awareness to authentically examine and answer such questions as: Why am I offended/hurt? Was the offense justified? What forces or situations could have motivated the offense? Do I share responsibility for this situation? What can or should be done to resolve the conflict? Exploring these two categories of inquiry quickly reveals why forgiveness is rarely the province of the closed-minded. Expansion of consciousness is required.

Those two categories of inquiry confirm the two most basic and overarching lines of competence needed for forgiveness practice:

1. the self-awareness to look deeply and accurately into the situation; and

2. the self-regulation to control/change your emotions, and execute your plan of forgiveness and reconciliation.

These are the same two most fundamental skills needed for expansion of consciousness. As we will see more clearly in the "How?" section of this chapter, practicing forgiveness is essentially practicing consciousness expansion.

How do we practice forgiveness?[38] There is a vast spectrum of wrongful conduct ranging from an act as mild as an unintended slight to horrendous acts such as physical and psychological torture, sexual abuse, and even mass murder. It is the horror of the unimaginable pain and suffering of the victims to such horrendous acts that causes me to begin this subsection with an apology. Since neither I nor anyone near and dear to me have ever experienced such pain and suffering, I feel compelled to apologize for presuming to suggest how such acts should or can be forgiven. I can only offer the consistent teachings of much more highly evolved persons who have experienced and witnessed such horrors. These teachers seem to be unanimous in their belief that forgiveness, even after such extreme circumstances, is beneficial for all who have so suffered. These include Mahatma Gandhi, Nelson Mandela, Desmond Tutu, and especially the purported speaker of the quote that begins this chapter.[39]

Forgiveness practice has more than arrived in the clinical practices of psychologists, psychiatrists, and therapists. Help from professionals skilled in the social science of forgiveness is readily available. As to self-help, the internet is plentiful with models, programs, and recommendations for forgiveness; many by highly qualified social science scholars.

Given our goal of consciousness expansion and the interrelated importance of meditation, allow me to offer a few examples of how forgiveness practice can be exercised through different meditation practices. We will consider the following nine steps on how to practice forgiveness with meditation:

1. Use meditation as your foundation. . .

2. Recognize the operative process. . .

3. Acknowledge your suffering. . .

4. Examine your emotions with non-judgement and non-attachment. . .

5. Consider the motivation of the offender. . .

6. Release yourself from negative thoughts and emotions. . .

7. Forgive the offender. . .

8. Explore reconciliation. . .

9. Use forgiveness as a fundamental practice opportunity. . .

1) Use meditation as your foundation to begin and continue the forgiveness process. . . . The forgiveness process can be optimized through the process of meditation.[40] Begin by slowing down the habit machine of the human brain which is constantly generating "filtered" thoughts, emotions, and actions. We know from research that after an offense is committed against you, the brain is already generating negative thoughts energized by powerful negative emotions and revengeful potential actions. Meditation allows you to begin the forgiveness process by slowing those powerful emotions.

You may have already developed a TF and SF that allows minor insults to bounce off your ego without negative response. You may even have developed an automatic forgiveness response sympathetic to why the offending person felt a compulsion to hurt you. If so, congrats! But if the offense is strong enough, and the hurt is deep enough, it's best to begin the forgiveness process "purposely" with meditation. This commitment gives the forgiveness process the gravity it deserves.

Beginning with meditation signals your brain that it's time to let all emotions and concerns go away for awhile (not only the offense at hand). Let calmness fill your thoughts and emotions even before you begin to attempt to tackle the hurt caused by the offense. Then continue to use the meditation process for all the following steps.

2) Recognize the operative process. . . The essential first step in attempting to change something is to first try and understand how that "something" works. You got this. You now have a meaningful understanding of such matters as: how the brain operates; the filters to consciousness; the power of emotions; and the ethereal nature of your sense of self. You are well aware of the benefits of forgiveness and the burdens of unforgiving. Hopefully, you have developed experience and skill with both calming and insight meditation. This knowledge is a precious tool that empowers you to then take the next steps of "transformance" through forgiveness.

3) Acknowledge your suffering. . . Condoning, denying, excusing, and trying to forget is not forgiveness. It only pushes the painful emotions of anger and hurt into non-consciousness. This is a dangerous place to attempt to hide emotions. As we know from Chapter Five, just because you are not readily conscious of powerful emotions like humiliation and anger does not mean these emotions are not festering and causing damage. Acknowledge the reality of your grief. Be willing to grieve. Recognize that dealing with your grief may last a long while. Forgiveness is a process, not a magic bullet. Sometimes the grief may even outlast forgiving the offender, but hopefully forgiveness will eventually help resolve the grief.

4) Examine your emotions with non-judgment and non-attachment. . . We tend to think that emotions are all psychological. Recall and appreciate that emotions have both psychological and physical manifestations. Often a person so suffering does not realize that an emotional hurt is manifesting somewhere in the body. They may be able to discern that they are sad, depressed, angry; but they are likely unaware that a sore back, stiff neck, headaches, shaky hands, or even a sore throat can be a physical manifestation of emotion. As you meditate, even before you focus on how you are feeling psychologically, take the time to focus on how your reaction to the offense may be affecting your body. This process is now commonly referred to as "body scan meditation".

There are numerous "guided" body scan meditations online where a teacher gently talks you through the process.[41] These typically last from ten to thirty minutes. During or after body scan meditation, you should try and decern "why" a specific bodily manifestation of emotion might be occurring. For example, why am I reacting to the offense with a tight chest or headache? It is not always easy to make this determination. If you are fortunate enough to recognize a connection as to why a particular body part/area/system is being affected, this often goes a long way toward healing, release, and forgiveness. Again, the essential first step in attempting to change something is to first try and understand how that something operates.

After you have worked with your physical manifestations, you next examine your psychological manifestations of emotion. It is fascinating to observe that after you have released (or at least calmed) the physical/bodily manifestations of emotions, the psychological manifestations somehow seem less overwhelming. As with physical manifestations, one of the most productive ways to gain a deeper understanding of the psychological manifestations is to examine during insight meditation the question of "why" you are suffering? This often involves looking at the relationship of the offense and your emotional response on the narcissism-humility spectrum. Reflect on how the offense affects your sense of self. Is your ego hurt? If so, why? Is the offense related to a false sense of self? As best you can, this questioning process should be engaged in without judgment or attachment. If you feel judgment (which you often will) ask yourself why? Is it likely because you are attached to some concept of "self" that feels threatened?

5) *Consider the motivation(s) of the offender.* . . Ask yourself questions such as: What would cause a person to act that way? Could you ever see yourself acting in a similar way? Have you ever acted that way? Do you bear any responsibility for the confrontation? Did the offender realize the harmful nature of the action? This questioning process should be engaged in without judgment or attachment. You may often find that this step makes it easier to release negative thoughts and emotions.

6) *Release yourself from negative thoughts, emotions, and any associated physical manifestations.* . . At the end of this questioning process, use the knowledge you've gained as well as the techniques learned from body scan and insight meditation to help release all judgment and attachment to any remaining negative thoughts, emotions, and associated physical manifestations. This is easier said than done. It may help to actually vocalize the release silently or out loud. Be specific in your release. Name each negative/harmful thought, emotion, and physical manifestation individually. If you are still having difficulty with release, return to insight meditation to explore why you might want to hang onto a particular emotion?

7) *Forgive the offender.* . . There is no requirement to rush this step. Allow time for the above steps (which you may need to repeat) to coalesce and support your act of forgiveness. Remember that forgiveness doesn't mean you are condoning, denying, excusing, or forgetting. Forgiveness may not be easy; but it can sometimes be made easier by (even selfishly) recalling that forgiveness is (at this point in the process) more for your benefit than the offender. Remember though that true forgiveness is an unconditional gift. No mental reservations are allowed, and the offender does not have to earn nor deserve it. It's perfectly understandable why true forgiveness can take time.

8) *Explore reconciliation.* . . Understand and accept that reconciliation may not be possible now or in the future. For starters, the offending party may not be willing to engage, much less cooperate. Reconciliation should be avoided where it would be dangerous to your emotional or physical safety. Reconciliation with the offending party is ideal, but not required for the forgiveness process to support consciousness expansion. The only requirement in addition to fully and freely forgiving the person within your own consciousness is that the potential for reconciliation be considered without judgment or attachment.

9) *Use forgiveness as a fundamental practice opportunity.* . . This suggestion is much easier with minor slights and grievances. Surprisingly, after practicing forgiveness for awhile, you may actually look forward to encountering minor slights and grievances just so you can practice. . . a similar situation to encountering people who irritate you as discussed in Chapter Six. Such practice not only strengthens your FS and FT, but increases competence in lines of virtues such as humility, compassion, self-awareness, and self-regulation.

Allow me to complete this chapter by describing a third forgiveness meditation practice called "Tonglen". It is a meditation practice found in

Tibetan Buddhism which is especially beneficial for developing and strengthening your FS and FT, as well as for developing empathy and compassion. It is a practice I often use.

The history, benefits, and practice instructions for multiple variations of Tonglen are easily found online. My particular practice of Tonglen usually occurs at the end of my daily meditation of following the breath, and when there is a person in my life with whom I'm not getting along. I begin by engaging in a sequence of three visualizations. First, I visualize a person I love such as a family member; and I visualize that person surrounded in a pink, blue, or white light/cloud of love. This is the easy part because feelings of love, protection, and care easily flow to such a person during this first visualization. Next I visualize a so-called neutral person such as someone from work or neighbor, and I surround them with the same light of love. Finally, I visualize the person with whom I am not getting along, and I surround that person with the same light of love. Over the years of engaging in Tonglen, it has become tangibly easier for me to develop feelings of empathy, compassion, and forgiveness for a person with whom I am not getting along. Often this change in my own consciousness from practicing Tonglen results in an easier and more successful mending of the damaged relationship with the person with whom I have a disagreement.

Contrary to the claims of some mystics, there is nothing "magical" about Tonglen. You can't send out some superpower of love to make the visualized people feel or act better. Not surprisingly, there is actually one study where scholars investigated Tonglen, and found no such distant psychological healing effect.[42] Tonglen only benefits you personally (unless Tonglen leads to reconciliation). The affects of Tonglen on your own FT, ST, and supporting lines of competence can be profound.

The challenges of forgiveness practice can and will be exceptionally difficult at times, but the potential consciousness raising benefits far outweigh the struggle. When forgiveness is practiced along with meditation, there may be no better way for reducing narcissism (both forms) and developing the humility needed to maximize consciousness. Humility opens consciousness. Expanded consciousness through forgiveness practice also helps us begin to see, understand, and accept many of life's deeper realities. In the next and final chapter, we will learn how the more than three thousand year old teachings of Buddhism also enlighten this search to better understand reality.

---

1 This quote can be found at Luke 23:34. It is not found in the gospels of Matthew, Mark, or John. Accordingly, biblical hermeneutics argues that Jesus likely did not actually say these words. Jesus son of Joseph (c. 5 BCE-30 CE) was the name of Jesus following his birth and for most of his life. At that time in history, Jewish men had only one name; but it was customary to add the name of the person's father or place of origin, which in this case would be Jesus son of Joseph or Jesus of Nazareth. Following his death, Jesus also became known as Jesus the Christ or Jesus Christ.

2 See, for example, "Forgiveness: Definitions, Perceptions, Contexts and Correlates" by Lijo K. J.; Journal of Psychology of Psychotherapy , Volume 8, Issue 3 (2019).

3 "Forgiveness *Theory, Research, and Practice*" edited by Michael E. McCullough, Kenneth I. Pargament, and Carl E. Thoresen, The Guilford Press, New York, 2000. (Here and after "McCullough".) McCullough also provides fascinating and educational blogs at social-science-evolving.com. (In this history, McCullough goes out of his way to list and honor the significance of the financial support from the John Templeton Foundation in advancing innovative scientific research into the process of forgiveness. I would like to take this footnote opportunity to also thank JTF for its financial support of many innovative scholars/programs that I have found both informative and inspiring over the years; in particular the funding of the National Public Radio Show "On Being" hosted by Krista Tippett, a true guru in her own right.)

4 McCullough at p3-4. McCullough notes that in 1932 Piaget did make a modest reference to forgiveness in Piaget's models of moral development. Many current scholars have published articles commenting on and further developing Piaget's models. These can easily be found online by searching "Piaget Forgiveness".

5 McCullough at p6.

6 Robert Enright, Ph.D., another pioneer and leading scholar in the scientific study of forgiveness, published the first empirically based study on which there was explicit focus on person-to-person forgiveness. See "The Adolescent as Forgiver" by R.D. Enright, M.J. Santos, and R. Al-Mabuk, J Adolesc. 1989 March; 12(1): 95-110. (Here and after "Adolescent".)A more current and lay-accessible article by Enright on the history of scholarly research on forgiveness; the problem of defining forgiveness; and the proved psychological health benefits of forgiveness can be found online. See "Reflecting on 30 Years of Forgiveness Science" by Robert Enright, Ph.D., posted by Psychology Today April 16, 2019. (Here and after "Enright".)

7 McCullough at p7.

8 McCullough at p8.

9 Everett Worthington is a clinical psychologist, one of the earliest pioneers, and still a leading scholar regarding the application of forgiveness practice in clinical psychology. McCullough was a graduate student of Worthington, and together with others developed the REACH model of forgive-

ness, which can easily be found online. Worthington's writings involve a strong dose of religion and what Worthington calls "spirituality". It is somewhat unfair of me to reduce the expansive writings of these scholars to these short definitions, but the quotes are in their words and reasonably representative of their writings.

10 McCullough at p8 citing "Dimensions of Forgiveness" by Enright, R.D. & Coyle, C. T. pp.139-161, Templeton Foundation Press, Philadelphia, PA (1998). Enright has a much lengthier definition in "Forgiveness is a Choice: A Step-by-Step Process for Resolving Anger and Restoring Hope" APA Lifetools, Washington D.C. (2001).

11 McCullough at p8.

12 "Forgiveness Is An Emotion-Focused Coping Strategy That Can Reduce Health Risks And Promote Health Resilience: Theory, Review, And Hypotheses" by Everett Worthington, Jr. and Michael Scherer; Psychology and Health, June 2004, Vol. 19, No. 3, pp385-405 at p387. (Here and after "Worthington/Scheuer".)

13 McCullough at p92.

14 McCullough at p93. Australopithecus afarensis ("Aa") was a hominid ancestor of ours, and the earliest hominid skeleton ever found. "Lucy" is a female skeleton Aa found in Africa, and dated back to c. 3.2 mya. "Ardi" is a male, also found in Africa, and dated even further back to c. 4.4 mya.

15 See Billingsley at p95. One of the most lay accessible and excellent scholarly article on the evolution and operation of the neural aspects of the process of forgiveness is "The Neural Systems of Forgiveness: An Evolutionary Psychological Perspective" by Joseph Billingsley and Elizabeth A. R. Lobin; Frontiers in Psychology 2017; 8:737. (Here and after "Billingsley".)

16 McCullough at p93. As discussed in Chapter Four, we now understand that emotions are not just reptilian reactions, but emerge in a complex manner similar to the emergence of consciousness.

17 McCullough at pp93-97.

18 McCullough at p95.

19 Billingsley at pp3-4.

20 Billingsley at p4.

21 A study that deals with the offender is "Neural Correlates of Receiving an Apology and Active Forgiveness: An fMRI Study" by Sabrina Strang, Verena Utikal, Urs Fischbacher, Bernd Weber, and Armin Falk; which can be found online at htts://doi.org/10.1371journal.pone0087654.

22 Billingsley at pp6-8.

23 Billingsley at pp9-14.

24 See "Association of DRD4 and COMT polymorphisms with anger and forgiveness traits in healthy volunteers" by Jee In Kang, Kee Namkoong, and Se Joo Kim; Neuroscience Letters 430 (2008) 252-257 which is available online at www.sciencedirect.com. (Here and after "Kang"); "Granting Forgiveness: State and trait evidence for genetic and gender indirect effects through empathy" by Charlotte VanOyen Wituliet, Lindsey M. Root Luna, Jill L. VanderStoep, Tre-

chaun Gonzalez & Gerald D. Griffin; The Journal of Positive Psychology, 15:3, 390-399, DOI: 10.1080/17439760.2019.1615108.

25 Nature of: "Trait forgiveness as a predictor of state forgiveness and positive work outcomes after victimization" by Madelynn A.D. Stackhouse. Published online by Elsevier Ltd. Volume 149, Pages 209-213 (2019). (Here and after "Stackhouse".) Measuring Forgiveness: "Measuring Forgiveness A Systematic Review" by Maria Fernandez-Capo et al, European Psychologist (2017), 247-262 https://doi.org/10.1027/1016-9040/a000303. Benefits: "Forgiveness Is An Emotion-Focused Coping Strategy That Can Reduce Health Risks and Promote Health Resilience: Theory, Review, and Hypotheses" by Everett L. Worthington, Jr. and Michael Scherer; Psychology and Health June 2004, Vol. 19, No. 3, pp. 385-405 (an older yet perhaps the seminal study on forgiveness benefits. . . numerous current articles can easily be found online by searching "benefits of forgiveness"). Also see, ForgivenessResearch.com for a bibliography of scientific literature about forgiveness.

26 Kang at p252.

27 "The New Science of Forgiveness" by Everett L. Worthington, Jr., published online (2004) at https://greatergood.berkeley.edu/article/item/the_new_science_of_forgiveness. (Here and after "Worthington/Berkeley".) Regarding workplace issues, see Stackhouse, supra.

28 McCullough at Chapter 8, pp. 156-175. See also, "Too Proud to Let Go: Narcissistic Entitlement as a Barrier to Forgiveness" by Julia Juola Exline, Roy F. Baumeisster, Brad J. Bushman, W. Keith Campbell, and Eli J. Finkel; Journal of Personality and Social Psychology 87(6):894-912 Jan. 2005, DOI: 10.1037/0022-3514.87.6.894. (Here and after "Exline".)

29 McCullough at p162.

30 Isaiah 14:12-15; Revelation 12:7-10. It's also interesting to note that "pride" is always listed first in the Catholic teaching of the "Seven Deadly Sins".

31 The McCullough at p161; See also, "Are We All Narcissists? 14 Criteria to Explore" by Leon F. Selize, Ph.D. published online by Psychology Today (2018) at https://www.psychologytoday.com/us/blog/evolution-the-self/201805/are-we-all-narcissists-14-criteria-explore.

32 The concept of narcissism was introduced by Freud in 1914. There are many types of narcissism; some of which are: Acquired Situational; Codependent; Closet; Conventional; Destructive; Exhibitionist; Medical; Sexual; and Narcissistic Personality Disorder ("NPD") (which used to be called "megalomania". The American Psychiatric Association puts out a manual called Diagnostic and Statistical Manual of Mental Disorders. The latest version is known as DSM-5, and contains the symptoms of NPD.

33 McCullough at p164.

34 See, "You Probably Think this Paper's About You: Narcissists' Perceptions of their Personality and Reputation" by Erika N. Carlson, Simine Vazire, and Thomas A. Ottmanns; Journal of Personality and Social Psychology. 2011 July:101(1); 185.201. DOI: 10.1037/a0023781.

35 Worthington/Berkeley; "Forgiveness: Letting go of grudges and bitterness" by Mayo Clinic Staff; published online at https://www.mayoclinic.org/healthy-lifestyle/adult-health/in-depth/forgiveness/art-2004692. "Forgiveness: Your Health Depends on It" by John Hopkins, published online at http://www.hopkinsmedicine.org/health/wellness-and-preventionalforgiveness-your-health-de-

pends-on-it.

36 Enright a p2; Worthington/Scheuer at pp394-400. There is also evidence that forgiveness practice is especially beneficial to elders regarding quality of life. See "Enhancing Forgiveness: A Group Intervention for the Elderly" by Berit Ingersoll-Dayton, Ruth Campbell and Jung-Hwa Ha; Journal of Gerontol Social Work 2009 Jan; 52(1): 2-16, published online at www.ncbi.nlm.nih.gov/pmc/articles/PMC3116269.

37 Multiple scholarly studies have demonstrated that choosing un-forgiveness has the very real potential of raising cortisol levels. Cortisol is a stress hormone that metabolizes fat for a quick response to stress. Unfortunately, after the stress abates, the fat is deposited around the waist since that is the bodily area where the fat is most easily re-accessible. Berkeley Blog at p6.

38 The often overwhelming problem of "self-forgiveness" is not specifically explored in this chapter, but the same meditation techniques will apply.

39 Numerous inspirational quotes, book excerpts, and wise teachings by Gandhi and Mandela can easily be found online by searching "Gandhi Forgiveness" and "Mandela Forgiveness". Tutu has written a book specifically on forgiveness following horrendously wrongful acts. See, "The Book of Forgiving" by Desmond Tutu and Mpho Tutu; HarperCollins Publishers, New York (2014).

40 One study found that meditation increases forgiveness in college students. See, "Meditation Lowers Stress and Supports Forgiveness Among College Students: A Randomized Controlled Trial" by Doug Oman, PhD et al; Journal of American College Health, Vol. 56, No. 5 March /APALL 2008, which can be found online.

41 At the time this chapter was written, there was an excellent guided meditation on YouTube by Jon Kabat-Zinn for a general relaxation body scan.

42 "A Randomized Controlled Trial of Tong Len Meditation Practice in Cancer Patients: Evaluation of a Distant Psychological Healing Effect" by Gioacchino Pagliaro et al; Explore, Volume 12, Issue 1, January-February 2016, pp42-49, which can be found online at www.sciencedirect.com/science/article/abs/pii/S1550830715001597.

CHAPTER TEN

BUDDHIST INSIGHTS FOR THE MODERN AGE

The coming of Buddhism in the West may well prove to be
the most important event of the twentieth century.
—Arnold Toynbee[1]

Buddhism has long been described as one of the "Five Great Religions". In rough numbers, these five are: 1) Christianity, representing 2.2 billion followers and 32% of the world's population; 2) Islam at 1.6 billion and 24%; 3) Hinduism at 1.2 billion and 16%; 4) Buddhism at 520 million and 7%; and Judaism at 15 million and 0.2%.[2]

Many impressive books describe the fascinating life of the founder of Buddhism, Siddhartha Gautama, whom scholars refer to as the "historical" Buddha.[3] Gautama lived sometime between the 6th and 4th centuries BCE, and traveled and taught for over 40 years in an area near the border of modern day Nepal and northeast India.

Scholars consider Buddhism a "non-theistic" religion. This means there is no transcendent creator. Scholars agree that the historical Buddha never intended to start a "religion" as such. Rather, the Buddha sought only to teach freedom from suffering through awakening to the true nature of reality. Yet the powerful human longing for: gods; a personal connection with the transcendent; revenge against wrongdoers; and promised immortality without suffering are such that, like all the "Great Religions", Buddhism soon fractured into competing branches and sects, each with their own power/ reward structure, esoterica, gnosticism, myths, and superstitions. Buddhism never developed a "creator" god, but it was not long until the Buddha and others were worshiped as gods. Magical powers were attributed to the Buddha as well as to a number of his highly regarded teachers. Statues, bracelets, bells, and relics became household talismans. Teachings and beliefs about mystical god-like figures (including more Buddhas); the promise of individual help from such transcendental figures; the rewards and punishments of karma; and the promise of immortality through reincarnation eventually leading to Nirvana hardened their insatiable hold on much of Buddhism.

Despite these predictable religious detours, Buddhism provides many precious insights into the nature of reality, as well as proved practices for gaining, understanding, and accepting such insights. The oft-heard claim that for millennia "the greatest minds of the East" dedicated their lives to developing such insights is of course an exaggeration, but it does have some truth behind it. An example of this is Nalanda University, which dates back to the fifth century, and which thrived in northeast India (modern-day Bihar province) as a center of Buddhist learning. "Great minds" from the far regions of the Eastern world made the challenging pilgrimage to Nalanda to study and teach.[4]

The depth and breath of Buddhist teachings are beyond the scope of this chapter. Fortunately, there are many thoughtful (superstition free) books on the numerous important teachings of Buddhism.[5] This chapter will focus on inviting aspects of Buddhism that may assist us in consciousness expansion. The areas we will explore are:

1. The "no fear" attraction of Buddhism. . .

2. Bottomline Buddhism is all about change. . .

3. The Buddha's practice path. . .

4. Way Out There Buddhism. . .

1) The "no-fear" attraction of Buddhism. . . Many chapters in this book have emphasized the awesome power of fear. We romantically and desperately tell ourselves that love is the most powerful emotion, but is this poetic belief supported by the data of life? It is fear not hate that is the opposite of love. It is fear not love that is the prime motivator in the competition of evolution, the so-called survival of the fittest.[6] If you look deeply enough, it is fear not love that motivates each level of Maslow's "Hierarchy of Needs" (although perhaps not the highest level assuming such a level exists). It is fear that compels us not to relinquishing our death grip on our primal narcissistic belief in an independent and intrinsic self in control of our own consciousness. If we want to increase our awareness of reality and corresponding ability to better control our responsive thoughts, emotions, and actions, it is critical that we appreciate the power of fear. This omnipresent reality of fear can be more than a bit depressing. At least for me, one of the optimistic and inviting attractions of Buddhism involves its welcoming "no-fear" facets.

These inviting aspects of Buddhism begin with the title of "Buddha" itself. "Buddha" derives from the Sanskrit word "budh" which can be translated into words such as "awaken" or "understand".[7] The historical Buddha was known as: one who is awake; one who is enlightened; or (my preference) one who see things as they really are. The Buddha was initially seen as a teacher or guide rather than as a master, a lord, or a god. The Buddha was someone to learn from and follow because he brought awareness of and practices for successfully navigating the difficult realities of life. As we will learn, the primary teaching of the Buddha was an awareness of the reality of suffering, and a path away from suffering toward the goals of wisdom and compassion. (Note that Buddhism often uses the terms "wisdom" and "compassion" together. This is done to emphasize that true compassion goes beyond mere empathy. While empathy is a wonderful virtue, in Buddhism true compassion as a goal and as a practice must include the wisdom needed to understand both the cause and how to alleviate any particular form of suffering.) Although admittedly a romantic simplification, I prefer to think of the historical Buddha more in the New Testament role of Jesus welcoming and teaching the little children, rather than the Old Testament (and Revelations) God of fire and brimstone.[8]

Another welcoming aspect of Buddhism is the "Charter of Free Inquiry" which we looked at toward the end of Chapter Six. This charter invites (and even encourages) a practitioner to question, challenge, and compare the teachings of Buddhism against personal experience and against non-Buddhist teachings. Contrast this fearless openness with the "creeds" of many Christian religions which require for membership belief in such phenomena as virgin birth, transubstantiation of bread and wine into the flesh and blood of the Jesus Christ, or a literal interpretation of the bible. To be sure and already noted, Buddhism has similar myths, and many sects have what could be considered creeds; but from its inception, Buddhism has actively encouraged not only questions, but the potential validity of other non-Buddhist teachings and practices. This openness continues into the present day as evidenced by the talks, books, and organizations of two of the most influential and active Buddhist teachers: the Dalai Lama and Thich Nhat Hanh.[9] A pointed example are the opening lines of the Dalai Lama's talk at the annual meeting of the Society for Neuroscience in 2005:

> The last few decades have witnessed tremendous advances in the scientific understanding of the human brain. . .with the advent of the new genetics, neuroscience's knowledge of the workings of biological organisms is now brought to the subtlest level of individual genes. This has resulted in unforeseen technological possibilities of even manipulating the very codes of life, thereby giving rise to the likelihood of creating entirely new realities for humanity as a whole.
> —Tenzin Gyatso, the Dalai Lama[10]

Perhaps the most welcoming "no-fear" aspect of Buddhism is the underlying Buddhist teaching that the deepest nature of a person is inherently good. Buddhists describe this as "Buddha nature". Each of us, no matter our talents, station in life, or prior bad conduct needs only knowledge and practice to move toward the goals of wisdom and compassion. Compare this to the underlying teaching of most Christian religions which hold that the deepest nature of person is inherently sinful (bad). These traditional Christian religions describe this as "original sin". Each of us needs to be saved (to avoid some type of hellish and eternal afterlife) through confession of sinfulness and committed/faith belief in the death and resurrection of Jesus Christ. It is not the purpose of this book to criticize Christianity or any other religion. There are so many beautiful and valued teachings in all religions. It comes as no surprise to me that almost all the Christians I know well enough to discuss such personal matters (including a number of Evangelicals) do not in the privacy of their own thoughts buy into the more extreme religious claims and creedal requirements. They choose instead to simply practice the more loving aspects of Christianity of which there are many. Yet the very real contrast in the two underlying visions of Buddhism and traditional Christianity is stark, and not unfairly represented in the following two quotes:

> Original sin is in us like our beard. We are shaved today
> and look clean; tomorrow our beard has grown again, nor does it cease
> growing while we remain on earth. In like manner original sin cannot
> be extirpated from us; it springs up in us as long as we live.
> —Martin Luther[11]

> Buddha-nature represents the extremely positive news that our essence, no matter how many mistakes we make, is not fundamentally flawed. It is the opposite of original sin and affords us the potential for true freedom.
> —Nalanda Institute for Contemplative Science[12]

2) Bottomline Buddhism reveals an ultimate truth that life is all about change. . . The teachings and practices of Buddhism are indeed expansive and complex, but the initial and bottomline teaching is that "all phenomena" within material reality are the result of change. All phenomena emerge into existence through change, and all phenomena continue to change until they cease to exist. "All" means all. "Phenomena" means everything you can think of including: objects (from birthday cake to people), thoughts, emotions, actions, sensations, concepts, consciousness, and what we think of as self. This reality of change gives rise to the first basic Buddhist teaching of "impermanence." All phenomena are impermanent.

To help us better understand impermanence, we can look at what could be called the second most basic Buddhist teaching of "interdependent co-arising". This teaching states that each phenomenon comes into existence because of causes and conditions of other phenomena. The traditional way of explaining interdependent co-arising involves the thought experiment of thinking of a piece of furniture such as a wood table.[13] Next think of all the phenomena that went into creating that table. It's easy to see how the single table arose in part because of wood from a tree and the work of a table builder, but you must go deeper. Think of the cutting down and milling of that tree. Go even deeper into the almost infinite phenomena that went into the growth of that tree, which would involve such phenomena as the quality of the earth surrounding the tree, which in turn would involve the insects and micro-organisms helping to create the quality of that earth. The same is true of the builder, the builder's effort in building the table, the professional training of the builder, and even the birth and child-rearing of the builder. The reality of interdependent co-arising gives rise to the Buddhist teaching of "emptiness". All phenomena interdependently co-arise, and are therefore empty of intrinsic existence.

Emptiness means an absence of "intrinsic existence". This means no phenomenon interdependently brings itself into existence. No phenomenon solely sustains its own existence. All phenomena change, but without complete control of such change. And all phenomena eventually cease to exist. This includes the phenomena of self. But before you let this teaching on emptiness bum you out, know that the teaching goes on to explain that "emptiness" is not simply the absence of the independence and permanence of intrinsic existence. To borrow and modify a metaphor from the Catholic mystic, Meister Eckhart,[14] this emptiness is a desert where your previous understanding of reality dies, but then this dessert of emptiness blooms into a new reality of freedom. Our previously fixed judgments and concepts; the pressures and fears from our perceived hierarchy of needs; and the filters to our consciousness die in the desert because their emptiness has been revealed. In their place blooms the promise of Buddhism which claims that understanding and accepting such emptiness reveals a new reality of freedom. It is a freedom from the suffering brought about by unnecessary "attachment" to those falsely perceived judgments, needs, and fears due to our inability to understand, accept, and release the powerful filters to our consciousness. It is the time of the true "Last Judgment" when we realize and accept the futility of unyielding attachment to any final judgment. This is the freedom of an "enlightened" consciousness which arises when we increasingly see reality in its true nature. There is great wisdom revealed by these insights about emptiness, but Buddhism does not stop there.

Buddhism goes on to claim that this enlightened consciousness further reveals that within each sentient being is an eternal essence (often referred to as "Buddha-nature") that emanates from and eventually returns to the Oneness of ultimate reality. This is the Buddhist promise of "Nirvana", the fourth basic teaching of Buddhism.

The promise of Nirvana seems more than a bit troublesome. What is this "eternal essence" that returns to Nirvana? Isn't this just another form of Dualism? As we will examine toward the end of this chapter, Buddhism attempts to reconcile this problematic issue along with the equally concerning Buddhist teachings of karma and reincarnation by proposing two realms of reality. As first mentioned in Chapter Eight on Meditation, these two realms of reality are often described with terms such as "physical reality" and "ultimate reality". Buddhism insists that these two realms do not amount to Dualism because Buddhism believes in only One reality. Later in this chapter we will see and evaluate how well Buddhism does in defending this seemingly "Way Out There" claim.

Impermanence, interdependent co-arising, emptiness, and Nirvana are the four cornerstones on which all of Buddhism is built; even though each of the various branches and sects have developed their own power/reward structure, esoterica, gnosticism, myths, and superstitions. Numerous subtle modifications to these four cornerstones have occurred over centuries of time, and continue through the present day, with many of the more inspiring developments due to Buddhism's openness to change. But let's now look at the very first teaching of the historical Buddha before his teachings became a religion. Although the Buddha might not agree with my description of his first teaching, it's not unreasonable to describe it as the Buddha's practice path for raising your consciousness.

3) The Buddha's practice path. . . Legends have it that the historical Buddha spent the first thirty years of his life in the city of Kapilavatthu, which was located in present-day Nepal. Earliest legends describe the young man known as Siddhartha Gautama[15] as the son of a wealthy tribal chief. Later legends elevate Gautama's status to being the princely son of a great king. Neither has been confirmed by scholars, but all agree that the beginning theme of all legends is that Gautama began life with all possible benefits that money and power could buy. This included material wealth and a loving wife and child. Later legends included and emphasized that Gautama's father was so rich and powerful that he was able to initially shield Gautama from experiencing sickness, death, and any other form of human suffering.

Although not specifically stated in the legends, it seems Gautama was blessed or cursed (depending on your perspective about such things) with a genotype/phenotype/consciousness that compelled him to search for and learn about the deepest meanings of life. All legends go on to describe that the wealth and privilege of Gautama's first thirty years of life were insufficient to stop his existential yearning. This is evidenced in part by the name Gautama gave to his only child and son, Rahula, which means "fetter". According to the legends, this name was given to demonstrate how even something as special as the love for a child can serve as an obstacle to the time and energy Gautama believed necessary to discover and understand reality. Later legends emphasize a consciousness changing event where Gautama was finally able to evade his father's over protections by sneaking out of the palace to view for the first time life as it really existed. It was then that Gautama first observed sickness, old age, and death. . .the reality that life inevitably involves suffering. This so moved Gautama that he made the decision to leave his privileged life and loving family so that he could further his existential search for the wisdom as to why reality existed as such.

Believing that the "way" of the pleasurable benefits of wealth, power, and family could not provide the answers he was searching for, Gautama chose to live his life in the most opposite and extreme "way" hoping this would provide the wisdom for which he was longing. Gautama chose to live the life of a wandering ascetic. The practice of asceticism involves the extreme discipline of self-denial. It is not simply giving up what we might think of as pleasure, but includes an almost total renunciation from how others live in society. Long before, during, and after Gautama's time, ascetics lived alone or in a group, usually away from a town, often in the forest, or simply under a tree. All minimally allowed food and clothing were obtained through begging. Ascetics ate only once a day. They slept outside without shelter, many forcing themselves to sleep in sitting positions. The legends agree that Gautama soon became the leader of a small group of ascetics, and continued these practices for six years.

Gautama reasoned that if he emersed himself deeply in such suffering, perhaps he would gain the wisdom of reality. Gautama had reason to believe that asceticism would provide the answers for which he was searching. Asceticism had long been a revered practice dating back more than a millennia before Gautama's birth. Ascetic practices could be found in the Vedas (which were first written down c. 1500-500 BCE, but oral traditions of the Vedas could be as old as 7000-5000 BCE) where it was suggested that the gods created the earth through the knowledge and power gained by such ascetic practices. Nonetheless, after six years of complete dedication to asceticism, Gautama began to realize that the second "way" of asceticism did not provide the answers he needed.

Gautama left his ascetic comrades, and against their angry protestations, struck out on his own. He then sat beneath a banyan tree in deep meditation searching for answers neither the way of privilege nor the way of asceticism had provided. Legends vary greatly as to how long Gautama meditated under the "bodhi tree" from a few hours to 49 days. All legends agree that Gautama emerged from this meditation as the Buddha. . . the one who sees things as they really are. The Buddha had discovered the "Middle Way". Neither great pleasure/power nor intense suffering/asceticism revealed the truth of reality. Reality could only be revealed to one who sees reality as a pure witness unattached to pleasure or suffering.

There are many versions of Gautama's meditation under the bodhi tree. This is mine. Gautama began to enter deep meditation by following his breath. He then slowed his spinning consciousness of thoughts, feelings, sensations, emotions, plans, and worries. When the spinning stopped, he was able to look more deeply, without fear, without judgment, and without attachment. Gautama was able to see reality as pure witness (as "pure witness" was described during meditation in Chapter Eight). As pure witness he saw the interdependent co-arising, impermanence, and intrinsic emptiness of all phenomena including the self. This emptiness did not frighten Gautama, because he saw that emptiness was not a negative. Emptiness was not just the absence of the independent permanence of such phenomena as thoughts, emotions, and self. Such emptiness was a reality of freedom. It was freedom from what we would call the filters to consciousness. It was a freedom from the suffering caused by grasping and attachment to falsely perceived needs, fears, and judgments. It was freedom to see reality in its true nature. As he witnessed more deeply, Gautama not only saw interdependent co-arising, impermanence, and emptiness, but he saw his deepest insight: the "inter-being" of all reality. This new wisdom of the inter-being, borderless, oneness of reality led Gautama into a state of compassion for all reality. He knew he would dedicate the remainder of his life to teaching this wisdom and compassion.

Gautama arose from his meditation under the bodhi tree as the Buddha, the one who sees things as they really are. He began to teach. His first teaching became known as "The Four Noble Truths."

The First Noble Truth is that the nature of existence is suffering. (Here the Buddha is referring to existence in the physical/material realm.) In ancient India/Nepal "dukkha" was the word for "suffering", and is the term used in Buddhist teachings today. It's important to understand that, just like the word "suffering" in English, "dukkha" can have many appropriate interpretations to fit the circumstances. In general, Buddhists speak of three types of dukkha. First is the suffering of pain (dukkha-dukkha). This includes the physical pain associated with events such as breaking your arm or stubbing your toe. It also includes emotional pain from events such as losing your wallet or the death of a loved one. Second is the suffering of change (viparinama-dukkha). This can occur when a desired event or experience comes to an end, such as having to return to work after vacation, or not being able to eat your cake and have it too. Finally, there is existential suffering (samkhara-dukkha). This is the conscious or non-conscious angst associated with our own mortality. From a deeper perspective, it includes suffering associated with clinging and attachment to a belief that each of us is an individual self with both intrinsic existence and total control over our own consciousness. The traditional insight of the First Noble Truth is that all aspects in the realm of physical reality involve some form of dukka/suffering.

The Second Noble Truth explains the causes of suffering. No matter the type of suffering, the Buddha's insight is that all suffering is caused by desire/grasping. This includes both the desire for pleasure as well as the desire to avoid any type of physical or emotional displeasure. Yet the Buddha knew (as we now know) that underlying this grasping is a consciousness which cannot see, much less understand and accept, the false filters to our consciousness.

The traditional understanding of the Third Noble Truth is the bold claim that "all" suffering can be eliminated through the practice of an eightfold path, which thereafter became known as the Noble Eightfold Path. Perhaps a better understanding of this third truth is that, while we can never completely eliminate all suffering (at least in the physical reality), we can learn to understand, accept, and somewhat control the desires and fears that cause suffering through practicing this Noble Eightfold Path.

The Fourth Noble Truth is the Noble Eightfold Path (which for ease of reading we will sometimes refer to as the "Path".) The names for the categories of the eight components of the Path have many different translations. Moreover, these categories (no matter the translation) are somewhat general, and therefore have been interpreted differently by different scholars and mystics over the centuries. The following is my interpretation, which largely tracks the spirit of Thich Nhat Hanh's interpretation:[16]

1.   Right View (deep reflection on why you are on the Path);

2. Right Speech (no verbal misdeeds such as lying, slander, negative speech);

3. Right Action (no physical misdeeds such as stealing, murder, or sexual misconduct);

4. Right Livelihood (no work that harms sentient beings or the environment);

5. Right Thinking (cultivating filter-free thoughts);

6. Right Diligence (committed effort);

7. Right Mindfulness (conscious attention to the present moment); and

8. Right Concentration (developing a consciousness free of attachment).

At first reading, one is tempted to dismiss the Noble Eightfold Path as just another ancient set of general rules of conduct such as the Ten Commandments or numerous other legal codes.[17] Indeed, the Path has some similar rules of conduct (in particular 2 through 4); but as we will see, the Path has many deeper implications for dealing with suffering through expansion of consciousness.

Each of the eight categories along the Buddha's Path is actually a "practice" as described in Chapter Six. As such, each requires stopping, looking, practice, and repeat. As you continue this process, realizations learned with each practice deepen and become more vivid in your consciousness. Although commentators frequently number the eight categories, they are not practiced sequentially. No single practice stands alone. They work together, where insights gained in one practice frequently lead to insights in other practices.

Right View... This practice is almost always listed first because it could be renamed "Right Overview" (or better yet, Right "Underlying" View). It asks the practitioner to stop and reflect on their current sense of reality as well as why they are engaging in the Path. You can begin on the Path as a complete agnostic about reality and the value of the Path, and then wait to see what happens. The only hard ask of Right View is that from time to time you stop and look closely at what your practices along the Path have indicated to you about the nature of reality and any benefits of the Path. Your insights will almost certainly change over time.

The next three practices along the Path started out as the same general prohibitions found in many ancient and modern codes of conduct. We will briefly look at how modern Buddhist thought leaders have deepened the subtleties of these three practices.

Right Speech. . . This practice tracks many ancient and modern codes of conduct. Initially, it prohibited what you might call the classic or obvious speech violations of lying and slander; but modern interpretations pointedly include a warning against exaggeration, especially any speech that seeks to aggrandize the self. Another modern development is Thich Nhat Hanh's teaching that a practice of "deep listening" is fundamental to Right Speech because it enables a person to be more productive and more compassionate when they speak in response.

Right Action. . . This practice also tracks traditional codes of conduct. Just like Right Speech, this practice initially prohibited the obvious wrongful conduct of stealing, murder, and sexual misconduct. Modern teachers such as Thich Nhat Hanh deepen the understanding of Right Action to include the affirmative obligation to stand up (perhaps by using Right Speech) to protect the disadvantaged. (It's interesting to note that in his 14th century epic poem, the "Divine Comedy", Dante Alighieri reserves a special place in hell for those, who in a period of moral crisis, maintain their neutrality by failing to speak or act.)

Right Livelihood. . . This practice asks that a person choose a line of work that will bring no harm, not only to other humans, but to all sentient beings. Modern commentators now include the environment. While all practices along the Path require periodic reflection, this practice will almost certainly involve numerous complex choices for which there are no easy answers. For example: Of course, you can't be a slave trader, but can you be a butcher? If you are a farmer, can you plow up your field if mamma mouse has just built her home there as we now know happened to poet Robert

Burns? In general, Buddhist teachers and mystics do not offer strict rules for the more subtle decisions regarding livelihood choices. (After all, the Dalai Lama not only eats meat, but in general will sometimes politely eat whatever food his hosts offer him.) The more important aspect of this practice is that a person make the commitment and take the time to reflect whether a work/business practice will bring unnecessary harm.

The remaining four practices differ from traditional codes of conduct. They look more deeply at both the self-awareness and the self-regulation of our thoughts, emotions, and actions. You will see how these four practices are closely related, but with subtle distinctions and benefits.

Right Thinking. . . This practice encourages taking responsibility for the way we use our consciousness. Right Thinking requires that we engage in practices to increase our awareness and control of our thoughts, emotions, and actions. (We now know that some of the most beneficial practices to develop these skills include changing perspective, meditation, and forgiveness.)

Right Diligence. . . This practice requires the type of "commitment" discussed in Chapter Six. More specifically, it requires engaging in each practice with the three-part core suggested by Kabat-Zinn in Chapter Eight on Meditation: on purpose; in the present moment; and with non-judgmental awareness.

Right Mindfulness. . . While teachings on mindfulness have been around since at least the time of the historical Buddha, the teaching, practice, and scholarly research on mindfulness have exploded since the early 1970s. This includes research from scholars of multiple professional specialties, mystics from many religious traditions, consultants in the business world, and purveyors of greeting cards and inspirational plaques. Not surprisingly, this has resulted in varying definitions and practices for mindfulness.[18]

Think of mindfulness as the same "conscious attention to the present moment" that we use for meditation, but now we are applying that conscious attention to our daily lives off the meditation cushion. This involves the practice of deliberately moving beyond the non-conscious autopilot of our habits and filters. Not surprisingly, scholars have demonstrated that mindfulness practice provides many of the same physical and psychological benefits as meditation.[19] Mindfulness practice is directed toward expanding our consciousness during our too often mindless state of attention while we engage in our routine workaday worlds. A perfect example of this may occur while we are mindlessly driving on a weekend errand, but suddenly find ourselves heading instead on the same commute that takes us to the office during the work week. Mindfulness is the opposite of mindlessness. Why restrict the consciousness expansion benefits of meditation we learned about in Chapter Eight to the meditation cushion?

There are numerous ways to practice mindfulness, but this is one of the simplest yet most productive. It involves using "bells of mindfulness" as taught by Thich Nhat Hanh. Ironically, perhaps the biggest challenge about being mindful is simply remembering to be mindful during our typically hectic days. You can solve this problem by using a bell to remind you to be mindful. This need not be an actual bell, but can be an activity or sound that you designate as your reminder bell. It can be something as simple as every time the phone rings, every time someone walks into your office, every time you go to the refrigerator, or every time you make your bed. When that bell goes off, focus on what you are doing or about to do. Focus with that same three-part Kabat-Zinn core: on purpose; in the present moment; and with non-judgmental awareness. For example: Really focus on the activities of deep listening and right speech to the person on the phone or who walks into your office. Think about why and what you are eating; and if you're making a meal, look closely at each task. Ha! Make that bed like you're in the army.

The point of Buddha's practice of mindfulness is to increase your awareness throughout the day, not just while you're meditating. Any practice of increased awareness is a practice of increasing consciousness. Why waste an entire day? It is during the day that we interact, not only with others, but with physically active life. Remember Piaget's insight from Chapter Three that knowledge is not automatically given to the passive observer, but is discovered through activity.

Right Concentration. . . This is the deepest of the eight practices. It is a commitment to work toward developing a consciousness of "pure witness" as described in Chapter Eight. This practice requires a commitment to developing deep meditation skills. As you learn this skill of pure witness during meditation, you will soon generate the "closely related" skill of engaging in life activities as a pure witness. This provides the freedom found in seeing things as they really are.

Practicing the Noble Eightfold Path is meant to increase your mindful engagement with reality, both during meditation and in living your life. The evidence from both scholars and mystics is strong that these practices will help to expand your consciousness regarding both the mundane and the profound aspects of life. These practices will strengthen both self-awareness and self-regulation over your thoughts, emotions and actions. Of that there is little doubt. On the other hand, it is fair to question whether such practices will eventually eliminate "all" suffering in your life. Let's take a look at how Buddhism handles this and other seemingly "Way Out There" claims.

4) *Way Out There Buddhism*. . . While the historical Buddha had many deep, moving, and impressive insights about the nature of reality (which are even more impressive given they occurred more than two millennia ago), unfortunately "Eastern" Buddha fell prey to the same cultural filters as did "Western" Descartes. This involves the Buddhist teachings of reincarnation, karma and Nirvana.

Long before Buddha's time, belief in reincarnation had deep roots in the writings of the Upanishads of the later Vedic period (c. 800-500 BCE). You can think of "reincarnation" as a subcategory of the umbrella term "transmigration" which contains various doctrines claiming that some essence of each sentient being (not just humans) survives after the death of the body. As we learned in Chapter One, this essence could be the Egyptian belief in "ka" which was the vital essence which animated the body, and which left the body at death for the eternal afterlife of darkness or the radically more desirable Field of Rushes depending on whether a person lived a righteous life. In more modern times and through the present, there is the Christian belief in the "soul" which after death transmigrates to heaven (purgatory?) or hell. This is similar in concept to the ka as well as to multiple other ancient cultural and religious beliefs, keeping in mind that many historical cultures had wide variations regarding the specific nature of the soul.

Both Buddha and Descartes were unable to see past the filter of the prominent religion of their day. For Buddha that filter was Hinduism which had flourished as far back as c. 2300 BCE. I suspect that, just like the ultimate doubter, Descartes, who could not fathom a reality without a soul ordained by God the Creator, so too the Buddha could not fathom reality without reincarnation. The same can be said about the Buddha's belief in "karma", which also preexisted the Buddha. Karma comes from the Sanskrit word "karman" which means "act". Karma claims individual sentient beings are punished or rewarded in subsequent reincarnations for conduct in previous lives. Karma answers the primal and longed-for need that the bad guys will eventually be punished even though not much can be done to stop or punish them at the present time. Reincarnation and Nirvana help assuage the primal existential fears associated with the finality of mortality. It is the primal appeal of all organized religions to offer hopeful answers to these compelling needs.

While the Buddha must be admired for having the insight and courage of consciousness to challenge a number of the fundamental beliefs of Hinduism, he was not able to expand his consciousness past the longstanding and omnipresent Hindu teachings of reincarnation and karma. Including reincarnation, karma, and Nirvana in the Buddhist understanding of reality not only has the "Way Out There" problem of returning us to Dualism, but brings into question whether the Buddha's Noble Eightfold Path will actually eliminate "all" suffering? After all, if the claimed Nirvana of the Oneness is not true, maybe the Path is not true? Let's take these problems one at a time.

Buddhism insists that reincarnation/karma/Nirvana is not Dualism because there is only One reality, even though in its teachings Buddhism uses the dualistic terms of the two realms of "physical reality" and "ultimate reality". Buddhism justifies this seeming Dualism as a metaphor to explain the very complex nature of the Oneness of all reality. This "metaphor" argument may be valid in justifying that Buddhism is not Dualism, but only if the Oneness of all reality is ontologically true. Unfortunately, similar to Christian apologists attempting to explain the ontological reality of heaven,

Buddhist apologists have been equally unforthcoming and unconvincing in explaining why Buddhism is not Dualism.

It has been interesting but frustrating that the great Buddhist teachers, from the historical Buddha through the present time, generally decline to discuss the specifics of their claimed ultimate reality. There are even several admonishments in the Buddhist Canon (including by the historical Buddha himself) against asking a teacher about such things. When finally forced to offer any kind of explanation about the nature of the essence that suffers karma, reincarnates, and/or returns to the Nirvana of the One, the great teachers frequently use two metaphors.

The first metaphor compares this transmigrating essence (Buddha-nature) during reincarnation to the flame on a candle. Reincarnation occurs when that flame is transferred to another candle by way of a taper. This is an excellent metaphor for the impermanent, independent co-arising, empty nature of physical existence (the flame); but it is far from satisfying in explaining what aspects of the eternal essence (of a person) transfers during reincarnation. We know from physics that zero part of that first candle flame actually transfers to the second candle because the flame is never the same from nanosecond to nanosecond. So what transfers if nothing actually transfers under this candle metaphore?

The second metaphor is more helpful. It compares the essence of an individual to a wave on the ocean. The wave gives the illusion of existing in physical space; for example, you can "physically" see it, feel it, even surf it. Yet when more closely examining a wave, it becomes apparent the wave is an impermanent, constantly changing, independently co-arising, and intrinsically empty unit. The wave continuously emanates from and returns to the One eternal ocean as it rolls along. The wave is never the same from nanosecond to nanosecond. The ocean is the "ultimate" reality, because the everchanging wave is always and only part of the One eternal ocean. The wave is always a temporary, changing, and "emerging" manifestation of the One eternal ocean.

In simple terminology, these great Buddhist teachers are saying with these two metaphors that the eternal Oneness has emerging properties.

These emerging properties include everything that exists in the so-called "physical reality": planets, gravity, people, consciousness, pain, pleasure, fear, and vodka, just to name a few of the infinite manifestations that make up "physical" reality. The argument goes that, just because the One manifests/emerges into the physical world, doesn't make this Dualism because the manifestations are always part of the One.

This emergent belief/theory is not new nor unique to Buddhism. Since before recorded time and through the present, there have been multiple myths attempting to explain why this One reality is not Dualism, but is Monism in another form. It is the form of Monism where all seemingly "physical" reality emerges/manifests as an inseparable part of the One "ultimate" reality.

This form of Monism can be found in numerous myths from ancient Hindu teachings that long preexisted Buddhism to current New Age claims. Examples of such myths were discussed in detail in Chapter One when we looked at Dr. Lanza's theory of "Biocentrism", and discussed again in Chapter Three when we looked at Ken Wilbur's "Kosmic Consciousness". While there are many versions of the myth, in general it proceeds as follows. The One and eternal Spirit/Godhead/Kosmic Consciousness goes through an eons long process of emerging in various forms such as a grain of sand, an aardvark, a supernova, a galaxy, and maybe even multiple universes. All manifestations are ultimately an indivisible part of the One just as the ever-changing wave is always an indivisible part of the One ocean. This is true even though there are degrees of seeming sentience emerging among the manifestations; and even though certain manifestations (humans) falsely believe they have intrinsic existence and are in control of their own consciousness. Most such myths go on to claim that all of the manifestations eventually engage in some sort of "return" process where the manifestations meld back into the eternal One just as the wave returning to the ocean in the classic Buddhist version of the myth. In many myths, the emergence and return then start all over again in an infinite cycle.

The appeal of this type of myth is that a return process implies some ultimate intelligence responsible for the whole process. Much more important to most people is their belief in some type of ultimate justice/reward/happiness at least after the return process. This gives the myth's adherents hope, not only for a non-suffering and eternal afterlife, but for meaning in their present lives. Yet the most troublesome problem with such a myth becomes whether this Oneness actually has any plan or concern for us mere manifestations, and whether this return/merging with the One is a good thing? Dr. Lanza offers no thoughts on any motivation by this One Consciousness for emanating, and it is unclear if he believes in any return process. Certain myths suggest that the reason for the manifestations is that the One is dreaming, or playing, or is bored, or has some grand purpose we cannot know without gaining insight via some special practice, ritual, or privileged gnostic secrets.

My agnosticism on such myths no doubt goes back to my dad's (previously discussed) "smartest man in the cave" warning where the smartest man in the cave thought the sun was God. Transpersonal myths about a fall and then return to the eternal source/Godhead/Spirit have been and continue to be in the minds of the smartest men and women since before recorded time and through the present. Some such thought leaders now argue that this continuous belief throughout the ages and across cultures is an important piece of evidence of the truth of such myths because such a continuous belief must represent a primal/deep memory we all carry as an inseparable part of the Oneness. Moreover, as we have learned, many highly regarded mystics and even some scholars claim to have actually experienced this Oneness through Altered States during meditation or with psychedelic drugs. These beliefs have great ego appeal because they imply that we are each part of the One/Godhead/Spirit. Not surprisingly, more than a few New Age movements use the mantra, "Be still, and know that you are God." (This, of course, is a tortured restatement of Psalm 46:10.)

Please let me be clear. I want Transpersonal myths to be true. I want to be eternal. Yet years of investigation, experimentation, and reflection about such matters have led me to my most basic reason for agnosticism: I am at my core an Occam's razor kind of guy.[20] The simplest explanation is usually the right explanation. The far more simple and therefore likely reality is that Transpersonal myths are beautiful but desperate dreams arising from our mutual, primal, existential angst regarding the historical Buddha's penetrating insights into the absolute truth of impermanence, interdependent co-arising, and intrinsic emptiness of our existence. It is this exact same angst that has existed in all human brains throughout history and across cultures that caused our cave dwelling brothers and sisters to dream, believe, and teach their children about such myths, beginning with the myth of Animism. We all share this angst; and we are all free to believe, deny, or simply doubt such myths of Oneness.

Let us complete this chapter (and book) with a look at whether, despite the ontological validity or non-validity of Buddha-nature or Nirvana, the Buddha's Noble Eightfold Path has value in our lives. We can begin with whether the Path can eventually eliminate "all" suffering as claimed by Buddhism. The answer is straight forward. Unless you mean that all suffering will disappear after the return to the Oneness, such a claim is patently false, and can easily be disproved by the plain observation and experience of life. More pertinent to our search is the question as to whether the Path can reduce suffering by facilitating meaningful expansion of consciousness.

The veracity and value of the Path for reducing suffering depends on what type of suffering you talk about. Consider the mundane suffering of the "physical pain" from a stubbed toe. Yes, skills developed from practice on the Path will likely keep you from overreacting to the pain. For example, if you have been practicing along the Path, it is unlikely you will pester everyone at work for days on end on how you have suffered because the idiot city didn't repair cracks in the sidewalks. But no, your toe will still hurt, and you will suffer similar pain the next time you stub your toe no matter how accomplished you are at following the Path. The Path does not prevent suffering from physical pain.

The Path will not eliminate the "emotional" suffering from certain types of loss. Yes, it will help you deal with the emotional burden of the loss, but it won't eliminate the pain, nor should it. You will still emotionally suffer from the loss of a job, a marriage, or a child. Buddhism has never sought to turn us into automatons without emotion simply waiting for Nirvana, confident in our denial of pain because we believe we are ultimately a manifestation of the One. There is no evidence nor example that emotional or physical suffering can be completely eliminated by the Path. The Path does, however, help us to cope with these types of suffering whether we are manifestations of the One or mere mortals. At times the Path even assists a person in seeing otherwise hidden aspects of beauty, growth, and opportunity in the midst and the mist of suffering. You feel the wonder of the rain.

The classic type of suffering that both the historical Buddha and most subsequent Buddhist mystics correctly claim can be greatly reduced is the suffering that comes from grasping and attachment. The Buddhist concepts of grasping and attachment are deeper that one might think. This human process does not just involve grasping for more money, promotion, good looks, or pistachio ice cream. It is the deeper and almost always non-conscious grasping created and exacerbated by the filters to our consciousness regarding our often falsely perceived needs. Examples of these powerful, yet largely non-conscious, attachments include compelling passions such as being part of a group or having our ego stroked as we studied in Chapter Three, Levels of Consciousness.

The true and invaluable teaching of the Noble Eightfold Path is that the suffering from such attachment and grasping can be greatly reduced and, at times, even eliminated by expansion of consciousness. Although the Path is thousands of years old, it is still the most productive way of expanding consciousness. It is a macro-point of this book that reduction of suffering through consciousness expansion represents an exciting new type of freedom. It is a freedom that is not defined by our looks, work, race, Cartesian gravity, genes, needs, family, or even by fear.

Let's do one last thought experiment to help understand how this new reality of freedom brought about by the Path helps reduce suffering. Think back on certain types of fear beliefs in your life which you now understand to be patently false. Those fears generated suffering even though you now know that they were based on ignorant beliefs which expanded consciousness would have helped you avoid. (This experiment works much better if you're older with decades of commonly held foolish and even hateful beliefs.) For example: Did you believe that you might not be alive in the morning if your parents failed to check under your bed for monsters? Did you suffer from not being popular in school? Did you believe you would burn in the eternal fires of hell for any number of so-called "mortal sin" offenses (think premarital sex)? Did you believe your life was over after the "love of your life" broke up with you? Did you fear your life would be ruined if you didn't get accepted into a certain school, job, or social group? Did you fear the country would be destroyed if you voted for a Republican or Democrat? Finally, think back especially on all the absurd and damaging beliefs and fears you had about the LGBT community and people of other races, religions, and nationalities, which most of us are too ashamed to even admit to ourselves decades later even though these beliefs and fears were born out of a consciousness of ignorance rather than malice. Meaningful expansion of consciousness provides a freedom from the suffering and confusion caused by attachment to false beliefs and fears. Simply let these false beliefs and fears die in the desert of an expanding consciousness.

Expansion of consciousness makes life's pleasures and even life's challenges more vivid, more real, more meaningful. We actually see and relate to the world and to ourselves as if from a different dimension. . .new values, new realities. . .a more authentic plain of awareness and existence. Consciousness expansion displaces false fears and needs, and welcomes us into "An Accessible Lightness of Being".

---

1 Arnold J. Toynbee (1889-1975) was a British historian and philosopher. You could argue that Toynbee was the world's most well known and admired scholar of the mid-twentieth century. He certainly was the most read, translated, and debated scholar of that time. His master work was the 12 volume opus "A Study of History", published 1934-1961. Although subsequent scholars found various faults with certain theories and conclusions of Toynbee, no one disputes that "A Study of History" is considered the most famous historical study ever written. Toynbee chronicled the rise and demise of 26 civilizations. A major thesis for Toynbee was that civilizations cyclically rise and fall based on their creative ability to meet societal challenges. Toynbee believed it was the "creativity minority" that rises to meet the challenges of civilization, and the masses follow. Beginning in 1929, Toynbee began to experience a profound spiritual attraction to the Japanese influence of Buddhism. An interesting article regarding Toynbee's relationship to Buddhist thinking is "Toynbee & Buddhism" by Philip Grant, which can be found online at worldculture.org. You can watch lectures and interviews of Toynbee on YouTube.

2 Judaism is only the 11th most populous religion on most surveys, but its affect on humanity is well described as "great". When I was a lad, there was a joke going around (with more than a kernel of truth in it) that the five most influential people in the history of the world were all Jewish: Moses, Jesus, Marx, Einstein, and Bob Dylan.

3 Two of the best books are: "Old Path White Clouds – Walking In The Footsteps Of The Buddha" by Thich Nhat Hanh; Parallax Press, Berkeley, California (1991); and "Buddha" by Karen Arm-

strong; Penguin Group, New York (2001). Armstrong's books are thoroughly researched and always insightful. It would be time well spent to read every book she has ever written.

4 Simply search "Nalanda" online for numerous sites regarding the history, archaeology, and wonder of Nalanda. At Nalanda's peak, there were around 10,000 students and 2,500 faculty from countries including modern day China, Greece, Iran, Indonesia, Japan, Korea, Mongolia, and Tibet.

5 The book I have used for years as a source and reminder of the numerous Buddhist teachings is "The Heart of the Buddha's Teaching" by Thich Nhat Hanh; Broadway Books, New York (1998). (Here and after "Heart".) An impressive young man recently gave me the book "Why Buddhism Is True - The Science and Philosophy of Meditation and Enlightenment" by Robert Wright; Simon & Schuster, New York (2017). I foolishly stuck it on a shelf for several months, mistaking the book for some trendy coverage on Buddhism. I was wrong. It is one of the better books introducing and explaining Buddhism to newcomers. I'm now in the process of reading and equally enjoying other books by Wright.

6 Although all organisms are by their nature competitive, it is both interesting and encouraging to learn that, since at least 2010, scholars are increasingly determining that "cooperation" and not just "competition" plays a vital role in the evolution of biodiversity. It's not difficult to understand how cooperation through reduction of fear leads to societal advancements both in human and other animal societies, but scholars are now demonstrating how such cooperation occurs even at the genetic level between species. For an introduction into this line of research see, "Cooperation, Conflict, and the Evolution of Complex Animal Societies" by Rubenstein, D. & Kealey, J. (2010) Nature Education Knowledge 3(10):78. "Cooperation, not struggle for survival, drives evolution, say researchers" Science Daily May 12, 2016. Both articles can easily be found online.

7 Sanskrit was the language of the upper classes at the time of the historical Buddha. Many scholars believe Sanskrit to be the oldest written language, with some dialects dating back to the Vedic period, possibly older than 3000 BCE. If the myth that the historical Buddha was a prince is correct, then Buddha would have spoken Sanskrit. If not, then he would have spoken Pali, the language of the common people of that time. The sacred Buddhist Canon, known as the "Tipitaka", is written in Pali.

8 For example, contrast Mark 10:13-16; Matthew 19:13-15; and Luke 18:15-17 with Genesis 19; Deuteronomy 29; Psalm 11; and Revelations 20.

9 Examples are numerous. Simply search online for "books on other religions" by either mystic/scholar. You will find books like "Living Buddha, Living Christ" by Thich Nhat Hanh, Riverhead Books, New York, 1994; and "Toward A True Kinship of Faith: How The World's Religions Can Come Together" by the Dalai Lama Three Rivers Press, New York, 2010. More than 30 years ago, the Dalai Lama founded the Mind & Life Institute which "brings science and contemplative wisdom together to better understand the mind and create positive change in the world" at midlife.org.

10 The Dalai Lama's talk can be found online at "Science at the Crossroads"; Science for Monks and Nuns at scienceformonksandnuns.org.

11 Martin Luther (1483-1546) was a brilliant and highly educated Catholic priest from Germany who rejected certain teachings of the Roman Catholic Church; in particular the power and efficacy of "indulgences" from the punishment due for sin. Luther subsequently left the Catholic Church, and became the leader of the German Protestant Reformation (1517-1643). Luther taught both salvation through "Faith" alone as well as an essentially literal interpretation of the bible, which Luther

translated from Latin to German for greater access to the lay populace. It's not unfair to argue that Luther's teachings on faith and the bible became the foundational beliefs of not only Lutheranism, but of most Evangelical religions.

12 The Nalanda Institute for Contemplative Science is a highly respected Buddhist educational institution in New York inspired by ancient Nalanda University. This quote was written by Scott Tusa in an article on the Nalanda Institute website entitled "Our Underlying Wholeness, A Reflection On Buddha-Nature", which can be found at nalandainstitute.org/2020/02/06/our-underlying-wholeness-a-reflection-on-buddha-nature.

13 There is a "visualization" meditation I have found to be both effective and enjoyable in helping to realize interdependent co-arising. Thich Nhat Hanh calls it "Tangerine Meditation", but I have always called it meditation on an orange. This is because an actual orange is used to bring your olfactory sense into play to help deepen the realization. It begins with the centering meditation of following the breath. Then close your eyes, and bring the orange up near your nose so that you can fully appreciate the fragrance of the orange. Take a few deep breaths through your nose so that the fragrance of the orange fills your consciousness. With eyes always closed, visualize the orange hanging from a small branch just before it is picked. Then trace in your visualization that small branch back to a larger branch, and then back to the trunk of the orange tree. Try and smell the bark of that trunk within the fragrance of the orange. (This will take a free imagination and perhaps some practice.) Then visualize the trunk of the tree going down into the earth with its roots spreading out into fertile soil. Now smell within the orange the fragrance of the orange, the bark and roots of the tree, and the fertile soil from which the tree and its orange receives its life-giving nourishment. When you sense each of these phenomena within the orange, congratulations! You have achieved a deeper realization of interdependent co-arising.

14 Meister Eckhart (1260-1326/7?) was a German, mendicant, friar of the Dominican Order of the Roman Catholic Church. He was without a doubt a true mystic in the sense we have been using that term in this book. He often used the metaphor of the desert in his teachings. A strong argument can be made that Eckhart believed in a One Consciousness reality. The Catholic Church brought proceeding against Eckhart to declare many of his teachings as heretical, but Eckhart died before this process concluded.

15 Most scholars believe that "Siddhartha" was Buddha's personal name, while "Gautama" was a family/clan name.

16 I have renumbered, modified, and reductively summarized Thich Nhat Hanh's teachings on the Four Noble Truths to fit the language and space limitations of this book. His specific teachings are best found in Part Two of his book "The Heart of the Buddha's Teaching"; Broadway Books, New York (1999). (Here and after "Heart".)

17 It is interesting to learn that the ancient world was replete with codes of legal conduct. Simply search online for "ancient legal codes" to find such codes as the Code of Ur-Nammu c. 2050 BCE; the Code of Hammurabi c. 1790 BCE. Of course we've all heard of Mosiac Law which primarily includes the Torah (first five books of the Hebrew bible); but did you know there was the Seven Laws of Noah (Noahide Laws)?

18 There are several somewhat older but accessible and instructive scholarly articles of the history, methods, and validity of mindfulness practice which can easily be found online. See: Mindfulness: Theoretical Foundations and Evidence for its Salutary Effects: by Kirk Warren Brown, Richard M. Ryan, and J. David Crewel; Psychological Inquiry 2007, vol. 18, No. 4,211-237. "Mindfulness=Based

Interventions for Physical Conditions: A Narrative Review Evaluating Levels of Evidence" by Linda E. Carlson; International Scholarly Research Network ISRN Psychiatry Volume 2012, Article ID 651583, 21 pages doe: 10.5402/2012/651583. "Mind the Gap in Mindfulness Research: A Comparative Account of the Leading Schools of Thought" by Rona Hart, Itai Ivtzan, and Dan Hart; Review of General Psychology 2013, Vol. 17, No. 4, 453-466.

19 See, "The benefits of meditation and mindfulness practices during times of crisis such as COVID-19" by C. Behan; Ir J Psychol Med. 2020 May 14: 1-3 doi: 10.1017/ipm.2020.38.

20 The Occam's razor principle is attributed to the English philosopher and Franciscan friar, William of Ockham (c. 1285-1349); which in plain English states: When there are two competing explanations for the cause of something, the simple and more direct explanation is more likely to be correct. The term "razor" is meant as a metaphor to shave away unnecessary assumptions. "Occam" is a longstanding misspelling of "Ockham".

EPILOGUE

Some people feel the rain.
Others just get wet.
—Unknown[1]

Thank you for taking this journey with me. Not surprisingly, we were unable to discover together the answer to the "hard problem", nor were we able to determine with certainty whether there is a Transcendent/Transpersonal level to reality. Yet if this book works as I hoped it would, you now have the foundational knowledge and practices to continue this adventure on your own, and eventually arrive at your own insights. (Ha! If you do confirm a Transcendent/Transpersonal level, please be sure and let me know.)

My final hope is that this book provides you with an ever-expanding freedom of consciousness. A freedom to challenge the powerful filters to consciousness, and leave behind the fears and mindless habits of closed consciousness. It invites you to pursue roads less traveled, and return to share the wisdom and compassion you discover. This freedom of expanding consciousness can perhaps best be described as an accessible lightness of being. It is a window of pure witness into the wonder of it all, both the so-called good and the so-called bad. When you walk in the rain, no longer will you just get wet. In celebration of that goal, the following is a piece of poetry dedicated to this new freedom. (The first and last few lines were shamelessly stolen from much better poets.)

Some people feel the rain
Others just get wet
Some people live in fear
Others do not fret

Some people group enclose
Others do not hide
Some people play it safe
Others open wide

Some people never doubt
Others want to know
Some people horde within
Others overflow

Some people never love
Others cannot wait
Some people close their minds
Others laugh at fate

Some people have cold hearts
Others hearts that sing
Some people never risk
Others fly with Wings

The wonder of it all, baby
The wonder of it all, baby
The wonder of it all, baby
Yeah, yeah, yeah[2]

—DJP

---

1 There is both a scholarly and an emotional dispute as to the author of this perfect quote that poetically reveals the nature of an open consciousness. Most attribute the quote to Bob Dylan, many to Bob Marley; but the best evidence of authorship points to Roger Miller, an American singer-songwriter known for his novelty hit songs like "King of the Road" and "Dang Me". See, quoteininvestigator.com.

2 If you missed the hint in the fifth stanza, the last stanza of this poem is an homage to the final lyrics of the song "Listen to What the Man Said" by Sir Paul McCartney from the Wings album "Venus and Mars".

ABOUT THE AUTHOR

David is the oldest of seven children from a loving and free-spirited Chicago family. At the age of 14, he entered the seminary planning to become a priest, but discovered this was not his path in life. He went on to law school where he served on the writing staff of the Law Review. Beginning in 1977, David practiced for nearly four decades as a trial lawyer in the medical- legal field. He regularly lectured to physicians and lawyers, published in both legal and medical journals, and was a guest lecturer at the University of Notre Dame Law School. During these years, he volunteered with the Legal Assistance Foundation of Metropolitan Chicago, and eventually became Chair of the Board of Directors.

In the early 1990's, David went back to school to earn a Masters Degree in Theology with a major in ethics, and for the next several years served on the Ethics Advisory Board ("EAB") of Children's Memorial Hospital in Chicago. While at Children's, he lectured to interns and residents on medical-legal issues, participated with the EAB in attempting to resolve heartbreaking medical situations, and was instrumental in organizing the first ethics retreat at the hospital.

In the late 1990s, David was invited onto the Board of Directors of Friends Without A Border, an American-Japanese charitable organization that provides medical treatment to the children of Southeast Asia; as well as formal training for local doctors, nurses, and other healthcare workers. (See "Friends" at www.fwab.org.) In 2015, David retired from the practice of law and stepped down from the Friends Board to volunteer full time as the Executive Director of Friends where he oversaw the founding and initial development of Lao Friends Hospital for Children in Luang Prabang, Lao PDR.

David has studied and practiced meditation for many decades, including training with recognized masters in Europe, Israel, Nepal, Tibet, and the United States. He has taught introductory meditation courses including seminars for lawyers at the Chicago Bar Association; and in 2006, served as one of four group facilitators at the "Compassion in the Rockies Retreat: A Meditation Retreat for World Peace" at which the Dalai Lama, Sakyong Mipham Rinpoche, and Rabbi Irwin Kula gave teachings.

David and his wife Joan have three adult children: Genevieve, Zak, and Tyler. In 2018, David and Joan moved to a lake house in Northwest Indiana where David writes, and they both enjoy spending time with their son, Zak, his wife Jeannie, and their grandchildren, Oliver and Eloise.